Children and Social Policy

Also by Paul Daniel

Social Work and Local Politics (with J. Wheeler)

Children and Social Policy

Paul Daniel and John Ivatts

MACMILLAN

First published 1998 by
MACMILLAN PRESS LTD
Houndmills, Basingstoke, Hampshire RG21 6XS
and London
Companies and representatives
throughout the world

ISBN 0–333–65207–X hardcover
ISBN 0–333–65208–8 paperback

A catalogue record for this book is available
from the British Library.

This book is printed on paper suitable for recycling and
made from fully managed and sustained forest sources.

10   9   8   7   6   5   4   3
07 06 05 04 03 02 01 00

Copy-edited and typeset by Povey–Edmondson
Tavistock and Rochdale, England

Printed in Malaysia

To our children and grandchildren
Andrew, Eleanor, Mark, Nicole, Oliver, Rachel and Simone

Contents

List of Tables and Figures

Tables

Figures

Acknowledgements

We are greatly indebted to the many Social Policy and Early Childhood Diploma students whose desire for understanding and acute concern for children's welfare have provided a rich source of ideas, and indeed the original inspiration for this book. To our colleagues in the Sociology and Social Policy Department at the Roehampton Institute we also owe a great deal. Their encouragement and fecund comments upon some of the original material contributed substantially to the development of the content of this text. Thus our particular thanks to Martin Albrow, John Baker, David Denney, Graham Fennell, Stephen Groarke, Robert Leaper and Lorraine Radford. To Jane Lambert, Peter Jackson, Arthur Ivatts, Simone Ivatts and Edith Le Riche we are also particularly grateful for their expert advice on specific subject matter. The completion of a book of this kind depends upon the works of innumerable writers and researchers. We gratefully acknowledge our debt to all those who have contributed to the store of public knowledge upon which we have been able to draw so copiously. The task of writing this text has also been greatly facilitated by the unfailing help and courteous efficiency of the staff of the Roehampton Institute libraries and of the Horsham branch of the West Sussex public library service; our appreciation in this connection to Pat Biggs, James Chislett, Julie Harrison and Maria Hisco, and to Andrea Peace and her colleagues at Southlands College Library. Finally, and above all, we owe an immeasurable debt of gratitude to Joanna Ball and Rose-Marie Ivatts who have not only shared the stresses of authorship with great patience, but have provided invaluable support and encouragement throughout.

PAUL DANIEL
JOHN IVATTS

The authors and publishers gratefully acknowledge the permission given by the Controller of HMSO and The Office for National Statistics to reproduce the material used in the figures and tables.

Introduction

Children's lives are to a considerable extent shaped by social policy. They are among the principal recipients of welfare services, and their experience in areas such as housing, health and education will do much to determine not only their present well-being but also their future life chances. Yet they make only shadowy appearances at best in most of the social policy literature. In the early 1980s it was suggested that:

> Children have been the companions of women in the closet of political science. A few short years ago women began to set up such a clamour that a few were released ... Children remain, with few exceptions, both silent and invisible. (J. Elshtain, 1982)

In recent years the study of social policy has been characterised by its concern to give greater prominence not only to the position of women but also to other 'hidden' groups such as ethnic minorities and people with a disability. Children, however, have remained relatively 'silent and invisible'.

Our intention in writing this book has been to produce a child-centred account of UK social policy since 1945. We use the term 'child centred' in this context to mean two things. First, the child is firmly in the centre of the picture. The aim has been to examine the impact of social policy over a number of areas such as health, housing and social security, not on adults, households or families, which are the conventional units of analysis, but on children.

Second, the framework used in the book is that of 'children's rights'. This will be discussed more fully in Chapters 1 and 9. As a brief indication of what we mean by this, however, we would simply say that children are viewed as 'human beings rather than human becomings' (Quortrup, 1994). Too often, social policies that are specifically directed at children are justified in terms of 'investment'. Children symbolise 'the future', 'social renewal', 'survival of the nation' or equivalent sentiments. As we write, in 1997, this is clearly encapsulated in the 'New Labour/New Britain' campaign which

1

stresses 'investment in human capital' as the key to future economic prosperity.

Child-centred social policy, on the other hand, starts from the premise that children have an inherent value as individuals in their own right and not merely, or even mainly, as future adults. In this respect, the United Nations Convention on the Rights of the Child (1991) provides a valuable basis from which to evaluate policy. The UK government's judgement on its own record contained in its first report to the UN Committee on the Rights of the Child (DoH 1994, p. 1) was that it could 'claim with some confidence to have a good record in general on its treatment of children'. The conclusions reached here are somewhat different.

A number of points need to be made about the scope and format of this book. First, although we have tried to use a wide lens in our discussion of children and social policy, inevitably the range of topics covered is selective and limited for reasons of space. In some sense or another, all social policies affect children and this is true not only of national social policy but also increasingly of global developments. Although some of these wider issues have been touched upon, especially in Chapter 3, our focus is mainly on the UK, and in some cases more specifically on England and Wales. The issue of the effects of 'globalisation' on social policy, and the impact of this on children, deserves a much fuller exploration and discussion than can be given here.

The definition of 'childhood' is similarly more limited than we would ideally have chosen. As is generally now accepted, childhood is a socially constructed classification and not one that is solely biologically determined. There are no natural cut-off points. Thus any age boundaries to do with social policy and children are arbitrary. In order to keep the project to manageable proportions, we have taken the socially determined transition age from primary to secondary schooling – eleven – as our boundary. Clearly, though, many of the issues covered in this book apply equally to older children, and where appropriate the data includes this group. In these cases we have indicated this fact; otherwise, data relates to the 0–11 age range.

It should also be stressed that although the unitary term 'children' is used, this should not be taken to suggest that children in the UK experience social policy in the same way. The royal princes, Harry and William, have little in common with the children of lone parents living on inner city estates! We recognise that there are many different childhoods in the UK and have tried to indicate, where appropriate, the circumstances of certain groups such as black children, traveller children and refugees. Nevertheless, within the framework of the child-centred perspective adopted for this study, there are common elements which unite all children in their relationship to the adult world.

The fact that the period since 1945 is taken as the time frame inevitably means that many significant social policy developments in relation to children are missing. Child protection, for example, has its origins in the late nineteenth century and many other contemporary issues and debates need to be placed in a longer historical context than has been possible here. For this earlier period reference can be made to Hendrick (1994).

Having said this, there is no doubt that 1945 was a watershed in UK social policy, and perhaps particularly so for children. Our own family histories (and the same will no doubt be true for many readers) reveal the extent to which children's life chances were transformed by the welfare reforms of the 1940s. At the same time, however, it must be recognised that:

> new and subtler forms of deprivation may have been caused by the profound changes occurring over the last forty years in labour markets, in environmental conditions, in family structure, in internal and international migration, in the organisation of society and in other aspects of life. (UNICEF, 1989).

It is hoped that this book will shed some light on what it has meant to be a 'child of the welfare state' and to consider what it will be like for its grandchildren.

Finally, we return to the issue of children's rights. The UN Secretary General has observed that, of all issues, 'none has the acceptance, or the power to mobilise as does the cause of children' (quoted in Newell, 1995). Our review of UK social policy since 1945 suggests that while children may frequently be invoked by politicians for their symbolism and power to arouse emotions, the reality is that 'the cause of children' rarely makes it on to the political agenda. The final chapter therefore includes a number of proposals for modest reforms of the policy-making process, aimed at making it easier to mobilise on behalf of children in the twenty-first century.

1

Social Policy and Childhood: An Overview

Every nation, implicitly or explicitly, has a policy towards its children.
(J. S. Bruner, 1980)

Introduction

Our aim in this chapter is to examine the principles and underlying assumptions that have guided British policy on children since 1945. It is not a straightforward task. British policy stands squarely at the implicit end of the spectrum. In the absence of a written constitution or Bill of Rights, there is no tradition in the UK of the state defining its obligations towards its citizens, whether adults or children. To use the terminology of the 1990s, the UK has no Mission Statement or Charter relating to children.

Indeed, there has been remarkably little public discussion of British fundamental values and aims in relation to children. A number of other countries have developed far more explicit policy frameworks and have stimulated wider popular debate about children and their needs. In Denmark, for example, Karin Vilien (1993) has described how:

> the government appointed a permanent committee of civil servants from 13 ministries, delegating to members responsibility for following all matters relating to the conditions affecting children's lives . . . Public debate has been very active and engaged . . . all in order to give children a high priority.

By contrast, in the UK civil service, responsibility for children is scattered and fragmented, and the public profile of children's issues

4

very low. This fragmentation of responsibility for services for children has long been recognised as one of the major barriers to developing effective and coherent policies, especially in relation to the early years. Linda Challis, for example, in a study of early years' day care in the early 1980s noted over twenty different departments of central and local government involved in the planning and delivery of the service in one London borough alone (Challis, 1980). If she had also included the many private and voluntary organisations providing day care, then her total would have been approximately doubled.

The fact that responsibility for children is diffused with no mechanism for co-ordination means that, apart from a number of voluntary organisations, there is no effective advocate for children's interests in the UK. Moreover, in the absence of any explicit framework of aims and principles, policy towards children is developed according to a set of implicit assumptions and values, often embedded in wider concerns such as the relationship between the state and the family, or the future of the nation.

Children come first?

If we were to judge the situation solely by the volume of legislation and policy initiatives ostensibly concerned with the welfare of children, then we might conclude that children in the UK do enjoy a relatively high priority. The Children Act 1989 was the sixth major piece of legislation since the Second World War relating specifically to the protection of children. However on closer inspection, it becomes clear that legislation that is enacted in the name of children frequently arises out of a variety of concerns that have little to do with the needs or interests of children.

A classic example of this was the introduction of Family Allowances in 1945. The campaign for family allowances had been a long and hard fought one which owed much to the work of Eleanor Rathbone before the war, notably in her influential text *The Disinherited Family* (Rathbone, 1924). Certainly, the need to tackle child poverty was a major concern in the campaign, but as Macnicol (1980) and Land (1975) have separately shown, this was just one of a wide range of issues raised.

In the event, other arguments appear to have been more decisive. Two, in particular, weighed heavily with the Beveridge Report and ultimately with the Treasury. The first was the need to arrest the decline in the birth rate and help to rebuild the nation's future following the devastation of war. The second attraction of family allowances was as an anti-inflation device. They enabled low wages to be topped up without a general increase in pay levels.

A more recent example of a policy initiative launched under the guise of children's welfare, but with other concerns dominant, is the Child Support Act 1991. Despite the fact that the White Paper preceding the legislation was entitled *Children Come First*, it is clear that other interests – such as the desire to cut public expenditure, to reinforce parental responsibility and to increase work incentives – were put before those of children. We shall discuss this more fully in Chapter 3, but would simply note here that a number of studies have demonstrated that the way the Child Support Act was framed has meant that children in low-income families have not benefited, and indeed may even have been made poorer in some cases (see, for example, Garnham and Knights (1994), and Daniel and Burgess (1994)).

If children have not enjoyed a high profile in their own right then they have certainly played a central part in one of the main themes of UK social policy since 1945 – the family. Fiona Williams has suggested that 'family' has been one of the three organising principles of post war welfare development, along with 'nation' and 'work' (Williams, 1989). Arguably, children are instrumental in each of these and we shall discuss the theme of children as 'the future of the nation' and 'the future workforce' later in this chapter. By far the most influential of these themes in relation to children, though, is that of 'the family', and it is to that we now turn.

The family: a dominant theme in UK social policy

We would suggest that no other factor is as significant in explaining British social policy towards children as the nature of the relationship between the family and the state. This claim is more than a simple recognition that most children spend most of their childhood within families: it is based on the view that children are virtually 'invisible' within the family unit, and they have almost no separate social policy identity. Not only is this reflected, as Jonathan Bradshaw (1990) has shown, in the way official data is collected and classified:

> While the UK has what constitutes an excellent national data base on family or household living standards, social conditions and social attitudes, children have not been the primary focus of attention.

Even our language frequently substitutes the word 'family' for that of 'child'. For example, we talk of 'starting a family' when we mean 'having a baby'. The question 'Do you have a family?' means 'Do you have children?'

The language of social policy is similarly family rather than child-centred. When financial support for children was introduced in 1945, it was termed 'Family Allowance' rather than child allowance. Although this was later renamed 'Child Benefit' the tradition of equating children and families was upheld by the introduction of 'Family Credit' as a benefit for households with children. Under the Children Act 1989, local authorities are required to provide 'family centres' as part of their support for children in need. By contrast, we have very few 'children's centres' in Britain.

Perhaps the most striking reflection of children's invisibility within a broader emphasis on the family is to be found within much of post war social work theory and practice. Ironically, a service whose objectives includes the protection of children has sometimes found it difficult to differentiate between supporting families and safeguarding the welfare of children. This point was strongly made by the inquiry report on the death of Jasmine Beckford:

> It is axiomatic that the protection of the child can usually be best achieved by working with the family, of which the child is an integral part. But the focus must invariably be the on the child . . . Jasmine's fate illustrates all too clearly the disastrous consequences of the misguided attitude of the social workers having treated Morris Beckford and Beverley Lorrington as the clients first and foremost. (London Borough of Brent, 1985)

It is arguable that Jasmine Beckford's invisibility within her abusing family was no more than an extreme case of the way children are seen by society generally. Social workers in this and other similar cases were pilloried and punished when they were themselves victims of a much wider failure to recognise children as individuals in their own right.

This failure to distinguish conceptually between children and families has been termed the 'familialization' of childhood by Quortrup and his colleagues (1994). It is clearly not a phenomenon that is unique to British social policy. But it is a factor that inhibits any impetus towards developing child-centred social policies. If children are socially 'invisible', it is unlikely that social policy will be developed specifically around their needs.

However, while the recognition that children are people with separate identities from that of the larger unit of the family is a necessary first step, it is not a sufficient condition for the development of policies which respect children's rights as individuals.

The state–family relationship

There is a far more significant barrier to child-centred social policy in Britain. This arises out of the particular set of assumptions about the relationship between the family and state that underpin British social policy. This relationship is one which has received detailed analysis, mainly from a feminist perspective and in relation to the position of women (examples include Wilson, 1977; Pascall, 1986; and Williams, 1989). We shall therefore deal with it only briefly here.

The crucial premise upon which all other assumptions are based is that the family and state are distinct and separate spheres. The family is seen as a 'natural' and 'private' institution outside the realm of the state. Variously described as a 'bulwark against the encroachment of the state' (Rogers and Clements, 1985) or a 'haven in a heartless world' (Lasch, 1977), the family derives its legitimacy from the belief that it is an autonomous institution.

In fact, as the feminist critiques referred to above have indicated, the idea that the family is in any way separate from the state is a highly dubious one. The particular form the family takes at any time is a social construction, and the state plays a significant part, through its legislative and social policy framework, in shaping family relationships and obligations. Janet Finch has provided a detailed and illuminating analysis of the way such obligations have been defined in British social policy (Finch, 1989).

Nevertheless, the idea of family privacy remains a powerful and resonant theme in social policy discourse. Moreover, as David Archard has suggested, it is an ideology that is self-perpetuating, 'For what the state will not intrude upon is defined as "private", and the "privacy" of the private is what then serves as the principal ground for non-intervention' (Archard, 1993, p. 113). The idea that the family is a separate sphere outside the realm of the state clearly has enormous significance for social policy and for children. Indeed, the 'privacy' of the family effectively defines the limits of social policy in this area.

Alongside, and bound up with, the privacy accorded to families is responsibility for dependent members. On the face of it, there has been no shortage of concern to 'support the family' in UK social policy since 1945. In the 1980s and 1990s in particular, political parties have competed for the mantle of 'the party of the family'. However, as Gillian Pascall has suggested, 'the real meaning of supporting the family is supporting family responsibility, as distinct from state responsibility' (Pascall, 1986, p. 38). The principle that social policy should not interfere with the family's responsibility to care for its dependents has been a consistent theme throughout the post-war period. We can trace it from the Beveridge Report's justification of family allowances through to Lord McKay's introduction to the Children Act 1989. Beveridge says:

> These proposals are based on two principles, first that nothing should be done to remove from parents the responsibility of maintaining their children, and second that it is in the national interest for the state to help parents discharge that responsibility properly. (Beveridge Report, Cmnd. 6550, 1942, p. 14)

And Lord McKay:

> The government is anxious to make it clear in the Bill that families should generally be left to sort out matters for themselves, unless it is shown that without an order the child's welfare will suffer. (Mckay, 1989).

Indeed, we can find clear evidence that every proposed social policy intervention relating to children – from compulsory schooling, through the provision of school meals, to day care for the under-fives – has had to contend with the claim that it will infringe the 'autonomy of the family'. This issue has never been far below the surface of political debate in the UK and USA in the post-Second World War era. With the rise of the 'New Right' in both countries in the 1970s and 1980s we have witnessed what one academic study has termed *The War Over the Family* (Berger and Berger, 1983).

One of the main features of the New Right's argument is that social policy support for families, and particularly that offered by social security programmes, has undermined the family's willingness and ability to fulfil its responsibilities towards its dependent members. Academics such as Charles Murray (1984) and Lawrence Mead (1986) in the USA, and pressure groups such as the Conservative Family Campaign in the UK have advocated a reduction in welfare support for families and a return to 'traditional values'. The impact of these arguments on social policy on both sides of the Atlantic has been considerable (see Abbott and Wallace, 1992). This was no doubt helped by the fact that these views on family responsibility corresponded with the dominant economic theory of the time, which stressed 'rolling back the state' and cutting public expenditure.

What is notable about the politics of the family in the 1980s and 1990s is that while the 'New Right' are undoubtedly more strident in their stress on 'family responsibility', there is no serious challenge to the basic principle. In the UK, 'New Labour' put just as much stress on the responsibility of families as does the 'New Right'. The main political differences over the issue of social policy and the family centre on the definition of 'family' and the extent to which welfare does, in fact, undermine 'family responsibility'. On the one hand, the 'New Right' see the 'family' in traditional terms, with two parents and well-defined gender roles, and argue that social policies have been instrumental in the disintegration of the traditional family form. On the other hand, the centre-left accept that there is a diversity of family type and believe that social policy can and should be used to enable families to fulfil their responsibilities more effectively.

This stress on 'family responsibility' and the consequent anxiety over the state of the family that has characterised political debate in the UK and USA is not a universal phenomenon. In much of Europe, notably France and the Scandinavian countries, the situation is quite different. There is much greater emphasis on social responsibility for children. In France, for example, as Cresy Cannan has argued:

The state's responsibility to ensure a high level of social protection is not debated. The family is seen not as separate from the state, but as part of a continuum of institutions which link the individual to society. (Cannan, 1992, p. 10)

To suggest, as we do, that the UK's emphasis on the family is detrimental to the interests of children is not in any way to imply that children's welfare is not best served within the family. It is rather to argue that the fact that children are subsumed within the term 'family' prevents them from becoming the primary focus of policy.

Indeed they can, instead, easily find themselves instrumental to the pursuit of broader 'family values'. Examples of this abound – from Beveridge's failure to provide within the National Insurance scheme for lone parent families, to the benefit penalty on lone parents who refuse to co-operate with the Child Support Agency. Even in the mid-1990s, the government is reported to be considering withdrawing the £100 maternity payment from single mothers who are claiming Income Support (*Guardian*, 31 March 1995). In each of these examples, policy has been framed in such a way as to reinforce paternal responsibility through mechanisms which make children worse off.

We have argued that 'family' has been the dominant theme in UK social policy and one that has distracted from the welfare of children as individuals in their own right. However, children are not entirely absent from social policy discourse. They do appear, but are confined to three distinct roles as Harry Hendrick (1994) has pointed out: these are; threat; victim; and Investment. We look briefly at each of these in turn.

Child as threat

There could be no more vivid reminder of the significance of 'the child as threat' as a potent force in contemporary social attitudes towards childhood than the response to the murder in 1993 of 2-year-old Jamie Bulger by two 10-year-olds. This, almost unique, incident evoked more concern and more debate than any other issue to do with children in recent history. Much of this debate centred on anxiety over the state of contemporary childhood and the perception that it constituted a threat to the social order. Peter Newell (1995) has described it as 'an outpouring of deep rooted adult suspicions, fears and venom; the *Lord of the Flies* nightmare'.

Marina Warner (1989) has suggested that the gap between the worlds of children and adults has been growing steadily, with the consequence that 'never before have children been so saturated with all the power of projected monstrousness to excite repulsion – even terror'. In fact, such concerns are by no means recent. Indeed, Dingwall and his colleagues have shown that 'the child as threat' is perhaps the earliest theme to surface in the development of social policy for children. They suggest that this first became an issue under the Elizabethan Poor Law when children of the vagrant poor were perceived as threats to the social order: 'Attention was focused first on protection from children and only latterly on protection of children. They are threats before they are victims' (Dingwall, Eekelaar and Murray, 1983, p. 214). A similar point is made by Nigel Parton in his important study of the emergence of child abuse as a social policy issue. He argues that the state's concern about the inadequate socialisation of children not only preceded but has also been more pervasive than the intermittent interest in the issue of children as victims of abuse (Parton, 1985, ch. 2).

The significance for social policy of the mass evacuation of children during the Second World War has been well documented (Titmuss, 1950). During this period nearly 900 000 children, mainly from working-class families, were moved out of the towns and cities. Contemporary accounts demonstrate the palpable sense of shock experienced by the middle-class hosts at the condition of many of the children. In part, the reaction was concern at the discovery of the poor physical state of the evacuees, but this was mingled with fear of 'the child as threat'. The following passage taken from a contemporary report gives a flavour of the attitudes of the time: 'Within this group are the "problem families", always on the edge of pauperism and crime, riddled with mental and physical defects, in and out of the courts for child neglect, a menace to the community' (Hygiene Committee of the Women's Group on Public Welfare, 1942). Around 15 000–20 000 evacuees were classified as unbilletable owing to behavioural problems (Hendrick, 1994, p. 5).

Child as victim

Jean Packman has shown how the two categories of 'deprived' and 'depraved' children increasingly came together in social work theory and practice in the period after the Second World War. Theories which linked delinquency to neglect and explained child mistreatment in terms of cycles of abuse served increasingly to conflate the categories of 'victim' and 'threat', while the Children and Young Persons Acts of 1963 and 1969 sought to deal with the two groups of children within the same legislative and policy framework (Packman, 1975, ch. 6).

Nigel Parton has suggested in his valuable study, *The Politics of Child Abuse*, that the theme of the child as purely and simply a 'victim' has made only fleeting appearances on the political agenda (Parton, 1985, p. 46). This tended to be the dominant motif, however, in UK child care policy from the 1970s, following the 'rediscovery of child abuse'. This will be discussed more fully in Chapter 8. It has also been dealt with admirably by Parton.

As a brief comment, however, and at the risk of oversimplifying a complex and multi-faceted development, we would suggest that the growing concern over child abuse had little to do with any change in the incidence of abuse nor in social attitudes towards children. Rather it reflected principally a change in the relationship between the state and family. Growing disillusionment with the policy of supporting families in a preventive capacity was accompanied by a more restricted and authoritarian emphasis on policing child abuse. The visual image of the 'child as victim' as exemplified by Maria Colwell also enabled the media and some politicians to mount an attack on the failure 'welfarism', and social work in particular.

Child as investment

The theme of the 'child as investment' is a pervasive one in the history of social policy. We have referred to the identification by Fiona Williams of the three 'organising principles' of UK social policy as 'Family', 'Nation' and 'Work'. Children occupy an important place as the 'future of the nation' and the 'future workforce'.

The development of child and maternal welfare services in the early twentieth century owed much to concern over the quality and quantity of the population, arising out of the poor condition of recruits during the Boer War (Lewis, 1980). Population anxieties have waxed and waned in the UK in subsequent years. Arguably, there has never been the level of concern seen in some other European countries, such as France (for a comparison of policy in Britain and France, see Baker, 1986).

In the UK, the tendency has been to view children more as a private indulgence than a public responsibility. Social policy concerns in Britain have focused just as readily on discouraging reproduction as on supporting it. (Notable examples include Keith Joseph's campaign in the early 1970s against the 'cycle of deprivation', and that of various cabinet ministers' in the 1990s directed at lone parents.)

Nevertheless, at times of national renewal or self analysis, the importance of 'investing in children' has reappeared as a powerful theme in UK social policy. We see this most notably perhaps in the Beveridge Report of 1942. Here, concern over the population was clearly a major influence in the proposals for post-war reconstruction. In a now infamous passage, Beveridge referred to his belief that: 'In the next thirty years housewives as Mothers have vital work to do in ensuring the continuance of the British Race and of British Ideals in the world' (Beveridge, 1942, para. 117).

Beveridge viewed the falling birth rate with alarm, claiming that: 'unless this rate is raised very materially in the near future a rapid and continuous decline in the population cannot be prevented' (ibid., para. 15). This led him to advocate family allowances as a 'signal of national interest in children', and to argue that 'it is imperative to give first place in social expenditure to the care of childhood and the safeguarding of maternity' (ibid.)

Over fifty years later the Commission on Social Justice, in its report subtitled *Strategies for National Renewal* put similar emphasis on 'children as investment'. This time the concern was less on the quantity of the population and much more on the quality – particularly its level of education: 'Children are not a private pleasure or a personal burden; they are 100% of a nation's future . . . the best indicator of the capacity of our economy tomorrow is the quality of our children today' (Commission on Social Justice, 1994, p. 311).

The liberal dilemma

These three often overlapping concerns with the child – as 'victim', 'threat' and 'investment' – challenge the view that the family is essentially a private, autonomous institution. Indeed, it is this challenge which produces what Dingwall and colleagues have termed the 'liberal dilemma'.

> For the liberal, however, the unresolved problem is how child rearing can be made into a matter of public concern and its qualities monitored without destroying the ideal of the family as a counterweight to state power, a domain of voluntary self regulating actions. (1983, p. 214)

The response to the 'liberal dilemma' is perhaps best described by David Archard (1993) as the 'liberal standard'. The basis of this approach is the belief that while the state has a legitimate interest in the rearing of children, this is best served if intervention is confined to the last resort.

Although there has been some slight shifting of the boundaries of responsibility between state and family from time to time, this stands as a reasonable description of the position in the UK throughout the post-war period. The dominant view, as Crescy Cannan (1992) has suggested, is that 'only abusive or "problem" families need services; the majority cope and therefore do not need them'.

In many respects the philosophy underpinning policy towards children in the UK is best epitomised by the Children Act 1989. Although widely seen as a progressive piece of legislation and frequently dubbed a 'children's charter', it is in fact (as we shall suggest in Chapter 8) a minimalist piece of legislation which reinforces the principle of family responsibility.

Far from offering any promise of a break with the 'liberal standard' which, as we have argued, has characterised UK social policy towards children in the period since 1945, the Children Act 1989 is very much a continuation of the implicit values we have outlined in this chapter. For an alternative set of values and principles, based on the rights of the child, we need to look outside UK domestic legislation to the 1989 United Nations Convention on the Rights of the Child. It is to this we now turn.

The United Nations Convention on the Rights of the Child

It has been suggested that 'the Convention of 1989 and the World Summit of 1990 are watersheds in the history of children' (Freeman, 1992). Although not everyone is so optimistic about its potential (Franklin, 1989) and it is clearly still too early to assess its full effects, the United Nations Convention on the Rights of the Child is arguably the most significant development in UK policy towards children since 1945. Ratified by the UK in December 1991, the Convention sets out a number of detailed standards and principles that are intended to govern the way states deal with children.

Under the terms of ratification, governments were required to 'make the principles and provisions of the Convention widely known by appropriate and active means to adults and children alike' (Article 42). Guidelines from the UN Committee on the Rights of the Child advocated the widest possible popular participation and public scrutiny of the whole process. In the event, there has been almost no debate in the UK and it is likely that very few people – adults or children – are aware of the Convention's existence. The response of the government in the UK has been justifiably described as 'more of a whimper than a bang' (Lansdown, 1992).

In its first Report to the UN Committee on the Rights of the Child, the UK government declared that 'ratification of the Convention did not require any amendment to UK legislation' (DoH 1994, p. 4). When it comes to the detail of the specific articles of the Convention this is an arguable position. Many of the provisions are fairly broadly drawn – deliberately so, to encompass the circumstances of all nations. The Convention accepts that due account should be given to 'the traditions and cultural values of each people' and makes allowance for 'the national conditions and means' of signatories.

This being so, it is not difficult to make out a case that UK policy is in line with most of the specific provisions of the Convention. Even at this level, however, the opposite can also be argued, and we shall examine a number of the specific provisions in later chapters. Certainly, the government's report on its progress in implementing the Convention has come under attack from a number of voluntary organisations (*Community Care*, 8 February 1995) and been dismissed as 'a deeply complacent document, dishonest by omission and providing no recognisable picture of the state of our children' (Newell, 1995, p. 196).

Whatever its direct impact on UK legislation and policy, however, we would argue that the Convention's real potential lies in its underlying principles and values. Because, despite the government's claim that 'the UK's perception of children's rights and needs is closely aligned with the philosophy of the Convention' (UK First Report to UN, 1994, p. 1), we would suggest that the core values of the Convention are significantly different from those that have shaped policy in the UK.

In particular, we would cite the following elements of the UN Convention which differentiate it from UK policy:

- children are visible and central
- children are *people* with inalienable human rights
- children have a right to special assistance
- children's own views should be given due weight
- greater emphasis on state rather than family responsibility.

Children's central position

Although it is the least tangible difference in emphasis, the fact that the UN Convention places children squarely in the centre of the picture is perhaps the most fundamental shift in perspective. The recognition of the child's position within the family is present in the Convention in the Preamble and again in Article 18. The latter outlines the duty of states to provide support for families to assist them in their child-rearing. But nothing in any part of the Convention detracts from the fact that it is the rights of the child that are at issue. As Bob Franklin (1989) has pointed out:

> It represents adult society's public declaration to children and young people that they are valued members of the community with shared civic obligations and deserving, as well as owing, respect to others. (p. 60)

Children are people

On the face of it, nothing could be more banal than the claim that children are people in their own right. In fact, the claim carries with it two important implications. The first is that children are valued for what they are now rather than what they might become in the future. In contrast with so much of the UK debate on policy for children there is no reference in the Convention to 'investment' as a justification for children's rights. The second is that children, as people, must be entitled to human rights on the same basis as everybody else. As Penelope Leach has argued, the phrase 'children's rights' is needed not because we are identifying a separate category of rights but because children have been excluded from those which are universally human (Leach, 1994, p. 204).

The importance of the stress on children's human rights, as opposed to other more frequently applied concepts such as their 'welfare' or 'needs', is that rights confer dignity and respect. As Freeman (1992) has suggested, 'because children have lacked the moral coinage of rights, it has been easy to brush their interests aside'. A good example of this is the case of corporal punishment. If children possess the same human rights as adults, then by definition they should enjoy the same protection from being hit by another person. Yet in the UK children have no protection from corporal punishment within the family – an issue we shall discuss further in Chapter 8.

Accepting children's rights as human beings does not mean that they should be treated as adults. The Convention differs from the more extreme children's rights perspectives which emphasise children's autonomy (examples include Farson, 1978; and Holt, 1975). Children's vulnerability is recognised with the consequent right of protection, including occasionally protection from the consequences of their own actions. Children are not, as Hafen (1977) put it, 'abandoned to their rights'.

A number of feminist writers have taken issue with the concept of 'rights', on the basis that it involves an individualistic and masculine view of the world (Gilligan, 1982). However, it is important to stress that the UN Convention, and the model of children's rights it espouses, goes a long way to meet this criticism in that it does not see children as autonomous individuals but rather promotes the fact that they have an important interdependent relationship with their family.

The emphasis (Article 3) on 'the best interests of the child' clearly preserves a strong element of paternalism within policy towards children. In this respect, the Convention does little to solve the dilemma of the conflict between the protection of children on the one hand and respect for their autonomy as human beings on the other. Indeed, some of its critics suggest that the Convention errs too far in the direction of children's welfare rather than their rights (Franklin, 1989).

We would agree with Freeman (1992), however, when he argues that protection and autonomy should not be seen as a dichotomy. Any programme of children's rights must recognise and reflect both principles. The virtue of a strong emphasis on children's rights to respect and dignity, which is central to the values underpinning the Convention, is that it confines paternalism, even if not totally eliminating it.

Children's right to special assistance

This principle, enshrined in the preamble to the Convention, was further endorsed at the 1990 World Summit for Children, where 159 nations assented to the proposition:

> That the lives and normal development of children should have first call on society's concerns and capacities and that children should be able to depend on that commitment in good times and in bad. (UN, 1990)

The idea that children should have first claim on society's resources is not a novel one. It would certainly be given lip service within UK social policy. The important point to stress, however, is that, by locating the principle within a framework of children's rights, it does not depend upon either a sentimental image of childhood or on an 'investment' motive. Children are entitled to have first claim because they are essentially victims of adults. As MacPherson (1987) put it: 'children are by definition weaker and more vulnerable than adults – their suffering is both greater and more clearly the responsibility of adults'.

The point is well underlined by the evidence, presented to UNICEF by Jonathan Bradshaw (1990), relating to the effects on children of social and economic policies in the UK during the 1980s. Bradshaw concluded: 'Children have borne the brunt of the changes that have occurred in the economic conditions, demographic structure and social policies of the UK.' Children's relative powerlessness to protect themselves from the consequences of decisions taken by adults justifies their right to special treatment. This is not a theme that is reflected either explicitly or implicitly in UK policy on children.

Giving weight to children's views

Article 12 of the Convention grants the child the right to have his/her views heard and be 'given due weight in accordance with the age and maturity of the child' and it is true that this principle has found its way into UK social policy and is enshrined in the Children Act 1989. As we have already indicated, though, the scope of the Children Act 1989 is relatively narrow. It certainly does not ensure that children's voices are heard in all areas of social policy. Indeed, the principle of giving the child a voice is remarkably muted in UK social policy – even in areas such as education.

The United Nations appears to have been unaware of the irony involved in producing the Convention without any reference to the views of children. But perhaps this serves to underline the fact that rights on paper are only a first small step in improving children's lives. Bringing about the institutional changes required to make the rights a reality is more problematical. This is particularly true when it comes to giving children a voice in matters that concern them. This is an issue we shall return to in our final chapter.

Emphasis on state rather than family responsibility

The Convention does, as we have already pointed out, recognise 'the responsibilities, rights and duties of parents' in relation to children (Article 5). The Preamble affirms the importance of the family to children's welfare – to an extent that some critics find unacceptable (Franklin, 1989). Nevertheless, there is a clear difference in emphasis, with regard to the respective responsibilities of family and state, between the Convention and the values underpinning UK policy. There is no sense in the Convention that the family is primarily a private institution. The responsibility of the state to support families caring for children is emphasised much more strongly.

The difference between the UN and UK philosophies is most clearly illustrated by comparing the approach to early years' childcare. This is cited specifically in the Convention as a service that should be provided as a right for all children of working parents, but

UK legislation and policy establishes no such right. Instead, as we shall discuss in Chapter 6, local authorities have a duty under the Children Act 1989 to provide day care for the much more restrictive category of 'children in need'.

Conclusion

There is considerable scope for debate as to whether in practice the UN Convention will advance the cause of children in the UK. Most of the sections dealing with substantive rights are necessarily unspecific and open to wide variation in interpretation. Children would have more to gain, perhaps, if the Convention were to open up greater discussion about the principles and core values that shape social policy in the UK. The contrast between the commitment to respect for the child, which is so central to the UN Convention, and the indifference to children which runs through UK policy is surely the key lesson.

Further reading

Quortrup *et al.* (1994) provides a wide-ranging, mainly sociological, discussion of contemporary childhood. Archard (1993) is a useful source for discussion of the relationship between state, family and child. The UN Convention on the Rights of the Child is contained in the appendix of Alston *et al.* (1992), which also contains some useful articles analysing theories of children's rights. Fox Harding (1996) examines the relationship between the family, the state and social policy.

2

Children in Britain Today

One child more or less in a family size of six is a change of seventeen per cent, but with an average family size of two it is fifty per cent. The erratic course taken by fertility since the 1930s has dominated the demography of the industrial world for the rest of the twentieth century and will dominate it well into the next through its effects on the age structure. (David Coleman, 1988, p. 48)

Introduction – population studies

Much of this book is concerned with the scope and effectiveness of social policies as these affect children's health and well-being – that is with the qualitative aspects of our present day child population. However, before we can address these issues it is first necessary to examine basic questions of quantity. In this chapter therefore we set out to provide an overview of the size and social diversity of Britain's child population.

Population is a continuous flow of people over time. Society in fact may be best conceptualised as a reservoir with a flow in of individuals at one end by virtue of birth and immigration, and an outflow at the other via death or migration. A population is therefore essentially a process of continuous metamorphosis and flux. Attempts to measure its total volume or particular dimensions freeze this process at a given point in time, so that we are left with what is in effect a snapshot view. If, of course, these 'snapshots' are taken regularly and reasonably frequently we may be able to obtain some indication of long-term trends taking place. But to state that a population is of a certain size and has certain characteristics, is merely to say that at the particular moment in time (for example, if we are using data gathered by the last census – on the night of

21 April 1991) the population was found to be of a particular size and to have certain attributes.

Indications of the size of the child population provide a case in point. We can state the number of children in Britain on 21 April 1991, but by the time this book is published the children indicated as being in the 0–4 age group will have moved into the age group above, while those in the 11–15 cohort will in fact have ceased to be classified as children at all. We assume in all this that the measurements of population taken in 1991 and subsequent estimates provide a reliable indication of the population process, and that consequently the child population will have been replenished in a numerically predictable way. We are thus in this section providing what are considered at the time of writing to be the best-informed estimates, but there is no complete certainty that these are wholly reliable and, as we indicate below, the suggestion that some sections of the population (and by inference, the size of their respective child populations) are under-recorded, if correct, has obvious policy implications.

Determinants of the size of the child population

Concern over population, its quantity and quality, has been one of the strongest motive forces in social policy relating to children; so population changes therefore have important consequences for the rights of children. Even relatively small fluctuations in the size of the child population have serious implications for governments, and are likely to incur wide social, political and economic effects. A large increase in the child population, as occurred in the twenty-five years following the end of the Second World War, posed immediate health and educational demands, which necessitated steady increases in resources to enable achieved levels of service and standards to be maintained. Yesterday's expanded child population moreover will be tomorrow's ageing population, with all the health and welfare implications this entails. Either way, an abnormally high (or low) birth rate for any period will alter the age group balance of the population.

Demographic analysis indicates that 'since 1750 the number of children in Britain has increased decade by decade, almost without exception' (Hair, 1982, p. 35). This steady increase has continued during the twentieth century, though more slowly, but it is likely, Professor Hair suggests, that we have now come to 'the end of a 200–year era of British history, an era of virtually continuous growth in child population' (ibid., p. 36).

Fertility

The major determinant of the size of the child population is the overall level of fertility of a society, and this is measured by *the total fertility rate* (TFR) – or *total period fertility rate* (TPFR), which refers to the average number of live births per female of a particular society or section thereof. The higher the fertility rate, clearly, the larger the child population will be. An average of 2.1 children per woman is defined as 'replacement level fertility', and a stable population size is only likely to result over time if the reproductive level of a society is around this rate (Craig, 1994, p. 20). However, for a period, increased life expectancy may offset any fall in fertility so that the total population size remains constant, or even continues to increase. In the case of the United Kingdom, at the time of writing, the population is projected to grow by a further 4.3 million by 2027, even though 'for all birth cohorts from 1950 onwards, their completed family sizes have been, or are projected to be, below replacement level' (ibid., p. 21).

In the past the main determinant of fertility trends was the control of marriage – its timing and avoidance. But while changes in the average age of marriage continue to affect fertility, the primary determinant during the twentieth century was the use of contraception (Coleman, 1988, p. 52).

It would, of course, be easy to assume from this that the widespread adoption of more efficient means of contraception in the post-war period and the increase in abortions since the passing of the 1967 Abortion Act have had a downward impact on the potential size of the child population in comparison with earlier periods. However, there are several reasons why this assumption has limited validity. For instance, in the case of abortion, there is no conclusive evidence as to the actual number of abortions prior to the 1967 Act – estimates range from 30 000 to 100 000 per year, so although there is circumstantial evidence of the widespread existence of the practice most went unrecorded (Coleman, 1988, p. 57). It is also impossible moreover to make a fair comparison between dissimilar historical periods – we are simply not comparing like with like. Contemporary survey evidence suggests, for example, that sexual intercourse has never been more popular and that 'sexual activity is certainly starting earlier' (Coleman and Salt, 1992, p. 121), so that, as one standard textbook notes, 'sex before marriage has become the norm' (Abercrombie, Warde *et al.*, 1994, p. 280). In contrast, pre-marital sexual relationships in Victorian times were likely to have been limited to a period shortly before marriage. Contraception of itself is neutral and, as David Coleman notes, 'merely allows family intentions to be translated more accurately into reality; it doesn't change these ideals or intentions' (1988, p. 57).

Neither contraception nor abortion can of themselves explain recent falls in fertility, which is a generalised phenomenon common to most Western societies. Although these may now be the principal means by which current fertility levels are achieved, they are what Coleman and Salt (1992) identify as 'proximate' or 'immediate determinants', and they cannot be the underlying causes for the significant changes in sexual mores and in the moral values underlying perceptions of family needs and interests that have taken place during the twentieth century.

Infant and perinatal mortality

A far more certain influence upon the actual size of the child population rather than on the underlying fertility rate is the dramatic decline of child mortality that has occurred during the twentieth century. Infant mortality refers to the number of infants who die within their first year of life, and the *infant mortality rate* (IMR) is the ratio of the total number of such deaths to every thousand live births in a given year.

The child population of the nineteenth and early twentieth centuries would of course have been far larger than it actually was had not the death rate of infants – and children in general – been so high. Thus during the twentieth century the decline in the size of the average family and in fertility has been partially offset by a marked and consistent decline in infant and perinatal mortality – from an infant mortality rate of 149 in 1900 to just over 6 in 1994 (CSO, 1996, p. 130). This subject is more properly an aspect of child health (see Chapter 4), but at this particular juncture it is worth noting that the changes in survival rates that have occurred during the twentieth

century have had a continuing impact on the size of the child
population.

Migration

The size of the British child population has always been affected by
patterns of migration. However, available data has been extremely
limited and has only accumulated slowly, partly as a consequence of
developments in British immigration policy since 1962. In terms of
the population totals involved, including children, we can conclude
from what evidence there is that Britain was a *net exporter* of people
over the century up to 1939 – especially to many of the countries
which now comprise the Commonwealth; that is to say that more
people left Great Britain for permanent settlement elsewhere than
entered from abroad to take up permanent residence here.

A similar pattern has been maintained since 1945 and only briefly
has the extent of inward migration been greater than the outward –
in the early 1960s, in 1973 and more recently between 1984 and 1987
(Coleman and Salt, 1992, p. 443). While there has been a steady
outflow of people from Britain throughout the period, what has
made the overall pattern of migration since the Second World War
markedly different from that of previous eras has been the settlement here of racially distinctive groups from the New Commonwealth Countries and Pakistan (NCWP). It is the non- European
racial distinctiveness of these groups that has raised serious racial
issues in British society during the past forty years.

This ethnic minority population comprises 5.7 per cent of the total
population of Great Britain. However, because of the age structure
of these groups and the differential fertility of the groups of Asian
origin, the child population of these racial minorities represents 9
per cent of the UK's present total child population. Some of the
characteristics of the ethnic minority child population are discussed
below, but it is worth noting in this present context that there is no
evidence that the population has been unduly inflated since 1945 by
the settlement here of 1.7 million Black British and Commonwealth
citizens and by the 1.3 million children born in Britain to these
communities. In economic terms, the original immigrants, who were
encouraged to enter this country to meet the labour shortages of the
1950s and 1960s, were in any case making up the labour deficit in the
British population caused by the low birth rate of the 1920s and

1930s. Thus in the context of the overall decline in national fertility, the presence of these minority group children, from a demographic point of view, has prevented and is continuing to prevent population decline and the more rapid emergence of an ageing population profile. Moreover, given the continuing loss of population via emigration since 1945, these children have only served to replace those children of emigrants from the UK who have been born elsewhere. The present generation of children of the racial minorities is in this way providing some youthful counterbalance to an ageing indigenous population, although whether British society can exploit to the full such youthful potential is a different matter.

Thus it is that the size of the present child population results from the interplay of complex and sometimes unpredictable forces created out of the currents of history; and these have deep roots, so that 'population growth rates do not just reflect today's vital rates. They also depend on those previous hundred years, which created the present age structure' (Coleman, 1988, p. 105).

Long-term fertility trends in the United Kingdom

The rapid expansion of population that accompanied the onset of industrialisation in the late eighteenth and early nineteenth centuries was associated with increased 'nuptiality' – that is earlier and an increasing number of marriages, especially in the centres of new industry (Wilson and Woods, 1991). Population during the nineteenth century in Britain was thus characterised by unusually large proportions of children and young people.

From the 1870s, however, 'a widespread and remarkably homogeneous decline set in, leading to replacement level fertility by the 1930s' (ibid, p. 399). By 1900 therefore the decline in the size of the average family had already become well established – from 5.8 children in 1870 to 3.4 in 1900.

Examination of the fertility rates for the twentieth century reveals that these have fluctuated at lower levels throughout, though with rises following both world wars. Thus for much of the century the TFR has hovered slightly above or slightly below the replacement level of 2.1, though since the 1970s it has fallen to its present 1.75 (1994). The annual numbers of live births and the TFR since 1944 are indicated in Figures 2.1 and 2.2.

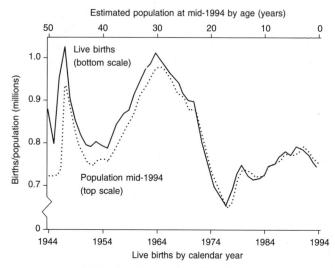

Figure 2.1 United Kingdom live births, 1944–94 and estimated population,
            mid-1994

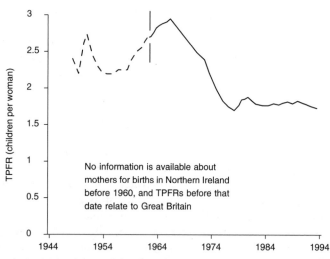

Figure 2.2 Total period fertility rate (TPFR) in the United Kingdom,
            1944–94

Source for both figures: Office for National Statistics (1996), pp. 7–8;
Crown copyright 1996. Reproduced by permission of The Controller of
HMSO and The Office for National Statistics.

The most recent period when the birth rate rose above replacement level was the baby boom period from the early 1950s to the late 1960s. The fertility rate peaked in 1964 in the UK with a TFR of 2.94 (Coleman, 1988, p. 49). This rise was associated with a noticeable increase in the prevalence of marriage and with earlier marriage. Perhaps surprisingly, the time lapse between marriage and the birth of a first child increased relatively little during the 1950s and 1960s – from 18 to 20 months – in comparison with the period 1900–9, in spite of the widespread adoption of family planning. At the same time the interval between the first birth and the last birth has been narrowing, especially for marriages since 1951.

Since the early 1970s, there have been marked changes from the early post-war patterns of marriage and fertility. The interval between marriage and the birth of the first child had widened to 28 months by 1985. Moreover, whereas in the first half of the period since 1945 women tended to complete their families within the first ten years of marriage, the trend in this second 25-year period is in the opposite direction. More women are delaying childbearing often until well into their thirties, and far more children are being born to unmarried couples and within 'reconstituted' families, while teenage births overall are less prevalent. Any possible revival in fertility since the low point of 1977 (1.69) has been largely due to older women and women who already had two children (including remarried women), who together have made up much of this recent increase (Coleman, 1988, p. 56).

The child population

So just how many children are there, and how many can we predict in the immediate future? Table 2.1 provides a breakdown of the child population figures for the period 1961–2001.

As the table indicates, since the end of the 1970s the numbers of children in each of the year groupings up to the age of 10 have been relatively constant; and once the children born during the bulge of the 1960s have reached 15 this has also become true of children in the adolescent years of 11–15. Since 1971 the number of live births has remained constant at about three-quarters of a million per annum. Current projections suggest that something of the order of

Table 2.1 Number of children, United Kingdom, by age and gender[1] (000s)

					All aged under 16		
	Under 1	1–4	5–10	11–15	Boys	Girls	Total
1961	915	3 359	4 585	4 289	6 737	6 410	13 147
1971	899	3 654	5 580	4 124	7 318	6 938	14 257
1981	730	2 725	4 553	4 533	6 438	6 103	12 541
1991	794	3 091	4 409	3 444	6 032	5 707	11 739
1992	787	3 123	4 434	3 503	6 083	5 764	11 847
2001	750	3 094	4 680	3 873	6 360	6 037	12 398

Note: 1. Data for 1961–92 are mid-year estimates; data for 2001 are 1992-based projections

Source: Central Statistical Office (1994), p. 7; Crown copyright 1994. Reproduced by permission of The Controller of HMSO and The Office for National Statistics.

700 000 live births will occur annually well into the twenty-first century (to 2031); thereafter they are predicted to fall to some 650 000. This means, therefore, that the numbers of children in each year of childhood are now roughly equal and likely to remain so. Thus if future projections in the event prove to have been reasonably accurate, social policy decisions can certainly be based on constant numbers of children.

In 1901 children under the age of 15 represented 32 per cent of the population, and in that year there were nearly 1.1 million live births for a total population of 38 million, so that live births as a proportion of the population represented 2.9 per cent of the total population at that time. By contrast, in 1994 there were 751 000 live births representing 1.3 per cent of a total population of 58.4 million. Thus in 1971, even at the end of the baby boom of the 1950s and 1960s, the 14.3 million children under the age of 16 represented no more than 25.5 per cent of the total population. Since then the numbers of children under 16 have fallen to 12.25 million, representing 21 per cent of the population (CSO, 1996, p. 39). If life expectancy had not grown throughout the century (that is, had the mortality rate not declined), these figures would have presaged an overall decline in the size of the population.

The geographical distribution of the child population

The figures above for the total child population, indicative as they may be in certain respects, do not tell us how children are distributed geographically, i.e. where they actually live; and this has important implications for social policy as well as for the life chances of children.

While national statistics have not focused directly on this question, any examination of such statistics reveals considerable geographical variation in the number of children growing up in particular regions and localities.

There have long been national differences in the UK between Northern Ireland, Scotland, and England and Wales. Until 1983 the birth rate in Scotland remained consistently higher than in England and Wales. However, because of a similarly consistent higher death rate, the natural increase of population in England and Wales has been higher than in Scotland since 1945. What this has meant is that Scotland has had fewer old people but a slightly higher proportion of children throughout this century (Coleman, 1988, pp. 42–3).

Northern Ireland has had a continuing higher birth rate, so that the current age profile is somewhat different from that of the rest of the UK. The 1993 birth rate figure of 15.3 live births per 1000 population is significantly higher than the 13.1, 12.6 and 12.4 recorded for the same year for England, Wales and Scotland respectively (OPCS, 1995, p. xviii). In consequence, Northern Ireland's age profile is untypical of the British norm. Although the province now contains a population bulge of young adults resulting from the high birthrate of the 1950s and 1960s, it also possesses at present a proportionately larger child population than other UK regions.

Regional and intra-regional variations

When the regional distribution of children – Northern Ireland apart – is examined, there appear to be few differences. However when we examine differences between sub-regional areas in the proportional size of their various child populations, some significant contrasts appear. The 1991 Census identified a number of demographic differences between local areas. These included, for example, the percentages of households in a district with (a) single parents; (b) at least one child aged under 5; and (c) at least three children aged under 16.

Geographical differences in the spatial distribution of the child population do have serious policy implications. In Newham and Tamworth, for example, approximately one household in six was shown to be rearing a child under 5, while in Christchurch, and Kensington and Chelsea only one household in twelve was doing so; and whereas in Blackburn, Luton, and Shetland one in thirteen households contained at least three children under 16, the comparable figure for Hove was 1 in 40 (OPCS, 1993, p. 4).

In the absence of closer analyses of age groupings by local authority it is difficult to discern any particular national pattern. Although as the evidence we adduce below indicates, there is a considerable concentration – one might more correctly say 'ghettoisation' – of ethnic minority children and single-parent families in certain urban metropolitan districts. David Coleman and John Salt also note in passing when they describe the concentrations of the elderly in coastal areas, that 'The young, too, display their own distribution characteristics', and that there is a 'massive concentration of 25–44 year olds to the north and west of London' (Coleman and Salt, 1992, p. 89). These are, of course, precisely the age groups of adults most likely to be bearing and rearing young children.

Gordon and Forrest's analysis of the 1991 census data provides some interesting evidence that elaborates on Coleman and Salt's point about the geographical distribution of children in England and Wales. They found a higher incidence of 'young families' – that is, with heads of households in the 16–34 age group – in northern industrial districts, 'with a band of districts running from Merseyside and Greater Manchester across to Humberside, Tyne and Wear in the north and with rural districts in Cumbria, Northumberland and Cornwall'. Older families – that is, with heads of household aged 35–54 – were found to be more typical in 'mixed urban/rural and new town districts in the commuter belt around London' (Gordon and Forrest, 1995, pp. 43, 45).

The children of ethnic minority groups

Question 11 on the 1991 Census form asked respondents to identify themselves as either 'white' or belonging to one of eight other non-white ethnic groups. Additionally, two of the eight groups so listed, 'black – other' and 'any other ethnic group', invited the respondent to describe their particular ethnicity.

Clearly, 'ethnic group' is here identified as being synonymous with racial group. But we should note that this association is of relative recent origin. Earlier studies of ethnic diversity in the UK identified a number of 'white' minorities of European, New World or Old Commonwealth origins (see, for example, Krausz, 1971; Watson, 1977). Racial minorities apart, the UK's Irish community still represents one of the largest culturally distinct groups in this country; some 559 000 people born in Eire were recorded as living in the UK by the 1987 Labour Force Survey. This survey also identified 110 000 United States citizens living in Britain, as well as sizeable communities from East European, Australasian and EU countries. However, in view of the 1991 Census evidence derived from their Question 11, we are restricting analysis in this section solely to those racially distinct ethnic minorities identified by the Census.

Fertility and the age structure of ethnic minorities

The age distribution of the ethnic groups identified in the 1991 Census is presented in Table 2.2. What is immediately striking from this data is the overall youthfulness of these communities. Almost a third of their total populations (32.6 per cent) comprise children and adolescents under the age of 16, and the proportions of children in the Pakistani and Bangladeshi groups are even larger. Conversely, these communities contain very few people in older age groups.

With regard to their fertility, as Coleman and Salt note, 'sparse data make the fertility of ethnic minorities difficult to analyse. Moreover, the tempo and quantum of their family building is changing fast and that makes it difficult to trust conventional summary measures' (1992, p. 508).

The available data indicates, however, that the fertility rates for women born in the New Commonwealth and Pakistan but whose own children were born in England and Wales during the period 1971–87 have varied considerably between the different minorities. The rate for West Indian women at 1.9 is very close to the national average of 1.75. For women from South Asia, however, the rate has

Table 2.2 Population, Great Britain, by ethnic group and age; Spring 1995
(percentages)

	Under 16	16–29	30–44	45–59	60 and over	All ages (=100%) (000s)
Ethnic minority group						
Black[1]	29.0	25.5	27.0	11.3	7.2	869
Indian	25.3	26.0	25.5	16.0	7.2	844
Pakistani/Bangladeshi	40.6	26.4	19.4	9.3	4.3	725
Other[2]	37.2	23.3	26.0	9.6	3.9	773
All ethnic minority						
groups	32.6	25.3	24.6	11.7	5.8	3 211
White	20.1	19.0	21.6	18.3	20.9	52 844
All ethnic groups[3]	20.9	19.4	21.8	18.0	20.1	56 072

1. Includes Caribbean, African and other Black people of non-mixed origin.
2. Includes Chinese, other ethnic minority groups of non-mixed origin, and those of mixed origin.
3. Includes ethnic groups not stated.

Source: Central Statistical Office (1996), p. 40; Crown copyright 1996. Reproduced by permission of The Controller of HMSO and The Office for National Statistics.

been very much higher although more recent data indicates, 'an overall decline to an average just below 3. But among the predominantly Muslim Pakistanis and Bangladeshis the TFR is still over 5' (Coleman and Salt, p. 509).

The present fertility patterns of British black minorities, though at different stages according to the timing and patterns of the particular migration, thus reflect continuing processes of acculturation and the transition from often non-industrial, non-urban backgrounds to the reverse in contemporary Britain. Such evidence of current demographic trends among these groups provides some indication that these communities are gradually adopting the low fertility norms of the host society. Inevitably however these minorities have for the present disproportionately large child populations.

The geographical concentration of the ethnic minority population

The 1991 Census also revealed that the minority communities are heavily concentrated in a limited number of geographical areas – particularly in the more urbanised parts of the country, especially London and the West Midlands. The 1991 census indicates that 44.6 per cent of the total non-white population live in Greater London, compared to only 10.3 per cent of the white ethnic group, while 15 per cent of the non-white population live in the West Midlands, although this area contains only 5 per cent of the country's total population (Owen, 1994, p. 23).

The degree of concentration in London is even more marked for certain groups and in certain districts than the above figure might suggest. Some 78 per cent of the Black African population live in the capital, as do 59 per cent of the Black Caribbean community, and 54 per cent of Bangladeshis. Only the Pakistani community is more evenly distributed through the English industrial regions.

Certain London boroughs have large settlements of minority groups with high numbers of children because of the age structures of these communities. London's children therefore come disproportionately from the racial minorities, though they are not evenly distributed across the capital. For example, although 20 per cent of the population of Greater London is from the ethnic minorities, only 5.5 and 4.7 per cent respectively of the populations of Richmond upon Thames and Bromley come from these groups; whereas well over a third of the inhabitants – large numbers of them children – of the boroughs of Brent, Newham and Tower Hamlets hail from racial minority backgrounds.

Detailed analysis at the national level certainly confirms that the situation in other parts of the country is similar to that in London. Thus David Owen, writing in a recent edition of *Population Trends*, stresses that because the ten ethnic groups identified by the 1991 Census each have their own distinctive geographical distributions, 'even where these groups do form a significant part of a local population, localities will vary in the number and magnitude of ethnic groups represented' (Owen, 1994, p. 25). This study concludes that the most ethnically diverse districts outside of London are Birmingham, Leicester, Slough and Luton. However, at the local ward level it is also noted that, over three quarters of the white population live in wards where the percentage of ethnic minority groups is below the GB average. There is a dramatic contrast with ethnic minority groups, for most of whom the position is almost reversed; three quarters of their population live in wards with more than the national average percentage of ethnic minority groups. (Owen, 1994, p. 28)

Clearly, for the present generation of children the experience of growing up in a supposedly multiracial and multiethnic society must be a very partial and segregated one.

Children growing up in lone-parent families

One group of children currently the focus of considerable popular and political concern are those who are growing up in single-parent households, nine out of ten of which are headed by women. Single-parenthood is of course not a new phenomenon, though compared to 1900, today's principal causes are very different – divorce and separation rather than the death of a parent. (It should also not be forgotten that two generations were massively affected by the absence and often loss or disablement of fathers in the two world wars.)

As a proportion of all households, the conventional family of two married parents with their natural offspring has declined since the 1960s from 38 to 25 per cent; and there has been in the same period a steady increase in the number of households containing only one adult caring for dependent children, from 2 per cent in 1961 to the present 7 per cent. Thus of all households with dependent children, 22 per cent are now headed by lone parents – 20 per cent by women and 2 per cent by men – which when translated into actual numbers means that there are approximately 1.5 million lone-parent families in Britain who are between them rearing 2.3 million children (CSO, 1996, p. 54).

Despite the post-1986 increase in the 'single mother' category (that is, women who have 'never married'), marital breakdown remains the commonest cause of single parenthood. Divorced and separated mothers together in 1992 constituted 11 per cent of all families with dependent children.

Births outside marriage

These recent increases in the numbers of lone parent families should not thus be seen as a direct and straightforward consequence of an increase in the numbers of children born to 'never married mothers'. It is true that the incidence of births outside marriage has been growing since the 1950s (although there had previously been wartime bulges during both the First and Second World Wars). 'Illegitimacy' (as it was previously termed until the passing of the Family Law Reform Act in 1987), however, accounted for no more than 5 per cent of live births until the 1950s; since then births outside marriage have risen to over 30 per cent of all births. However, a large proportion of these births appear to be occurring within stable relationships, with 55 per cent being registered jointly by mothers and fathers (with different surnames) living at the same address; a further 21 per cent are registered jointly by both parents living at different addresses; while only 24 per cent are reported as being registered solely by one parent (CSO, 1994, p. 9).

The incidence of births to teenage mothers

To judge from the comments of some politicians, even cabinet ministers, Britain's contemporary social ills are attributable in part at least to the birth of children out of wedlock to teenage mothers. So what, then, are the facts?

Contrary to popular misconception, teenage births are in general rarer now than in the 1960s and 1970s. Coleman's calculation is that although there was some increase in births outside marriage to teenage mothers between 1975 and 1985, these amounted to only an additional 2000 registered singly by the mother (Coleman, 1988, p. 56).

With the trend towards earlier marriage and the growing popularity of marriage in the immediate post-war years, there was a steady increase in the total number of teenage births between 1938 and 1960; this total peaked in 1966 at 87 000 and declined to 58 000 in 1976, at which level it has remained relatively constant ever since. Since the 1960s the number of teenage births within marriage has fallen sharply, and these are now only approximately a third of the 1966 level. Commensurately the number of births to unmarried teenage mothers has risen considerably, and these now represent two out of three of all births to teenage mothers. However, 57 per cent of these births were registered by both parents, so that, as already noted above, the actual increase in the number of births of children to teenage mothers outside a stable partnership has increased very little. As Coleman comments, 'a great part of these births can be regarded as a replacement for earlier marital fidelity' (Coleman, 1988, p. 62).

Single-parenthood among ethnic minorities

The higher fertility rates, especially among groups of Asian origin, have already been discussed. With regard to the incidence of single-parenthood among black minorities there are marked contrasts between the West Indian and the Pakistani and Bangladeshi communities.

The Asian minorities stand apart from the host population. Among these groups, 'marriage is typically early and universal, and among Asians usually arranged; fertility outside of formal marriage is typically very low. Neither, in many of these cultures is there a tradition of nuclear families living in separate households after marriage – various kinds of extended family connections usually prevail creating large household sizes' (Coleman, 1988, p. 97). In 1984–6, 45 per cent of Pakistani and Bangladeshi men in the 16–29 age group were married, as were 76 per cent of women in the same age grouping; the comparable British figures for these years was 29 per cent and 45 per cent, respectively (Coleman and Salt, 1992, p. 512).

In contrast, the West Indian community 'breaks most of these generalisations. One-parent families and visiting relationships are normal' (Coleman, 1988, p. 97). Thus during the 1980s whereas only 3 per cent of Indian, Pakistani and Bangladeshi households were headed by a lone parent with dependent children, nearly half the births in England and Wales to West Indian born mothers were outside formal marriage (Coleman and Salt, 1992, p. 509).

The geographical concentration of lone parent households

The growing housing segregation of the population and the implications for children are discussed in Chapter 5, but it is perhaps worth recording here that lone parents are one of the social categories that have tended to become in recent years geographically concentrated.

There are significant regional differences in the distribution of lone-parent families, ranging along a continuum from 30 per cent of all families with dependent children in the North West and 28 per cent in Greater London, to East Anglia with 14 per cent (CSO, 1996, p. 55).

But the census evidence also reveals that the representation of single-parent households varies considerably between different local authority areas. So, for example, of all inner London households, 6.4 per cent are headed by a lone parent with dependent children under 16. Yet in Southwark and Hackney, 8.2 and 8.4 per cent respectively of households are headed by lone parents, whereas the comparable figure for Westminster is 3.7 per cent. While nationally the degree of concentration of single parents in particular local authorities varies from 9 per cent of all households in Knowsley on Merseyside and 8.6 per cent in Manchester to 1.5 per cent for Mole Valley, and 1.7 per cent in Derbyshire Dales (Forrest and Gordon, 1993, p. 29; OPCS, 1993, p. 4).

'Reconstituted' families

A growing number of today's children are also likely to be living in, or to be born into 'reconstituted families' – that is, into families based on remarriage or a new partnership following the break-up or dissolution of an earlier marriage or partner relationship for one or both of the partners in the new pairing.

Recent analysis based on the General Household and Omnibus survey data suggests that there were 500 000 stepfamilies in Great Britain in 1991 – that is around 1 in 15 (or 7 per cent) of all families. These stepfamilies, moreover, were found to contain about 800 000 dependent stepchildren and a further 300 000 dependent natural children. Thus there now exists a complex range of stepfamily situations, so that an increasing number of children are moving through a sequence of single-parent and related stepfamily situations during their childhoods. It is further predicted, on the assumption that the trends observed in 1991–2 remain constant, that 5.5 per cent of all children will become the stepchildren of a married couple and

6.7 per cent the stepchildren of a cohabiting couple at some stage
before reaching their sixteenth birthday (Haskey, 1994, p. 24).

Taking single-parent families and stepfamilies together, Clark
(1992) predicts that in the future, based on current trends, up to
half the child population will be growing up in one kind or another
of non-traditional family milieu. Yet even if this is the case we might
note in concluding this section that Laslett (1977) in his historical
study of nineteen English communities in the period 1595–1811
found that 16 per cent of all children were orphans living with
one parent only (see Murphy and Berrington, 1993). In earlier
periods of the twentieth century much smaller proportions of
children were living in lone-parent families than are at present,
but if the above historical evidence is valid, then the variations in the
contemporary familial structures within which children are growing
up today represent more a reversion to times past than any
unprecedented disintegration of the family caused by the forces of
modernisation of the late twentieth century.

Other child minorities

The diversity of household type and circumstance within which
British children are currently growing up is greater than the data
presented in this chapter has indicated. We thus conclude the
chapter with some mention of three additional, though smaller,
child minorities.

Children with disabilities

An OPCS Survey of Disability published in 1989 estimated that
360 000 children were suffering from some degree of disability at
that time (OPCS, 1989). This represents a rate of 32 per 1000
children under 16, which is approximately 3 per cent of all children.
The OPCS survey classified the degree of disability on a scale from 1
to 10 (10 being the most severe). According to this classification,
approximately half the children (174 000) came in the top half of the
scale (that is, have more serious disabilities), with the remainder
(186 000) coming in the lower ranges and having less severe forms of
disablement).

In view of these figures it is perhaps surprising that Department of Health figures for 1993 show that only 27 717 children 'were registered as 'substantially or permanently handicapped' by Social Service Departments in England' (NCH Action For Children, 1995, p. 28). The vast majority of disabled children live in the community in their own homes. In fact the 1989 OPCS survey found that only 5 565 children (or 1.5 per cent of all disabled children) were at that time living in communal establishments. This means, of course, that although there may be a limited overlap between disabled children and those children living in institutions, the latter are growing up in communal situations for the most part for reasons other than disability (see Chapter 8 below).

The children of refugees

In comparison with its partners in the European Union, Britain in recent years has accepted relatively few refugees, either for a limited stay or for permanent residence. Britain as a stable democracy has a long history of providing refuge for persecuted minorities, which stretches back to the influx of Huguenots in the seventeenth century. In the post-war period, among others, we have seen groups of refugees fleeing Communist repression in Hungary and Czechoslovakia, and 27 000 Ugandan Asians who were expelled by the Amin government in 1972–3.

All Western countries have received growing numbers of applications over recent years from asylum seekers, although the number of applications received by the UK has been relatively small compared to those received by other European countries, especially by Germany, France and Sweden. The United Nations High Commission for Refugees calculates that there were more than a million applications for asylum to European countries during the 1980s.

It is, however, impossible to say at any given time just how many refugees are resident in the UK, and how many households these represent. The UN High Commission for Refugees suggests a figure of 140 000, but, as Coleman and Salt comment, 'it is unknown who is included in the figure' (1992, p. 464). Most of those admitted in the period 1980–7 as 'refugees' came from seven countries: Iran, Iraq, Sri Lanka, Poland, Ghana, Ethiopia and Uganda. Figures for 1992 indicate that the principal source of asylum seekers during 1992 was the former Yugoslavia, but of the 22 370 applications received by the Home Office for UK asylum during 1993, 46 per cent came from Africa; and of the total number of applications either accepted for refugee status or granted exceptional leave (12715) only 22 per cent were jointly from Europe and the Americas (CSO, 1995a, p. 25).

Given these complex changing patterns of international migration (and persecution), it is difficult to estimate the numbers of children involved. According to the Refugee Council, there were 23500 refugee children attending British schools in March 1994, 85 per cent of whom were thought to be living in Greater London: 'The largest communities were Somalis, Sri Lankan Tamils, Zaireans and Turkish Kurds' (Rutter, 1994, p. 45). Individual London schools certainly reflect the diversity of the refugee population; thus 54 refugee children, representing 20 per cent of the total school roll, were in 1993 attending Anson Primary School in the London Borough of Brent. These children came mostly from Iran, Iraq, Somalia and Afghanistan, but no fewer than 34 different home languages were being spoken by the children attending this school (ibid, p. 54).

More generally some groups will share English as their first language with the host community; many others will not. The degree of integration will be exceedingly varied, with earlier groups having largely been assimilated within mainstream society. More recent arrivals, however, will be experiencing the trauma of culture shock and probably economic hardship, all of which may be exacerbated according to language, race and religion, and with the children sharing such hardships and difficulties to a greater or lesser extent.

Traveller children

The term 'Traveller' is an umbrella term used officially (by the Department for Education and Employment (DfEE), for example) to denote a number of diverse groups within the population who are associated with a nomadic lifestyle or who have been so in the past. Such groups include Gypsy travellers, fairground or showground people, circus families, bargees and other families living on boats, and 'New Travellers' or, as better known to the media, 'New Age Travellers'. These groups have their own distinctive lifestyles and traditions, but there may well be a considerable overlap and interchange between them.

Estimates as to the numbers of children belonging to these communities are notoriously difficult to obtain and likely to be unreliable. The 1996 OFSTED (Office for Standards in Education) report, *The Education of Travelling Children*, notes the limited nature of current knowledge of the child population of Travellers. Since 1970, the Department of the Environment has undertaken twice-yearly counts of Gypsy Traveller caravans; and that undertaken in July 1994 recorded the existence of 12595 such caravans. This, however, is considered to be an underestimate of the number of inhabited caravans and excludes 'at least two numerically significant Traveller communities' (who do not reside in mobile accommodation).

Under Section 210 of the 1988 Education Reform Act, local education authorities can apply for specific grants from the DfEE towards the additional costs of meeting the educational needs of Traveller children. LEAs in receipt of these grants are required to produce an annual report for the DfEE. Analysis of such reports covering 73 projects for the year 1994–5, revealed a total of 26408 Traveller children between the ages of 5 and 16 residing in or resorting to the areas of eighty-two LEAs. A similarly derived estimate of the number of children under 5 suggested there are nearly 7000 in these LEA areas. Noting that twenty-five LEAs did not receive grants for Traveller children and other possible limitations upon the coverage of this data, OFSTED concludes that a more realistic estimate of the total number of Traveller children under the age of 16 would be of the order of 50000 (OFSTED, 1996, p. 16).

The seasonal patterns of movement and the unpredictability of the mobility of certain of these groups makes it impossible to provide any precise information on the geographical location of Traveller children. Locally based surveys and reports would appear to indicate that these communities form clusters in different parts of the country, but that such groupings are variable in size and location according to the uncertainties of site availability, police action and local residents' negative reactions.

For example, the 1993 Gypsy Survey of sixty-three Gypsy families undertaken across the Northern region under the auspices of the Northern Gypsy Council, found that common problems included a lack of available sites and a denial of access to a site place in the region. Similarly, the Children's Society report, *Out of Site, Out of Mind*, based on interviews conducted in Somerset and South Avon with ninety-eight New Age Travellers, found that two-thirds 'had been forced into travelling' because of their previous circumstances, especially homelessness. However the Travellers were already finding it difficult to obtain secure sites, even though as the survey revealed thirty-eight children were present on the sites where the interviews were held, and three of the female interviewees were pregnant. The authors conclude that the then impending 1993 Criminal Justice and Public Order legislation would only serve to increase the number of evictions and make any normal living even less secure than it was already for both adults and children (Davis *et al.*, 1994, p. 14).

By way of contrast, on the other side of the country in Essex and neighbouring counties there would seem to be a centuries'-long tradition of Gypsy and Traveller presence and settlement. In 1990 an HMI survey, *The Educational Provision for Traveller Children in Essex*, found 391 Traveller children registered with schools in the county; and a further 589 children not registered with schools who were living on sixty-two unauthorised sites. These latter children had been visited during the preceding year by two mobile teaching units (DES, 1991).

As in the case of refugee children, the children living in Traveller communities are growing up under widely differing circumstances. Yet their relative invisibility in comparison with the majority of British children may make their needs all the more acute and at the same time often, by default, overlooked.

The changing experience of childhood since 1945

Since 1945 there have been two partly contrasting demographic phases that have determined the size of the contemporary child population and the experience of childhood.

From 1945 to 1970, against a background of full employment, rising real wages and consequently rising living standards, and of growing state-provided health and welfare services, there occurred a steady growth in the size of the child population. This was associated with earlier marriage and an increase in the number of births to married teenage women – while marriage itself appeared ever more popular with a higher proportion of people of both sexes marrying and a high rate of remarriage (approximately 75 per cent) following the break-up of a previous marriage.

Children, therefore, during these early post-war years were likely to have youthful parents, to have one or two siblings, and for these to be born in relatively close succession following the first birth. They were also likely to be part of an expanding school population, with all the pressures on educational and other welfare resources this may have entailed.

What this demographic pattern meant for parenting was that parents married young and generally bore children in the early years of marriage. Inevitably, with increased life expectancy, this child-rearing phase was completed by the time most couples had reached their mid-forties, so that for women in particular quite new vistas of active life lay before them in early middle age. Richard Titmuss eloquently summed up this new post-war situation when he wrote in 1958:

> the typical working-class mother of the 1890s, married in her teens or early twenties and experiencing ten pregnancies, spent about fifteen years in a state of pregnancy and in nursing a child for the first year of its life. She was tied, for this period of time, to the wheel of childbearing. Today, for the typical mother, the time so spent would be about four years. (1958, p. 91)

In the second phase of the post-war period – from about 1970 – rather different trends have manifested themselves: later marriage and a longer delay before the birth of a first child; increased 'common-law' marriage; a growing incidence of divorce and separation and therefore of single-parenthood and remarriage; a decline in births to teenage mothers; and a growing number of women of child-bearing age who are choosing not to have children. These are the demographic characteristics since the 1970s that have shaped the size of the present day child population, and the contemporary experience of childhood and parenthood.

However, throughout the whole post-war era the consolidation of the small nuclear family has continued and there has been a continuing decline in the number of large families. Children born in the late 1990s therefore are typically born as a member of a one- or two-child family (44 per cent being born as the first or second sibling of a two-child family, and 23 per cent as the only child, though with 24 per cent born as one of three or more siblings).

Those born as members of a two-child family are likely to be born close together, although their parents are likely to be somewhat older than those of the previous generation and the mother and father are less likely to be legally married. Children in the late 1990s, moreover, are likely to be growing up in a greater variety of family situations.

Since the 1960s there have been changes in sexual mores – changes that appear to be general to a varying extent throughout the Western world. Certainly, in the particular instance of Britain, since the early 1970s, with a rising age of marriage, the incidence and duration of cohabitation has increased markedly, which is consistent with the current prevalence, noted above, of the joint registration of children at birth by unmarried parents.

Indeed, it is suggested that cohabitation prior to marriage is becoming 'normal'. Thus whereas 5 per cent of women married in the 1950s said they had lived together with their husbands before marriage, by the late 1980s half of all couples marrying for the first time, and three-quarters of those marrying for the second time, reported having previously cohabited. In addition, it is suggested that, 'couples are increasingly choosing not to marry before having children, even if they may marry later' (Abercrombie *et al.*, 1994, pp. 279–8).

Conclusion

Maintaining a balanced age structure in the future

Data on the size of the present child population and future projections of this suggest that the United Kingdom has reached some kind of population equilibrium with regard to its child population. However, we note David Coleman's point that the chief characteristic of contemporary reproductive processes is their volatility, and it may well be that current economic and social developments in the United Kingdom threaten the present reproductive equilibrium. Indeed alarm bells are already being sounded in the press at the greater number of women who are predicted to remain childless in the future – from 13 per cent of women born in 1949, to 20 per cent or more of those born since 1964. If this prediction proves to be accurate, the British population will begin a downward trend from the year 2025, possibly for the first time since the Black Death in 1347–51 (ONS, 1996).

Of course there are those who might argue – on environmental grounds, for example – that a decline in the size of the British population is desirable; but this would no doubt present other problems such as a more rapid ageing of the population, and a potential loss of social vitality and a blunting of the forces of youth for change and progress; and perhaps also the dominance of an unhealthy political conservatism in a society top heavy with the elderly.

As has already been emphasised, the recent fall in the numbers of children being born means there are now at any given moment fewer adults involved in parenting and child-rearing; and this may already be lessening the social and political influence of parents as citizens in general, and hence be leading to a weakening of our society's concerns for the needs – and perhaps the rights – of children. The smaller contemporary family also means that the experience of parenthood is now limited to fewer years for most parents, and this period for a growing number of parents may now be no more than a relatively brief interlude during an extended lifespan focused more significantly – for both mothers and fathers – upon careers, adult relationships and the opportunities of extended retirement. Children themselves, unlike their counterparts in the Victorian era, may grow up in relative isolation from other children and largely insulated from the adult crises of normal humanity. And it might also mean fewer adults having any experience at all of the bearing and rearing of children.

The international context

The more recent trends occurring in the United Kingdom mirror broad international population developments. Similar trends are also affecting developing countries, so it is now widely accepted that 'fertility declines appreciably and probably irreversibly as traditional, non industrial, usually agrarian societies are transformed by modernisation or development into bureaucratic urban societies' (Jones, 1981, p. 88). This trend has been a general one across the developed world so that even a traditional non-Western society like Japan saw in the 1950s 'the most concentrated fertility reduction ever achieved in the world' (ibid., p. 107). Social class differences in fertility moreover have diminished, and the rise in fertility in the UK noted between 1950 and 1970 was widely mirrored in other developed societies, as also has been the decline since the late 1960s. The formative influences in this country on family size and structure, which consequently determine the size of the current child population, appear to be part of global population developments. Differences in these trends between the UK and other advanced societies thus represent no more than variations on a theme rather than startling – and undesirable – differences in specifically British familial mores, fertility patterns and child-rearing experiences.

The experience of childhood at the end of the twentieth century compared to its beginning has thus been transformed, and even in the more limited period since 1945 considerable changes have continued to take place. No developed nation can now take for granted a large child population to provide for its future manpower – and womanpower – needs with abundance. Nor can any government ignore the welfare needs of a country's children, or treat them with profligate disdain simply because children represent such a large proportion of the population.

Children in all the developed countries are now a more limited, precious resource, and each generation of children may well be called upon in turn to carry a heavier burden of aged dependents. This could behove any government to implement social policies for children with concern and generosity. But on the other hand, parents themselves, as an interest group, may be far less influential politically than they were during periods of high birth rate. This circumstance might equally tempt governments to ignore the specific policy needs of the young. Either way, it is clear that there are difficult and conflicting choices to be made. In the following chapters we examine just what policy choices *are* being made at the present time and how Britain's children are faring in key areas of welfare-state provision.

Further reading

Data on children is contained in *Social Trends* and the NCH's *Factfile* (both published annually). The most comprehensive analysis of post-war demographic change is Coleman and Salt (1992). Accounts of racial minorities and lone parents can be found in Abercrombie *et al.* (1994). David Mason (1995), Jill Rutter (1994) and OFSTED (1996) provide, respectively, accounts of ethnic minority, refugee and Traveller children.

3

Childhood and Poverty

State parties recognise the right of every child to a standard of living adequate for the child's physical, mental, spiritual, moral and social development. (UN Convention, Article 27)

Introduction

The child's right to an adequate standard of living is the most fundamental of all rights in a world where, according to the World Health Organisation's annual report for 1995:

Every year in the developing world 12.2 million children under five die, most of them from causes which could be prevented for just a few U.S. cents per child. They die largely because of world indifference but most of all they die because they are poor. (WHO, 1995)

Not surprisingly in the face of such devastating statistics, in the UK today, as elsewhere in the developed world, the imagery of child poverty is dominated by the suffering of dying children in developing nations. Alternatively, it is given a nineteenth-century backcloth through the children who populate the novels of Charles Dickens, Charles Kingsley and others. Either way, the phrase 'child poverty' is much less likely to evoke images of contemporary childhood in the UK. Indeed, it has been a striking feature of UK policy towards children for most of the post war period that poverty has been barely acknowledged, either officially or by the public at large.

Nowhere is this more obviously the case than in the UK government's First Report to the UN Committee on the Rights of the Child (DoH, 1994). There is not a single reference in this document to 'poverty'. No mention is made of the fact that 4.1 million children were living at levels below half of the average income (DSS, 1994).

No attempt is made to assess whether or not children in the UK are guaranteed an 'adequate standard of living' as specified in the UN Convention. The clear implication is that this is not an issue which applies in the UK.

The end of the line for poverty?

The denial of the existence of poverty in the UK is implicit in official documents which, as Carey Oppenheim has pointed out:

> no longer use the words 'poverty' – instead the tame language of 'low income', 'below average income' and 'bottom ten per cent' has replaced the reality of 'deprivation', 'poverty' and 'hardship'. (Oppenheim, 1990, p. 14)

Occasionally, government ministers have been more explicit about the fact that in their view poverty is no longer an issue in the UK. For example, in 1989, John Moore, then Secretary of State for Social Security, claimed that living standards had improved so much that they ensured 'the end of the line for poverty' (Moore, 1989). Similarly, an earlier Secretary of State, Keith Joseph, had argued:

> An absolute standard of means is defined by reference to the actual needs of the poor and not by reference to the expenditure of those who are not poor. A family is poor if it cannot afford to eat . . . by any absolute standards there is very little poverty in Britain today. (Joseph and Sumption, 1979, p. 27)

What Keith Joseph explicitly suggests, and what is elsewhere implicit in much government thinking, is that poverty can be defined in terms of an absolute standard based on physical survival needs. In this respect it would, of course, be justifiable to claim that children's poverty in the UK in the 1990s could in no way be compared with that of either their counterparts in the 1890s or their contemporaries in the developing world.

However the idea of 'absolute poverty' is one which has very little academic credibility, or indeed much political support outside the UK. Almost all social scientists who have concerned themselves with the subject have defined poverty in terms of the standard of living in a particular society at a particular time. One of the best-known of such definitions is that of the eighteenth-century economist Adam Smith, who wrote:

> By necessities I understand not only commodities which are indispensably necessary for the support of life but whatever the custom of the country renders it indecent for creditable people, even of the lowest order, to be without. (Smith, 1776, p. 693)

A more contemporary version of the same argument has been expressed by Peter Townsend, who claims that people could be said to be poor 'when their resources are so seriously below those commanded by the average individual or family that they are, in effect, excluded from ordinary living patterns, customs and activities' (Townsend, 1979, p. 31).

In fact, it is not difficult to establish that even basic survival needs are relative to particular societies at particular times. Let us take an example which relates to the physical health of children. It is perfectly reasonable to argue, given what was known in 1995 about the depleted ozone layer and the dangers of skin cancer, that sunblock cream could be considered a necessary item for all children. Yet it would not have been so regarded twenty years before, nor would it be allowed for within contemporary measures of absolute poverty. More important, as we shall argue later, the cost of such an expensive necessity is in no way reflected in current levels of benefit for families with children.

Poverty as social exclusion

The idea that poverty can be defined in terms of an 'absolute' subsistence standard is, then, intellectually unconvincing. More important, however, is that it is also clearly at odds with the way 'adequacy' is intended to be interpreted within the UN Convention on the Rights of the Child. It is true that Article 27 does not offer any guidance on the meaning of 'adequate standard', but in the context of the Convention as a whole, it is clear that what is envisaged is a standard that would enable a child to participate in the full range of social and cultural activities normal in his/her society.

Article 4 underlines the point that 'adequacy' is to be assessed in relation to the resources of the particular society, specifying that 'with regard to economic, social and cultural rights, States Parties shall undertake such measures to the maximum extent of their available resources' (UN Convention on the Rights of the Child, 1989).

As Thomas Hammarberg, one of the members of the UN Committee on the Rights of the Child, has emphasised:

> This has interesting implications. One is that countries with more resources should offer services to children on a higher absolute level than is possible for poor countries. The Convention should not only be seen as a list of minimum requirements. Richer countries should ask more from themselves, and should also put in the 'maximum extent' of their resources. This makes the Convention more relevant in the affluent societies. (Hammarberg, 1995, p. xii)

The idea that poverty should be defined in terms of social exclusion enjoys wide international acceptance. Perhaps the most explicit example is to be found in the approach of the European Union. In 1992 the European Community Commission issued a recommendation to member states:

> To recognise the basic right of a person to sufficient resources and social assistance to live in a manner compatible with human dignity as part of a comprehensive and consistent drive to combat social exclusion. (European Community, 1992)

A recommendation of the European Commission is not binding on member states, and the UK government has not so far accepted the need to establish a minimum income standard. Indeed, governments of all persuasions in the UK have steadfastly refused to set an official poverty line. As Veit Wilson has pointed out, the UK is now one of the few countries in the developed world that fails to define its view of minimal adequacy (Veit Wilson, 1994, p. ii).

The adequacy of income support

In the absence of an official minimum income standard or poverty line, we need to use other sources to establish the scale of child poverty in the UK. One widely used approach is to take the social assistance level – that is, the government's own safety net – as a surrogate for the poverty line. Since 1988 the relevant benefit has been Income Support (termed National Assistance from 1948–66, and Supplementary Benefit from 1966–88).

Perhaps the main advantage of using the Income Support level (and its predecessors) as a measure of poverty is that the data is published annually, is therefore reasonably accessible, and provides the opportunity to chart trends in the numbers of poor children over a period of years. It is also a benchmark as to what the government of the day regards as a politically acceptable standard of living for poor children, and in this sense is sometimes regarded as a quasi-official poverty line.

There is considerable controversy, however, about what the relationship is, if any, between this product of a political decision and a more objective measure of adequacy. When the safety net was first established by Beveridge it was based on the 'subsistence standard' developed by Seebohm Rowntree in 1936 (Bradshaw, 1988). However there is evidence that the rates introduced in 1948 were below even the minimal subsistence levels proposed by Rowntree (Veit Wilson, 1992).

Certainly, in the period since 1948 benefits have been uprated without any attempt by the government of the day to relate the level set to evidence of adequacy. Whatever the position in 1948, it would be a matter more of luck than judgement if Income Support levels corresponded to any objective measure of minimum standards, whether based on subsistence or social participation criteria. Moreover, if the scale rates for adults within Income Support and its predecessors have in general borne little relationship to need, children's allowances have been even more markedly inadequate. As Joan Brown has indicated, the history of child dependency additions within the social security system has been a chequered one. Her analogy sums it up well when she likens the performance of the state to that of

> a distracted parent, darting in and out of the nursery, administering a slap here and a bag of sweets there, without ever ensuring that the varying needs of the children were actually being met. (Brown, 1984, p. 92)

It is not surprising, then, that there is a considerable amount of evidence that the Income Support level for children is insufficient even for a minimally adequate standard of living in the UK in the 1990s. The evidence comes from two main sources, the first deriving from a number of household budget studies. We consider two in particular: Piachaud (1979); and Oldfield and Yu (1993).

Using a variety of techniques, these studies involved estimating the cost of bringing up children of different ages in the UK. In the case of the York Family Benefits Unit study (Oldfield and Yu, 1993) a choice of standards was provided – 'modest but adequate' and 'low cost'. In neither of the studies were the standards proposed anything other than 'adequate' in the terms laid down in the UN Convention. In Piachaud's study, the cost of his budget was 50 per cent above the then current Supplementary Benefit rates. The 1990s study revealed a similar picture. Even the low-cost budget, for example, was around 30 per cent higher than the 1993–4 Income Support Rates, while Child Benefit met only 35 per cent of the total cost of a child. For a family of two adults and two children under 11, an extra £34 per week would be required to meet even the modest standards used in the York study (Oldfield and Yu, 1993).

The second source of evidence of the inadequacy of benefit rates for children arises out of a wealth of studies over many years based upon the first-hand experiences of families living on social assistance (Burghes, 1980; Bradshaw and Holmes, 1989; Cohen *et al.*, 1992; Walker, 1993; Middleton *et al.*, 1994). The latter study, in particular, provides vivid accounts from children themselves of what it means to experience poverty. This and other work by the Child Poverty Action Group demonstrates the extent to which the education system places additional financial burdens on families, in the shape of school trips and other essential extras. As Middleton *et al.* conclude:

> The almost daily requests for money which are a manifestation of the new financial world in which schools are forced to operate, are seen by parents as unfair pressure on their own, often limited budgets. (Middleton *et al.*, 1994, p. 72)

What is clear from all the research is that, despite the emphasis by the government in targeting families with children in its social security reforms of 1986, it is precisely this group for whom the safety net benefit levels are least adequate in the 1990s.

Measuring the extent of child poverty

In the light of the evidence, there can be very little doubt that the number of children living at or below Income Support levels would be an underestimate of child poverty. More seriously, it means that the 3.2 million children of families receiving Income Support in 1994 (DSS, 1994) were living at levels that are inadequate to maintain social participation.

Despite this caveat about its usefulness as a true measure of poverty, the Income Support/Supplementary Benefit (IS/SB) level formed the basis of the government's own poverty count from 1979 to 1985 – the Low Income Family (LIF) statistics. This series was subsequently extended to 1989 by the Institute of Fiscal Studies. What these figures reveal is a dramatic increase in the levels of child poverty. Altogether, the number of children in families at or below IS/SB levels almost doubled between 1979 and 1989 from 1.5 to 2.8 million. As a proportion of all children, the figure rose from 1 in 8 to 1 in 4 (Kumar, 1993).

In 1985, the Low Income Family statistics were discontinued by the government to be replaced by a new measure – Households Below Average Income (HBAI). Although the government is careful not to use the term 'poverty line', a figure of half the average (mean) income is taken as the measure of low income. This corresponds to the measure of poverty widely used throughout Europe and recommended by the European Union. In this sense it is useful for comparative purposes. It is, however, more accurate to see this as a measure of income inequality than of poverty. There is certainly no a priori reason why 50 per cent of average income should constitute a poverty line. Indeed, there is evidence that this figure may understate poverty. Peter Townsend's work, for example, suggested that the minimum income level required to guarantee social participation in the UK was around two-thirds of the average income (Townsend, 1979).

Despite this reservation, the evidence of the HBAI figures also provide a clear indication that the UK is not a child-centred society. They show that children are significantly over-represented among the poorest members of society. Official data published in summer 1994 reveals that 4.1 million children (or 32 per cent of the total) were living below 50 per cent of average income in 1991–2. This contrasts with a figure of 25 per cent for the population as a whole (DSS, 1994). A similar picture emerges from the Joseph Rowntree Inquiry into Income and Wealth. This indicates that children comprise 30 per cent of the poorest decile (tenth) in the UK, whereas they constitute only 22 per cent of the total population (Hills, 1995).

What is also clear from the government's own data is that the relative position of children was subject to considerable deterioration during the 1980s. In 1979, the proportion of the child population living at below half the average income was 10 per cent, compared with 9 per cent for the population at large. So although even at that time children were slightly over-represented at the bottom of the income scale, the gap was very much narrower than in 1991–2. It is hard to square all this with the pledge at the World Summit for Children in 1990 that children should have 'first call on society's concerns and capacities' (see Chapter 1).

Child poverty since 1945

The link between childhood and poverty in the UK is not a recent phenomenon. Indeed, there was strong and clear evidence produced in 1945 that children were particularly prone to poverty. Inter-war research by Rowntree in York was just one of a number of studies which showed that between 20 and 30 per cent of children lived in families with incomes that were insufficient for even the bare necessities (Rathbone, 1949).

In what became a very influential model, Rowntree had earlier pointed out that for the working-class child, poverty was almost an inevitable feature of the life-cycle:

> During early childhood, unless his father is a skilled worker, he will probably be in poverty; this will last until he, or some of his brothers or sisters, begin to earn money and thus augment their father's wage sufficiently to raise the family above the poverty line. (Rowntree, 1901, p. 170)

The fact that an unskilled worker's wage was generally too low to support children led Rowntree to propose a minimum wage as an antidote to child poverty (Rowntree, 1918). Eleanor Rathbone argued that a more effective means of tackling this problem was a system of child allowances, and eventually Beveridge was persuaded to endorse her proposal and recommend in his 1942 report the introduction of 'family allowances'.

It was widely believed that this new benefit, together with the introduction of universal national insurance cover against unemployment in 1948, would largely eliminate the problem of child poverty. Historically low levels of unemployment in the 1950s and 1960s contributed to the understandable, even if somewhat misplaced, mood of optimism.

This was strongly challenged by the publication in 1965 of *The Poor and the Poorest* by Brian Abel Smith and Peter Townsend. The main significance of this study is that it played a major part in the 'rediscovery of poverty' in the 1960s, and led to the birth of the Child Poverty Action Group. Using the National Assistance rate as a basis for their poverty line, Abel Smith and Townsend revealed that around 2.5 million children were still living in poverty at that time.

Two other equally important, if politically less influential, studies will now briefly be considered. They are Peter Townsend's *Poverty in the UK* (1979) and the *Breadline Britain* survey (Mack and Lansley, 1985).

Townsend's book is arguably the most important contribution to the study of poverty in the UK since 1945. Its main significance lies in its innovatory use of a standard of poverty based on an index of social participation. Taking this as his benchmark, Townsend found that almost a third of the population were living below the poverty line in the late 1960s. Although the focus was not primarily upon childhood, this was shown to be one of the main risk factors. Children in unskilled manual working-class families had a 77 per cent chance of being poor, and this rose to 93 per cent when there were three or more children in the family. What also clearly emerged was the link between poverty and race. Almost half of those who were 'non-white' were classified as being poor, compared to the overall proportion of nearly a third.

The *Breadline Britain* survey, which was conducted for a television documentary, also adopted a social participation standard for its poverty line. Where it differed from other such approaches was to base this on popular views as to what constituted necessities. Those who lacked three or more of the socially approved necessities were deemed to be poor. The 1983 survey revealed that 2.5 million children (22 per cent of the total) were in this category. When the survey was repeated in 1990, this had risen to more than 3 million (around 28 per cent).

The evidence as we see it therefore is that a significant number of children continued to experience poverty throughout this period. Nevertheless, by the standards both of the pre-war and the post-1979 periods, there is little doubt that for thirty years or so after the Second World War there was a reduction in inequality and a fall in the proportion of poor children in the UK (Bradshaw, 1990, p. 7).

The causes of child poverty

As in Rowntree's studies earlier in the century, the two most significant causes of child poverty in the UK in the late 1990s are high levels of long-term unemployment together with growing numbers of low-paid jobs. Since the late 1970s there have been profound changes at both the global and the UK level that have made employment more precarious and driven wage levels down for those in insecure jobs.

Although it may seem remote and abstract in the context of a discussion about poor children in Belfast or Liverpool, the impact of changes in the global economy have been so enormous as to make national programmes of social welfare appear almost irrelevant. As John Gray has argued, the practically instantaneous movement of capital across continents has 'made the survival of communities everywhere conditional on changes in a world market which cares nothing for the stability of the societies it exists to serve' (Gray, 1995). This has led to a new instability of employment in developed economies as production is moved around the globe in search of cheaper labour costs.

Moreover, in the case of the UK, this has been accompanied during the period since 1979 by a concerted policy of labour market deregulation. A whole series of measures ranging across the fields of trade union rights, employment law, and welfare benefit regulations have meant that workers in the UK have fewer rights, and employers greater flexibility in hiring and firing, than anywhere else in Europe. The effect of these twin developments has been to create much greater instability in UK labour markets than existed in the 1970s.

The impact of this on families with children has been marked, and is the main reason for the substantial increase in child poverty over this period.

Although data on the number of children in unemployed families is not routinely collated in the UK, latest estimates based upon Labour Force Survey returns in Summer 1994 indicate that over 1.1 million children fall into this category. In nearly two-thirds of these families the breadwinner had been unemployed for more than twelve months (CPAG, 1995). It is also worth noting that unemployment is far from equally distributed. There are significant regional variations. In 1992, for example, rates of official unemployment ranged from 14.7 per cent in Northern Ireland to 8 per cent in East Anglia (Kumar, 1993).

Moreover, there are even more dramatic variations if we consider the position of different local authority wards (neighbourhoods with an average population of 5 000 people). Here we find that a number of wards in Liverpool and elsewhere on Merseyside have rates of unemployment of over 40 per cent, or four times the average (Hills, 1995). It is also clear from the evidence that, although there has been considerable continuity in terms of areas which experience high and low levels of unemployment, there has been a greater polarisation during the 1980s (ibid., p. 83).

If unemployment is distributed unequally on an area basis, it also disproportionately affects minority ethnic groups. Although the standard unemployment statistics do not contain information on the ethnic origin of claimants, evidence from the Labour Force Survey suggests that, in general, the unemployment rate among minority ethnic groups is around twice that of the white population. Within this there is some variation between different black and Asian groups (Kumar, 1993).

There is a close link between unemployment and low pay. In a report for the Policy Studies Institute, Bill Daniel (1990) described a pattern of recurrent unemployment interspersed with low-paid jobs:

> so long as the unemployed flow as a whole are concerned, they tended to work in low paid, low skilled, and manifestly insecure jobs. They lost them with little notice and little or no compensation . . . for those who found new jobs relatively quickly, those new jobs proved to be only temporary in most cases.

With no legal minimum wage in the UK, low pay is endemic, and has spread rapidly throughout the 1980s. The Council of Europe defines the low-pay threshold as two-thirds of full-time mean earnings. On this basis, there were 3.4 million children living in households where the head was low-paid in full-time employment in the UK in 1991. Almost one and a half million of these children were in poverty (defined as less than half of average earnings) (Kumar, 1993).

As in the case of unemployment, there appears to be a disproportionate number of families from minority ethnic groups among the low-paid. So, although there is no direct data on the ethnic background of children living in poverty, we can assume from their families' over-representation among the unemployed and low-paid that children from minority ethnic groups have a greater propensity to poverty than their white counterparts.

This shift in the labour market towards precarious employment – be it part-time, temporary, self-employment, or casual work – has had a somewhat mixed impact on child poverty. On the one hand, it has led to an increase in the number of families headed by a low-paid worker, as we have seen above. On the other hand, it has provided the opportunity in many families for both partners to work, albeit at low wages. As a recent Joseph Rowntree report, *Family and Parenthood* concluded:

> The advertisers' stereotype of prosperous dual-earner parents combining successful careers and active leisure time with the responsibilities of child rearing bears limited comparison with real life . . . The unglamorous truth is that had married women not joined the labour market in such numbers, the gap between rich and poor families would be even wider than it is today. (Utting, 1995, p. 26)

If unemployment and low pay continue to be the principal causes of poverty among children in the UK, it is demographic change that has received most attention from politicians. The increasing incidence of lone-parent families offer a convenient scapegoat for those who wish to adopt a 'victim-blaming' approach to poverty. The early 1990s, in particular, witnessed a concerted and virulent political and media campaign in the UK against lone-parent families.

Certainly, as we showed in Chapter 2, there has been a significant growth in the numbers of children living in lone-parent families in the UK, as elsewhere in the developed world. However, the rising number of lone-parent families is only part of the story. Just as significant, if not more so, when it comes to explaining child poverty is the fact that lone-parent families are increasingly likely to be poor. Indeed, 70 per cent of lone-parent families are in receipt of Income Support, which indicates that they are either not working at all or are working for fewer than 16 hours a week. This compares with a figure of just over a third of such families receiving Supplementary Benefit twenty years ago. If we take the figure of half the average income as our 'poverty line', then by 1992–3, 58 per cent of lone-parent families were living below this level compared to only 28 per cent in 1979 (Oppenheim, 1993).

There can be no doubt then that children are significantly and increasingly represented among the poorest people in the UK, and that this results, to an extent, from economic and demographic changes experienced throughout the developed world. In the following section we shall consider the impact of UK tax and social security policy on childhood poverty.

Family Allowance Child Benefit

When the Family Allowance was introduced in 1945 it was regarded by Beveridge, as we have seen, as an 'expression of the community's direct interest in children' (Brown, 1984, p. 34). As such, the subsequent history of the Family Allowance and its successor, Child Benefit, indicates an interest that has waxed and waned but never been much more than lukewarm. Introduced at 5s. (25p) compared to the 7s.6d. (37.5p) envisaged by Beveridge, Family Allowances were uprated only twice in the years from 1948 to 1967 and during this period they declined significantly in value when measured as a percentage of average male earnings (Brown, 1984, p. 48). The fact that they were not paid for the first child further reduced their value and contributed to the impression they were aimed mainly at encouraging population growth.

K. Banting suggests that the Family Allowance was regarded as a vote loser by politicians of all parties because it was widely believed to encourage irresponsibly large families or to be spent on cigarettes, alcohol and bingo (Banting, 1979). The post-war baby boom reduced the 'community concern' identified by Beveridge.

Child Benefit was introduced in 1975, as a replacement for both the Family Allowance and child tax allowances, and it has enjoyed an equally chequered career. Not only has it been frozen on a number of occasions, its very existence – at least in its present universal form – has been widely questioned (Brown, 1988). In the late 1990s as we have seen earlier, Child Benefit meets only about a third of the cost of keeping a child, even using a low-cost budget standard.

The failure of Child Benefit to secure widespread support as a universal benefit in part reflects the tendency for it to be considered from an adult's rather than a child's perspective. It is remarkable, for example, how far this benefit has been bound up with women's issues, and the position of motherhood in particular. Indeed, when the Child Benefit Bill was introduced to the House of Commons by the minister it was not as a benefit for children but as a contribution to International Women's Year (Brown, 1984, p. 64).

In this respect, Child Benefit and its predecessor have been the objects of considerable ambivalence. On the one hand, this benefit has been valued as an important part of the income of mothers. Indeed one pamphlet produced by Child Poverty Action Group in support of Child Benefit was entitled *Mothers' Lifeline* (CPAG, 1985). On the other hand, it has been viewed with suspicion by some women as a means of paying women for motherhood. Thus Ada Nield expressed her opposition in the 1930s, arguing that 'the children must be cared for, and women must care for them, but not by paying poor women to be mothers' (quoted in Field, 1982, p. 11).

If, as Hilary Land has suggested, 'the majority of women's organisations, even those representing employed women, have never made Family Allowances one of their major preoccupations' (Land, 1979, p. 19), then the trade union movement has also had reservations. This has come about partly because family allowances have been seen as an alternative to wage increases or the development of a 'family wage', and partly because they have involved a shift in resources from 'the wallet to the purse'.

Frank Field has claimed that 'the failure to win widespread grass roots support within the trade unions and women's organisations helps to account for the political vulnerability of today's child benefit scheme' (Field, 1982, p. 12). While this is no doubt true, we would argue that the real problem lies in the fact that Child Benefit is evaluated in terms of its impact on adults' lives rather than those of children.

Moreover, in so far as Family Allowance/Child Benefit have been viewed as benefits for children, the emphasis, as we saw in Chapter 1, has been on children as investments. This continues to be the position of those who defend Child Benefit (for example, Brown, 1988). But quite apart from our general objection to seeing children in these terms, this is in our view an insecure basis upon which to build support for Child Benefit. For while concern about the future population was strong in the 1940s, as we have seen, this concern soon dissipated. Future investment is always vulnerable to short-term financial pressures, and politicians are notorious for fixing their horizons on the next election rather than 16–18 years in the future.

The significance of Child Benefit lies not in what it can and cannot do for adults, but rather, it should form the cornerstone of children's rights, reflecting society's obligations towards its children as individuals in their own right. Child Benefit is, in Ruth Lister's words, the child's 'badge of citizenship' (Lister, 1990, p. 59). In this respect, the existing principles of universality and equality are important. They should be accompanied by the principle of 'adequacy'. A children's rights perspective would require all children to have an equal right to an adequate basic income whatever their parents' circumstances. Child Benefit is potentially the best way of ensuring this. It is a moot point whether or not this should lead to payment being made directly to the child – a largely symbolic change in the case of young children. Certainly it is a strong argument for ensuring that payment is not transferred from mothers to fathers as has been proposed on a number of occasions in its history.

Although the function of Child Benefit, with its universal basis, is not primarily the relief of child poverty, it is arguably the most effective way of accomplishing this objective. By providing a basic income for children whatever the circumstances of the family, it could go a long way to protecting children from the economic and demographic upheavals described earlier in the chapter. As Joan Brown (1988, p. xi) put it:

> It is flexible enough to cope with instability in family relationships, and provides some security and stability to children and their parents in the changing labour market of the late twentieth century, with its growing proportion of part-time and temporary jobs and the hazards of increasing self employment.

Other benefits are often dependent upon judgements made about adult behaviour – for example, the Job Seekers Allowance (and its predecessor, Unemployment Benefit) can be suspended if the bread-winner is deemed not to be actively seeking work. Child Benefit is unconditional – a recognition, according to Joan Brown again, that 'whether sympathy or blame is accorded to the parents for the difficulties they find themselves in, the child is *always* the innocent party' (ibid., p. 45).

There are, then, strong arguments in favour of a significant increase in the level of Child Benefit in the UK. The main counter-argument is the high cost. Given that it is universal and non-taxable, the cost of Child Benefit is relatively high – even a modest £5 per week increase would cost in the order of £2.5 billion per annum (Commission on Social Justice, 1994, p. 316). However, we should note that there is clear evidence that since the 1960s families with children have been paying relatively higher proportions of their incomes in tax and National Insurance compared with single people and childless couples (see, for example, Field, 1982; Utting, 1995). In the light of this, a good case could be made out for a significant increase in Child Benefit to redress the balance by shifting resources back to children.

One group of the poorest children who would not be assisted by any increase in Child Benefit consists of those whose parent(s) receive(s) Income Support. In their case, Child Benefit is currently deducted pound for pound from the Income Support entitlement. To counter this there would either have to be a change in the rules, allowing Child Benefit to be disregarded as income, or else Income Support child allowances would have to be substantially raised. Indeed, it would require a doubling of the allowances to bring children's incomes up to the modest but adequate budget level indicated by the York Family Benefits Unit study quoted earlier in the chapter.

A minimum wage

We have seen that, following the First World War, Rowntree proposed a minimum wage as an antidote to child poverty. However, the Beveridge reforms, influenced by Eleanor Rathbone, adopted the Family Allowance (Child Benefit) as a more 'targeted' approach to the relief of child poverty in families with a working head of household. It is arguable that such is the scale of low pay among families with children in the UK in the 1990s that both mechanisms are needed: 'Earnings inequality is now greater than at any time since 1886'. (Commission on Social Justice, 1994, p. 200). During the Thatcher years regulations governing wage levels were gradually dismantled, leaving the UK as one of very few developed economies without any minimum wage legislation. Although this is an issue which is wider than the question of child poverty, nevertheless the correlation between family responsibilities and low pay ensures that a minimum wage would be of particular significance for children.

Since the early 1970s UK governments have chosen to soften the impact on families of low wages through the social security system rather than by legislation on wage levels. Family Income Supplement (FIS), introduced in 1971 (and replaced by Family Credit in 1988) was designed to provide means-tested assistance to low-paid families. Conservative governments since the mid-1980s have explicitly favoured this more selective approach, not only over a minimum wage but also in preference to the universal support of families through Child Benefit.

Quite apart from any misgivings there might be over the principle of using the social security system to subsidise employers who pay poverty-level wages, Family Income Supplement/Family Credit has proved to be an inadequate response to the problem of poverty among children in low-paid families. To begin with, the benefit has always suffered from a relatively low take-up rate. Family Credit has never reached more than two-thirds of those eligible, and its predecessor Family Income Supplement hovered around the 50 per cent take-up level. Second, both benefits illustrate one of the problems inherent in means tested benefits – the poverty trap. In other words, as families' incomes rise, the combined effects of their reduced entitlement to benefit together with an increase in tax liability means that they are little, if any, better off.

A minimum wage would offer greater potential as a mechanism to combat child poverty. It would also be more in tune with the rest of the European Union though, of course, the level at which any minimum wage was set would be crucial. In fact, the York Family Benefit Unit's low-cost budget standard, discussed earlier, would suggest that, in order to support a partner and two children, a full-time worker would need to earn just over £5 per hour at 1993 rates.

If the partner also works, the couple would need to earn over £7 per hour between them to cover child-care costs as well (Veit Wilson, 1994). This would suggest that a figure of £3.50 to £5 (1993 rates) would be the lowest acceptable minimum wage if the intention is to tackle child poverty among working families.

Benefits for families out of work

If low pay is one of the main causes of child poverty then, as V. Kumar points out, 'mass unemployment is the biggest threat to a child's right to an acceptable living standard' (Kumar, 1993, p. 197). Full employment was one of the basic pillars on which Beveridge's post-1945 social security system was erected, and no policy initiatives to tackle child poverty at the end of the twentieth century can be complete without a commitment to end long-term unemployment. Clearly, detailed discussion of employment policy is beyond the scope of this book, but it is important to restate the principle of full employment since it has carried so little weight in UK policy since the 1970s. Norman Lamont's claim, made when he was Chancellor of the Exchequer, that 'rising unemployment was a price well worth paying for the defeat of inflation' (*Hansard*, 16 May 1991) sums up government policy throughout this period. What the work of Bradshaw and Kumar demonstrates is that the price has been a heavy one for children.

We should stress that full employment in the 1990s is a somewhat more complex question than it was for Beveridge. Whereas the employment model used in the 1940s was one of stable, 40 hours a week male jobs lasting forty years, this pattern is not only unrealistic in the 1990s, it is also arguably an undesirable model from a child's perspective.

A more realistic and child-friendly objective should be for policies which sustain a pattern of full employment that enables men and women to combine work with responsibilities for children and other dependents. We touch upon this briefly in Chapter 6. However successful our employment creation policies prove to be, there will also continue to be a need for benefits for families outside the labour market. It is to this subject we now turn.

Much has been written in recent years about the problems of the Beveridge scheme which has formed the basis of UK social security policy since the 1940s (Baldwin and Falkingham, 1994; Walker, 1993; Alcock, 1987). None of this analysis, however, has pointed out that the Beveridge scheme has never worked particularly well for children: there are several reasons why the Beveridge model of social security is an inadequate mechanism for tackling child poverty.

The first is to be found in the structure of benefits favoured by Beveridge and persisting in the late 1990s. Beveridge put forward a two-tier model of social security. The primary tier is based on the principle of social insurance. In return for contributions paid while working, people would be entitled to claim a range of benefits when out of work. Below this, as a 'minor but integral' part of the system would be the safety net of social assistance for those who were not eligible for social insurance. It was envisaged that few people would need to rely on social assistance, certainly for any length of time, and benefit levels were intended to be less generous than those governed by social insurance.

The reality is that the majority of children within the benefit system are consigned to the social assistance benefit – currently Income Support. This comes about partly because lone-parents, with the exception of widows, were never included in Beveridge's scheme of social insurance, and they have remained excluded ever since. Given the very substantial rise in the number of lone-parent families since 1945, this has meant that Income Support (and previously Supplementary Benefit) is having to perform a function for which it was never designed.

Similarly, families who are unemployed were only entitled to claim the insurance-based Unemployment Benefit for twelve months. After that, those who were long-term unemployed were required to fall back on social assistance. The replacement of Unemployment Benefit by Job Seekers' Allowance in October 1996 reduces the period of entitlement to the non-means-tested benefit to six months. The most recent available figures indicate that, of the 1.1 million children living in families with unemployed parents in 1994, in nearly two-thirds of the cases the unemployment had lasted over twelve months (CPAG, 1995).

All in all, around 3 million children under the age of 16 were receiving Income Support in February 1994, and for most of them this was less a safety net than a first resort. This brings us to the second respect in which the Beveridge system fails children. The benefit rates (or premiums) set for children are, as we indicated earlier, woefully inadequate when compared even with low-cost budget standards.

Perhaps the simplest, if rather defeatist, solution to these problems is to accept the reality that Income Support is now the first port of call for the majority of children whose parents are out of work, and to adapt it accordingly. As a minimum this would require a substantial increase in the childrens' rates. An alternative approach, favoured by the Commission on Social Justice and many academic commentators (for example, Baldwin and Falkingham, 1994) can be characterised broadly as 'back to Beveridge'. This starts from the premise that the insurance principle is a valuable one which should be retained and strengthened. While it would be inappropriate to go into details here, if it is to address the problems outlined above it would require measures to remove lone-parents from the means-tested part of the scheme through the introduction of a new non-contributory benefit such as that recommended by the Finer Report in 1974 (DHSS, 1974).

A more radical approach to reforming social security is to be found in 'basic or citizen's income', sometimes called 'social dividend' (a fuller discussion of this approach is provided by Hermione Parker, 1989). Citizen's income is defined by the Citizen's Income Trust as follows: 'For every citizen the inalienable right regardless of age, sex, creed, labour market or marital status to a small but guaranteed income unconditionally.' In other words, it offers a non-means-tested and non-contributory income. In this respect, Child Benefit can be regarded as a form of citizen's income. If our proposals earlier in the chapter for a substantial increase in the level of Child Benefit were to be implemented, this would be very much in line with the citizen's income philosophy.

Certainly any analysis of post-war benefit levels for children makes it apparent that they have been set at levels designed not to meet the needs of children but rather to preserve the incentive of adults to work. The desire to ensure that families should not be better off while receiving Income Support than while working inevitably ensures that social security systematically imposes poverty upon children. A minimum wage set at a realistic level would undoubtedly go some way towards eradicating this problem. However, it is hard to see how children's poverty could be totally eliminated without a radical restructuring of the benefit system along the lines proposed by exponents of basic or citizen's income.

Child support

Our discussion so far in this chapter has concentrated on the role of social policy in providing assistance to the *families* of poor children. Even Child Benefit is not directed at children themselves. The financial arrangements within families and their impact on children's welfare raises more complex issues for social policy. The UN Convention affirms the right of the child to be financially supported by his/her parents and the obligation of the state to secure the recovery of maintenance for the child (Article 27, Section 4).

As far as UK social policy goes, so long as families are still functioning and making no demands upon Income Support, then they are assumed to be fulfilling their child support obligations and are left to get on with it. It has been suggested that:

> Historically, children's financial interests have not been well served by the law; there was, in theory, a common law duty on a father to maintain legitimate children, but no procedure was available to reinforce the right. (Bainham and Cretney, 1993, p. 291)

The work of Jan Pahl has revealed that it cannot be taken for granted that male breadwinners will always meet their obligations in this respect (Pahl, 1989), and the periodical campaigns to ensure that Family Allowance/Child Benefit is paid to the mother reflect this concern.

On the whole, though, it is when families break down, or where a child's parents have never lived together, that the primary policy concerns have arisen. This is particularly so given the extent of the changes in marriage and family patterns in the UK since the 1970s (see Chapter 2). As Jane Millar (1993) has indicated:

> The question of how best to support children is becoming a key policy issue: what role should be taken by fathers, mothers, stepfathers, stepmothers, separated parents, parents who have never lived with the children, parents who have started second families? And what role should the state play in this?

The Child Support Act 1991 was an attempt to legislate in this delicate area. Described by the House of Commons Social Security Committee as the 'most far reaching social reform to be made for forty years' (House of Commons, 1993), it has proved, in its early stages at any rate, to be one of the most controversial and unworkable pieces of legislation in living memory. From the point of view of children's welfare, perhaps the most remarkable feature of the legislation and the subsequent responses to it has been the extent to which the focus has been almost entirely on adult interests. Indeed, the Child Support Act 1991 is a classic example of a social policy initiative that has been enacted in the name of the child (the White Paper preceding it was entitled *Children Come First*), but which in practice subordinates children's interests to those of adults.

The central principle of the Act – that parents who live apart from their children should provide realistic financial support for them – is an important one, and commands widespread support (Daniel and Burgess, 1994). It is also enshrined in Article 27 of the UN Convention on the Rights of the Child. Moreover, research by Bradshaw and Millar in 1990 shows that prior to the Act only 30 per cent of lone mothers and 3 per cent of lone fathers received any sort of regular maintenance. Amounts tended to be low, with the modal (that is, the most common) award being only £10 per week. Even so, over half of all maintenance orders were in arrears at any one time, and as many as 70 per cent at some time or other (DSS, 1990).

There is no doubt, then, that children's rights to maintenance was not being safeguarded by the courts, and this certainly helped to contribute to the poverty of children in lone-parent families. However, when we examine the case for legislation put forward in *Children Come First*, we find no reference to child poverty. This contrasts with the Australian child support scheme which provided one of the models for the UK legislation and which puts strong emphasis upon the relief of poverty among children (Millar and Whiteford, 1993).

In the UK, the objectives of the Child Support Act, as set out in *Children Come First*, include reinforcing parental work incentives and reducing 'dependence' on Income Support. It is no surprise, then, that the decision was taken to withdraw Income Support pound for pound from families receiving Child Support. This ensures that many of the poorest children will not benefit financially from the Child Support Act. A still more blatant example of children's interests being sacrificed to the government's adult-focused objectives is the 'benefit penalty' imposed on lone-parents who refuse to name the absent parent.

It is very hard to square the reduction of income of even a small number of children, who are in any case living on inadequate benefit levels, with the claim that 'children come first'. The government would claim that the aim of the legislation is to change parental attitudes and behaviour, and that children will benefit in the long run. In the short run, the Child Support Act as it is currently structured is likely to make some of the poorest children in the UK worse off (for evidence on this point, see Garnham and Knights, 1994; Daniel and Burgess, 1994).

As a postscript to the discussion of this legislation, it is worth noting that the furore it subsequently provoked among both the public and politicians arose not from concern about children's welfare so much as anger at its impact on non-custodial parents. Indeed, this episode is one of the clearest and most striking examples in recent UK policy of the way in which children's welfare has been drowned out by the clamour of adult voices.

Asylum seekers

In February 1996, UK policy changed in such a way as to create a new category of destitute children. This will be the effect of the decision to withdraw entitlement to social security benefits from refugees who fail to declare that they are seeking asylum at the point of entry into the country. It is true that the number of refugees entering the UK, and therefore the impact of this policy change, is relatively small (see Chapter 2). Nevertheless, we believe the significance of this policy goes well beyond the numbers involved. It highlights a number of notable features of contemporary policy towards children.

First, it is another example of the global dimension in social policy. The issue of asylum seekers owes much to the scale of global conflict at the end of the twentieth century. It poses problems, and not just for the UK, which the traditional social policy framework based on national borders is ill-equipped to tackle.

Second, it demonstrates the fact that the UK government pays little more than lip service to its obligations under the United Nations Convention on the Rights of the Child. Article 22 of the Convention requires that states take all appropriate measures to ensure that a child who is seeking asylum receives humanitarian assistance.

Finally, it is yet another indication of the willingness of the UK government to enact legislation which inflicts poverty upon children in the pursuit of other objectives. Whatever the merits of the government's claim that many asylum seekers are bogus, it is open to question whether it justifies withdrawing social security benefits from families with children, many of whom arrive in the UK in a highly traumatised state.

Conclusion

When the Child Poverty Action Group was first established in 1965, its founder members saw it as a short-term campaign. They believed that the shocking nature of the issue would force the then Labour government into prompt remedial action. Indeed, so optimistic were they that they did not even open a bank account for the organisation (Field, 1982, p. 24). Over thirty years later, the organisation is still campaigning strongly. Meanwhile, child poverty has escalated to levels never imagined in 1965. Perhaps the only thing to have diminished is any sense of public or political outrage. The fact that, as we have shown, children are so much more liable than adults to experience poverty reflects their greater vulnerability. It is also testimony to the neglect of children's interests by the policy process.

Child poverty in the UK in the late 1990s is not a product of famine or war; it lies within government control. Indeed, the extent and speed of the increase in child poverty during the 1980s owed much to deliberate policy choices by the Conservative government. When Margaret Thatcher declared, 'Let our children grow tall, and some grow taller than others if they have it in them to do so' (Thatcher, 1972), she was endorsing the view that inequality is beneficial to society. Thus UK economic and social policies in the 1980s were premised upon the belief that income and wealth inequality are necessary to stimulate economic growth, which then 'trickles down', so that all, including the least well-off, ultimately benefit.

The reality was that income inequality increased more substantially and more rapidly in the UK than in any comparable country (Hills, 1995, p. 65). But not only did the gap between rich and poor widen in the 1980s, in addition those in the bottom 10 per cent of the income distribution scale in fact became worse off in real terms. In other words, the poorest children were becoming both absolutely as well as relatively poorer. There was no evidence of any 'trickle down', and little opportunity for the rapidly rising numbers of poor children to 'grow tall'.

Child poverty is not a discrete phenomenon which can be confined to a single chapter in any account of contemporary social policy; it pervades every aspect of policy dealt with in this book. Children's housing, education, health experiences, and even their likelihood of spending all or part of their childhood in public care, will all be crucially affected by whether or not they are poor. Irrespective of changes in other areas of social policy, no other factor will have such a significant impact on children's life chances. If, as Peter Golding has suggested, 'poverty is most comprehensively understood as a condition of partial citizenship' (Golding, 1986, p. xi), then it is clear that children, above all, are experiencing exclusion from full citizenship in the UK at the end of the twentieth century.

Further reading

There is a large literature on poverty, but the following are among the most relevant to child poverty: Oppenheim (1996); Kumar (1993); and Bradshaw (1990). Middleton *et al.* (1994) gives a vivid picture of child poverty in the 1990s, including first-hand accounts from children. Baldwin and Falkingham (1994) is a useful review of current issues in social security.

4

Child Health and Health Care Policy

Health is a state of complete physical, mental and social well-being and not merely the absence of disease or infirmity. (Constitution of the World Health Organisation, 1948, Preamble)

Introduction

Even the best health care provision is only likely to ensure 'good' health if other circumstances of life provide an environment conducive to this, and to obtaining maximum individual benefit from the prevailing systems of medical care. Good, or indeed *bad*, health is thus at least partly dependent upon factors outside the competence of doctors and beyond the scope of the institutions of health care. This is patently so in the case of children for whose health, for example, adequate nutrition and a tobacco-smoke-free atmosphere may be far more important than elaborate medical facilities at the nearest hospital, critical as these may well be on occasion. Therefore to limit discussion to health care policy may serve to ignore other far more significant influences on child health.

This is widely acknowledged in health studies literature, so the dramatic improvements in health standards that have taken place in all industrialised countries during the twentieth century are attributed to a number of causes, of which advances in medical knowledge and in the treatment of disease are seen as only one factor. Thus McPherson and Coleman suggest, for example, that other factors include increases in real income, improvements in nutrition and housing standards, and higher levels of education (1988, p. 408).

Few people today would deny a child's right to health care through public provision. But, for better or for worse, this right is mediated by a child's parents, so that children cannot be seen as 'consumers' of medical care, since any choice for them is almost universally mediated through their parents and other adults. With young children in particular it is principally mothers who decide whether or not to seek medical help and advice if their child is unwell. In fact, as Wyke and Hewison point out, 'up to 90 per cent of minor illness episodes are diagnosed and treated at home' (1991, p. 1). This, of course, means that a proper study of child health care needs to take into account parental health education and the reciprocal attitudes of doctors and parents.

Allowing for the inherent limitations of any account of child health, we discuss in the first section of this chapter health care policy for children within the context of a changing National Health Service (NHS). In the second section we identify existing health inequalities within the child population. In the final section we examine briefly the wider policy implications of four major contemporary health risks to children – accidents, asthma, smoking, and diet.

Health care policy and children

The inauguration of the National Health Service on 5 July 1948 achieved more for the health of women and children than any previous measure of health reform. Free access to health care, which was then established, has of course long since been taken for granted. Complaint and dissatisfaction there may well be, but the principle of open access has since 1948 been carved in stone. Indeed the NHS has become a permanent feature of the British post-war way of life, an institutional pillar of our national identity and sense of pride (Widgery, 1988, p. 28).

The development of health care policy before 1946

Improving standards of health during the twentieth century and the parallel rising living standards have been matched by growing intervention by the state in the provision of health care services. However, for women and children in particular, unimpeded access to these was long delayed and provision generally until 1948 was piecemeal, fragmented and restricted.

It was only at the dawn of the twentieth century that governments began to develop policies aimed directly at improving the *personal* health of individuals, in contrast to a nineteenth-century emphasis on public health. A major landmark in the provision of health care was the introduction in 1911 of a scheme of 'National Health Insurance' for certain categories of employed male workers. This provided both sickness pay and free medical treatment from a general practitioner (GP) – but not specialist hospital treatment; and nor was any provision made for the dependants of an insured worker.

The advent of the First World War further focused public attention on the nation's health needs, but despite further reforms and the establishment of a separate Ministry of Health in 1919, glaring deficiencies remained. Hospital services, for example, were particularly chaotic, with four different categories (charitable voluntary hospitals, private nursing homes, municipal hospitals, and Poor Law infirmaries), and precious little co-ordination between them.

The exclusion of dependants from National Health Insurance

The greatest deficiency in health care remained the exclusion of dependants from the National Health Insurance scheme. By the outbreak of the Second World War, although around 21 million people were covered by the scheme – around half of the population of Great Britain, families were still excluded. Thus as one contemporary commentator put it, 'The [National Insurance] scheme is, of course, primarily designed for the industrial population . . . But the wives and families of insured workers . . . cannot normally get free doctoring' (Robson, 1948, p. 94).

Little wonder, therefore, that in spite of some improvement since the beginning of the century, so much ill-health persisted among young children and their mothers. Health standards were particularly poor before the Second World War in the depressed industrial areas. Thus the infant mortality rate varied from 42 per thousand live births in the home counties to 76 in Durham, 72 in Scotland and 114 in Jarrow (Iliffe, 1983, p. 22). Local investigation undertaken in 1930 by the then Board of Education into maternal and child health in South Wales found that, 'out of 749 children examined at

30 centres 240, or 32 per cent, were found to be more of less defective in the sense that their physical condition had been impaired by malnutrition, anaemia or rickets' (Dr. Dilys Jones, Public Record Office, File ED50/83). Such internal Board of Education reports also noted that children's nutritional levels would have been far worse had it not been for the self-sacrifices of their mothers. Aneurin Bevan, the architect of the NHS, was himself later to acknowledge that, 'The records show that it is the mother in the average family who suffers most from the absence of a free health service. In trying to balance her domestic budget she puts her own needs last' (Bevan, 1952, p. 75).

The Second World War served to highlight such deficiencies. The Emergency Medical Service (EMS) established at the beginning of the war revealed a grossly ill-balanced distribution of GPs and hospital specialists. Hastings, for example, had one GP for every 1178 people, while South Shields only had one for every 4105. Some counties were without a single gynaecologist before the war and the Eastern counties had no paediatricians (Titmuss, 1950, p. 493).

The National Health Service

The creation of a comprehensive medical service had been proposed as early as the Dawson Report of 1920, but it was the Beveridge Report which pronounced that the creation of a comprehensive health service was one of three indispensable conditions for the successful implementation of broader proposals for social security reform. Following extensive discussion, a White Paper was published in 1944, though the task of presenting the legislation to Parliament fell to Bevan as Minister of Health in the newly elected Labour government led by Clement Attlee.

The form in which the 1946 Act was finally implemented was strongly influenced by the medical profession and reflected more the outcome of a protracted negotiated compromise between external interests and political pressures than any purely Parliamentary deliberations and modifications (Ham, 1992, p. 15). Control and direction of the new NHS was based on a tripartite structure consisting of the newly nationalised hospitals, the family practitioner services, and the local-authority-run services which included maternity and child welfare clinics, vaccination and immunisation, the midwifery and health visitor services, and the School Medical Service.

Children and the new NHS

Whatever the inherent weaknesses in the original formulation of the new health service, few would dispute either the boldness or the ambitiousness of the scheme. Upon Bevan's insistence, the service was free at the point of delivery and was to be paid for largely out of general taxation to avoid any taint of a tax upon the sick; all citizens were to have equal access to the full range of available health facilities included under the service; and the highest quality of care possible should be ensured for all, or, as Bevan called it, 'universalising the best'.

The insistence in the new NHS on these principles served to remove those pre-existing barriers to primary and specialist health care for mothers and children, so that there can be no doubt that, in any comparison with the haphazard arrangements which preceded it, the NHS has made a significant contribution to improvements in child health since the Second World War. Thus whereas in 1948 1394 deaths were recorded from diphtheria, polio, measles and whooping cough, there were only sixteen such deaths in 1986; and deaths from the most virulent pre-war killer – tuberculosis – fell between 1938 and 1986 from 25 623 to 376. A consequence of this general improvement is that long-term in-patient care for children 'is now unusual', and there is less demand for specialist children's hospitals (Levitt *et al.*, 1995, p. 156). However, as we noted earlier, these improvements are associated with steady increases in living standards, and cannot therefore be simply attributed to the medical advances made available to our child population through the NHS.

The changing political and economic context 1948–89

Debate and subsequent reform since 1948 have centred on three principal problems, all inherent in the structure and organisation of the NHS from the outset: first, problems of cost, which have been compounded by steadily continuing advances in medicine as well as by demographic increases in those categories of people who, from the point of view of health care need, are more expensive; second, problems arising out of the structure of the NHS and the necessity to ensure effective co-ordination between the disparate elements of the service; and third, those stemming from the need to achieve an efficient system of management for a multi-faceted organisation employing nearly a million people.

Public enquiry, policy proposals and the subsequent reform of the NHS have taken place throughout its post-war history. But for the first twenty-five years of its existence these problems did not inhibit the steady expansion of the service. Thus by the mid-1970s the personnel employed had doubled since 1948; and the NHS was absorbing close to 6 per cent of national GDP compared to 3.25 per cent in 1953–4.

In response to the oil crisis of 1973, however, when oil prices quadrupled, government restrictions on welfare spending were tightened; and in 1976–7 'cash limits' on health authority expenditure were imposed by the then Labour government, a brake on NHS expenditure, which, as one authority notes, 'was never again more than momentarily relaxed' (Webster, 1993, p. 128).

In a colder climate for social welfare, the election of a new, more ideologically predisposed Conservative government in 1979 led by Margaret Thatcher, foreshadowed a new era for British post-war social policy. However, influenced though social policies have been since then by the ideology of the New Right with its emphasis on the efficacy of an unfettered private market and the need to reduce the burden of taxation, what is perhaps most surprising about the fortunes of the NHS under Conservative governments since 1979 is the degree of continuity. The NHS, in the words of one commentator, 'finished the decade [the 1980s] battered round the edges but largely intact' (Ranade, 1994, p. 49).

'Working for Patients' and the 1991 NHS reorganisation

The stringent cash limits on the hospital sector and the working through of the effects of a long-term reallocation of resources between the regions, and between primary care and the hospital sector, led to an apparently deepening crisis in the late 1980s, manifested – to wide public dismay – in ward and hospital closures, lengthening waiting lists, and children's scheduled operations postponed. To allay the not unnatural growing public anxiety, Margaret

Thatcher, following her third election triumph the previous June, instigated in January 1988 a Prime Minister's review of the NHS. The recommendations that flowed from this review were published in 1989 as a White Paper, *Working for Patients*. To the surprise of many, the financial tensions and problems within the NHS were not to be resolved by the radical adoption of a self-financing health insurance scheme, but by the introduction of an untried system of 'quasi' or 'internal markets', inspired by the American economist, Alain Enthoven, within the existing state run, tax financed and largely free NHS. The continuing search for efficiency gains would also be based on the further development of the enhanced management structures that had been implemented following the recommendations of the 1983 Griffiths Report. These proposals were given parliamentary sanction in the NHS and Community Care Act of 1990, and implemented in April 1991.

Central to the reforms is the separation of functions between 'providers' and 'purchasers'. In this, the hospitals are identified as the main providers, and the practices of 'GP fund-holders' and the district health authorities the principal purchasers. Practices with more than 7000 patients are now eligible to be fund-holders and, experimentally, 'consortia of practices as small as 3000'. GP fund-holder budgets exclude the costs of emergency treatment, and any treatment costing more than £5000 is paid for in full by the local district health authority. Budgets however cover other costs including the costs of prescriptions and those for the staff employed by the practice (Levitt *et al.*, 1995, p. 73).

Hospitals, moreover, are able to apply for 'self-governing NHS Trust' status, which as major providers gives them far greater local autonomy over staffing, specialist facilities and the control of the hospital's finances. The funding, weighted for the age and morbidity of the local population, is allocated to the district health authorities (DHAs), now called 'health authorities' (HAs), and to the family health service authorities (FHSAs) as the principal purchasers of health care on behalf of their respective population and patients. This finance can be used to purchase health care from the range of providers, including private hospitals, according to what appears to management and to the medical staff to represent the best value for money – and therefore presumably for patients. This 'purchaser-provider split', it is assumed will introduce an element of real competition among the suppliers who will no longer be assured of a fixed income and captive patients irrespective of their erstwhile performance.

These latest reforms are now shaping the nature and operation of the 'reorganised' NHS. In the following sections we consider some of the issues concerning child health care that appear to have arisen as a result of the reforms.

Child health care within the reorganised NHS

As is widely acknowledged it is too early to fully assess the effects of these reforms. Thus any conclusions concerning their implications for child health care must at the time of writing be somewhat speculative. It should be said, however, that the child population is almost wholly dependent on the services provided by the NHS. Nearly all private medical insurance policies specifically exclude pregnancy, childbirth, chronic illness and disability from being insurable conditions. Additionally, even though about 11 per cent of the population are covered by some kind of private medical insurance, most policies exclude dependents except where an additional premium is paid.

Children also absorb a relatively high proportion of health expenditure. Together, children and the elderly account for 60 per cent of the total expenditure on hospital and community health services (Baggott, 1994, p. 219). Though it might also be noted that women, because of their twin roles as child-bearers and child-rearers, are 'the biggest users of health-care facilities' (Abercrombie, Warde *et al.*, 1994, p. 399).

What all this means of course is that women and children and the very elderly are the groups whose health care needs are most immediately and intimately affected by NHS reform and any consequent changes in the state provision of medical services.

Primary health care and GP fundholding

The term 'primary health care' refers generally to those health services available within a local community – GPs, dentists, pharmacists, opticians, community nurses and midwives, and health visitors. 'Secondary health care' would thus refer to hospital services within a wider district.

Children are now less likely to be hospitalised, but many suffer from chronic conditions. Thus for children within the health care services good *primary care* is of particular importance. This is also true, of course, for pregnant women and nursing mothers. Policies since the mid 1980s to shift the emphasis away from acute hospital medicine towards primary care could therefore be seen as being of considerable advantage to children.

In 1993 there were approximately 30 000 GPs – an increase of 5000 since 1980, and practices have gradually become larger. However, although by 1990 60 per cent of practices consisted of four or more doctors, 10 per cent of practices were still provided by a single GP, and 30 per cent were shared by two or three doctors. For mothers and children, of course, this has the advantage of accessibility since, for most areas, there is a practice within 'pram-pushing distance' (Allsop, 1995, p. 201). At the time of writing, some 90 per cent of illness is managed outside hospitals and there has been a steady increase since 1979 in the number of GP consultations and the number of prescriptions issued. This growth was reflected during the 1980s in an increase in real terms in the funding for general practitioner services of more than 3 per cent. In a general sense this is good news for children, and there are some signs that the institution of fundholding will further enhance the role of primary health care. For example, in one investigation, the respondent GPs said they viewed fundholding as a means of maintaining their autonomy to refer patients and as a way 'to increase the leverage they had over hospitals to improve services'. These trends could represent, it is suggested, 'a shift in the balance of power back to general practice for the first time this century' (Glennerster *et al.*, 1994, pp. 167, 179).

One issue that does have considerable significance for health care provision for children is the geographical distribution of fundholding practices. Fundholding now covers half of the population, but the general picture is of fundholding having been taken up 'by the better organised practices in more affluent areas of the country. Poor inner city GPs are least likely to be fundholders' (Allsop, 1995, p. 185). So, for example, fundholding coverage was reported to be 4 per cent in Camden and Islington, compared to 84 per cent in Derbyshire, the Isle of Wight, and Kingston upon Thames and Richmond in Surrey (*Guardian*, 20 July 1995). Thus if improved services for patients do result from the introduction of fundholding, then clearly the disadvantaged areas will not share in such progress and, as we have already noted, some of the least advantaged groups of children are heavily concentrated in precisely these areas. Furthermore, any potential widening of the quality of health care between more affluent and less affluent areas will only increase those inequalities of GP medical care which existed before the 1991 reforms.

Hospital care

Parents with children are particularly dependent upon the accident and emergency services of their local hospitals. The instant availability and access to hospitalised care in the case of serious injury make 'casualty' a highly valued part of the NHS for parents. Moreover, some of the least privileged British parents have considerable difficulty in registering themselves and their children with a GP. It is also in casualty departments that children with unexplained injuries may first appear – like, for example, the children of Fred and Rosemary West, who attended the Gloucester Accident and Emergency Department on no fewer than thirty-one separate occasions. Hospital casualty departments for all children can be critical, so recent policies to rationalise hospital provision and to close A and E departments again have implications for child health. The substitution of 'minor injuries units', open during weekday office hours, though helpful for some, is no substitute for the 24-hour availability of a full medical team. Parents whose children suffer accidental injury may thus now find that their nearest A and E department is far less accessible than it was ten or fifteen years ago.

The issue of emergency health care provision was discussed at the 1995 annual conference of the National Association of Fundholding Practices. The then Health Minister, Stephen Dorrell, said he foresaw the end of the traditional hospital A and E unit. Instead, the main role in treating emergencies would pass to primary health care teams, with the most serious cases being treated in 'high tech, regional trauma centres'. However, fundholding GPs expressed some anxiety that they would be expected to assume this additional emergency role 'without adequate resources or reward' (*Guardian*, 19 October 1995). In light of the frequency and unpredictability of accidents to children, it would seem that such a proposal must cause alarm to many parents, particularly in view of the reservations being expressed by doctors. It is none the less possible that financial pressures within trust hospitals will lead to some continuing reduction in the present distribution of A and E services, in spite of what has currently been described as 'the relentless surge of emergency cases' which, according to a study by the King's Fund published in September 1995, are across all ages and diagnoses (reported in the *Guardian*, 20 September 1995).

One consequence within hospitals of the purchaser–provider split that does have implications for child health care is the growing visibility of the purchasing process and the rationale for 'commissioning' (or purchasing), even though the available information for reaching a decision may often be inadequate. This increased transparency of the process of health rationing and any restrictions on particular forms of treatment certainly raise the question of what priority should be given to a child's needs for health care. This question was illustrated agonisingly in the recent case of 'Child B' (more recently identified as Jaymee Bowen), whose Health Authority (Cambridge and Huntingdon), after consultation with her doctors, decided not to fund a second bone-marrow transplant as further treatment for her leukaemia. (Sadly, following subsequent private treatment financed by an anonymous benefactor and some months remission of her illness, Jaymee died on 21 May 1996.)

It may thus be that the case for increased health care expenditure on similar cases, and on children in general, may be strengthened by the greater openness of the debate about rationing now taking place within the NHS.

Discussion

There are further general issues arising out of recent NHS reforms that have implications for child health care. First there is the question of the administrative costs of the reforms and the enhanced management structure. The 1991 changes entailed a sharp acceleration of such costs in both the primary care and hospital sectors of the NHS. Clearly, if in a context of continuing financial restraint the administrative costs and burdens imposed by the reforms are allowed to demoralise medical staff, then the quality of health care for children especially, as main users, will be adversely affected.

A second issue concerns the status of children as 'consumers' or 'customers'. Since children cannot be viewed as 'consumers' in any meaningful sense of the word, changes in health care designed to increase consumer choice may not be wholly sensitive to children's health needs and may by a verbal sleight of hand avoid the issue of children's rights to the best available care regardless of cost. Children certainly are among those least likely to have the relevant medical knowledge to make informed choices. It is others – parents, clinicians, health service managers, indeed politicians – who have to make judgements about the most appropriate forms of health care for children's health needs, as in the case of Jaymee Bowen mentioned above.

In this particular context we should mention a highly significant House of Lords judgement in 1986. The 'Gillick judgement', as it has become known, concerned the question as to whether or not a girl of less than 16 years of age could seek contraceptive advice without her parents' consent. The Lords conclusion was that, where a child had sufficient understanding, s/he should have the right to make his/her own decisions in medical matters.

Despite this decision, there is little evidence that the health services have advanced very far in involving children, especially younger ones, in decision-making relating to their own treatment. In this respect G. Lansdown (1995, p. 12) points to the national campaign in 1994 to immunise school children against measles and rubella as an example of where the focus was on the parents rather than on the children themselves.

When the Patients' Charter talks of 'rights', these would appear essentially to be those that adult consumers might expect: to be able to register with a GP or to 'have the right to change your GP easily and quickly', for example. However, it makes only limited mention of the substance of what children's rights to health care might actually consist, except to say that everyone can expect the NHS to make it easy to use its services 'including children, elderly people or people with physical or mental disabilities'. The *Charter* does additionally spell out what parents can expect if their child is admitted to hospital – 'to be cared for in a children's ward under the supervision of a consultant paediatrician'(p. 6). Yet there is no mention of any right to the availability in a child's local area of accident and emergency hospital care – as we saw above, the commonest form of hospital treatment for children – nor of a child's right not to be a main carer when a parent is disabled.

A third concern is that the relegation of financial management to individual hospitals and local GPs will lead to a greater unevenness of standards and nationwide disparities in the standards and quality of health care available. Thus, as Baggott (1994) observes, 'The extension of Trust status and GP fundholding produces fragmentation and difficulties in the planning of services' (p. 199). Mohan (1995) goes further and asks whether it is meaningful to talk of a truly 'National' Health Service. He throws considerable doubt on the proposition of a truly 'national' service, and suggests that a combination of the new 'localism' together with the very varied resources available in contrasting areas, now threatens the original NHS principle of 'equal treatment for those in equal need', and may presage a widening division of welfare in the field of health care (p. 223).

Finally, there is the question of the overall funding of the NHS. It is widely recognised that the UK spends a smaller proportion of its GDP on health services than do other comparable nations. Thus OECD data for 1990 shows that whereas France spent 8.8 per cent of its GDP on health, and the OECD average was 7.6 per cent, Britain spent 6.2 per cent. Given the UK's achieved standards of health, the NHS clearly represents excellent value for money, but this does pose the question as to whether Britain's health services are not underfunded generally. We might thus ask whether, in terms of health care, Britain is not short-changing its children and bequeathing a legacy of poorer health for their later years.

Inequalities in health care among children

Child health in the 1990s – a century of progress

In 1901, for every thousand babies born, 149 would have died within their first year of life and a further 80 would be dead before reaching the age of fifteen. Malnutrition, poor housing and the absence of any proper health care for the large proportion of the child population ensured an early demise for many children, and chronic ill health for many others. One stunted generation succeeded another, as the early poverty surveys revealed.

Since that first decade of the twentieth century there has been a quite extraordinary and continuous improvement in child health. Thus since the end of the Second World War, for example, infant mortality rates have fallen sharply – from 50 per 1000 for 1941–5, to the lowest ever recorded figure of 6.2 for 1994.

Children do still die in infancy and before reaching adulthood, but death under the age of twenty has become a relatively rare occurrence. Over half (58 per cent) of all deaths under the age of twenty occur in the first year of life, but thereafter the 99.24 per cent of babies who survive their first year of life face a diminishing risk of premature death until later adolescence, when traffic accidents take a growing toll.

However, considerable long-term and short-term illness among children, though being due to changing and therefore different causes than before, appears to be widespread and serious in varying degrees. Thus the amount of chronic illness among children more than doubled between 1972 and 1991, so that some 15 per cent of infants and children (0–15 years) are now reported to be experiencing chronic illness at any one time; and of these more than 5 per cent find their lives restricted by their illness. Respiratory conditions – especially asthma – represent over half of all such reported longstanding illness (Woodroffe *et al.*, 1993, p. 39). Such an increased incidence no doubt partly reflects better access to improved medical care, but there is also now, of course, a greater chance of survival of very low birthweight babies and other infants with serious disabilities (ibid., p. 54).

Despite this qualification it remains true that in most respects the health standards of British children are now higher than they have ever been. However, the enormous improvements in child health that have occurred during the twentieth century have not eliminated differences in health standards between different sectors of the population, so that obstinate health inequalities continue to exist between the different social strata. A 1991 government Green Paper acknowledged this fact, when it noted that not all social groups had shared equally in these improvements, adding somewhat coyly, that there are 'significant variations in health – geographic, ethnic, social and occupational – within England as in other countries'; and that 'this is a cause for concern and a challenge' (Dept of Health, 1991b, p. viii).

The Black Report

In 1977 the then Labour government agreed to the setting up of a working group on inequalities in health. The resultant Black Report met with 'a frosty reception' when presented to the Conservative government in April 1980, but it nevertheless generated wide public concern (Townsend and Davidson, 1992, p. 3). In the words of one recent commentator, the Report showed that

> the lower down the social scale you are, the less healthy you are likely to be and the sooner you can expect to die. Furthermore . . . if you are working-class, then your *children* will also be at greater risk of injury, sickness and death. (Abercrombie, Warde *et al.*, 1994, p. 396)

The Health Divide

The evidence upon which the Black Report was based was updated in 1988 in *The Health Divide* – again officially disregarded. This confirmed the Black Report's findings of significant class differences in mortality that apply 'at every stage of life from birth, through to adulthood and well into old age' (Whitehead, 1992, p. 228).

Social class and childhood mortality

While infant mortality rates have improved steadily for all social classes, marked class differences still remain, so that infant mortality rates for social classes IV and V (semi-skilled and unskilled manual workers) are as much as 40 and 60 per cent respectively higher than for social class I (professional). (Woodroffe *et al.*, 1993, p. 86).

The pattern of child mortality above the age of one year displays a similar social class gradient. The major cause of death among children aged 1–14 remains 'injury and poisoning', which accounts for about a third of all such deaths. Boys are at greater risk than girls at all ages, but the sharp increases in child mortality by social class affect both sexes, so that children in social class V are nearly four times as likely to die from this cause (especially road and 'fires or flames' accidents) compared to children in social classes I, II and III (non-manual).

Social class and childhood morbidity

Evidence on childhood illness indicates that social class differences are less pronounced than they are for child mortality. However, recent analysis of the available data has shown that 'a higher proportion of children and teenagers in manual groups than the non-manual groups [are] . . . suffering from a longstanding illness limiting their activities' (Woodroffe *et al.*, 1993, p. 92).

Unemployment and health inequalities

Possible connections between unemployment and health have long been investigated, and it is widely recognised that unemployment among male workers in particular is associated with an increased incidence of a variety of illnesses – for example, lung cancer and heart disease (see Whitehead, 1992: 253). Moreover, there seems to be a direct association between unemployment and mental health, with unemployed people 'displaying consistently higher levels of distress than other people' (Harris, 1984, p. 89).

The children of families in which one or both parents are unemployed are thus doubly disadvantaged in that they are likely to suffer all the deprivations associated with low household income, and at the same time to be living in homes where their parents may be affected by poor health. Fagin's (1981) study, for example, found that unemployment affected families rather than just the male 'breadwinner', and that financial worry and family tension affected husbands, wives and children, all of whom displayed 'signs of distress – depression headaches, asthmatic attacks, loss of appetite' (quoted in Abercrombie, Warde *et al.*, 1994, p. 406).

The health of child minorities

The recorded incidence of mortality and morbidity is markedly higher among the children of unsupported mothers, ethnic minorities, and Traveller children. While these groupings cannot easily be located within the Registrar-General's classification of social class (which is widely used in measuring health inequalities), they do share many of the lifestyle attributes commonly associated with economic and social deprivation, so that their life chances relate to the socioeconomic hierarchy upon which measures of social class are based.

Unsupported mothers

The highest levels of infant mortality are associated with low birthweight. Official data reveals that babies born weighing less than 2500g (5.5lb) are twice as likely to die in their first year as babies born over this weight. Only 7 per cent of all deliveries in 1991 weighed less than 2500g, though these 'accounted for 59 per cent of all perinatal deaths' (Raleigh and Balarajan, 1995, p. 85); but the higher the social class, the less likely the baby is to have a low birthweight. The risk to the children of unsupported mothers is especially high, with an infant mortality rate of 13 per 1000 live births.

The health of children from ethnic minorities

Because of the limited data available, relatively little is known about the overall health picture of minority-group children. However, data is available about the health of children born of mothers who were themselves born outside the UK in New Commonwealth countries and Pakistan. Thus babies of 'mothers born in Pakistan, the Caribbean, and Africa other than those from East Africa, show excess mortality throughout infancy' (Raleigh and Balarajan, 1995, pp. 85–6).

Certain illnesses have in the past been far more common among the ethnic minority child population than among the child population as a whole. These include rickets and tuberculosis among children of Asian origin, and sickle-cell anaemia among children of Afro-Caribbean descent (Whitehead, 1992, p. 257). The OPCS Decennial Supplement concludes generally:

> Such information as is available suggests that morbidity and mortality is higher in ethnic minority children than in others . . . Most of the ethnic minority populations are in low paid employment and reside in inner city areas, with overcrowded, poor quality housing and restricted access to outdoor facilities. (Raleigh and Balarajan, 1995, p. 92)

Traveller children

If our available knowledge about the health of ethnic minority children is limited, even less is known about the state of health of Traveller children. What little we do know, however, should give great cause for concern. A majority of Gypsies are now thought to live in permanent housing, but large numbers of Travellers still retain their traditional nomadic life-style and live in various kinds of trailers and caravans, or other mobile accommodation such as barges (OFSTED, 1996, p. 14).

For the maintenance of good health, particularly among mothers and their children, the Traveller life-style thus requires two basic pre-conditions: first, satisfactory living conditions on the sites of residence; and second, access to the same standards of health care as are available to the settled population in an area.

Unfortunately, the fragmentary evidence suggests that for many Travellers neither of these health need prerequisites are being met adequately. There are constant reports of Travellers being summarily evicted and moved on so that a proportion of this community – with their children – would appear to live a life resembling a game of hide and seek, moving surreptitiously from one unauthorised site to another.

The 1968 Caravan Sites Act obliged local authorities to provide adequate accommodation (that is, sites) for Travellers residing in or resorting to their area. Unfortunately, no time limit has ever been imposed for meeting this obligation. Thus Hughie Smith, the National Gypsy Council President, at a National Conference held under the auspices of Save the Children and other organisations in 1991, concluded that, 'the [1968] Act has failed, because we've *still* got a situation where over one-third of all Gypsies in this country are forced to camp illegally . . . There is, he continued, an element of cruelty towards Gypsies in this country which is evident from the harsh eviction policies employed by many Local Authorities' (National Conference, 1991, pp. 12–13).

The limited amount of evidence from local studies would certainly confirm this situation. J. Pahl and M. Vaile's study of Kent Gypsies found that, of the 263 mothers interviewed (by health visitors), 26 per cent were living with their families on unauthorised sites which 'were mostly fields but included waste land and roadsides' (Pahl and Vaile, 1986, p. 16). Of this sample, 14 per cent of families had no access to mains water, while 21 per cent had no mains electricity on their sites and 33 per cent no lavatories (ibid., p. 18).

Inevitably, Traveller children suffer from poor health. Thus, according to Pahl and Vaile's evidence for the 814 Gypsy births to their sample of mothers, the overall infant mortality rate (IMR) was 17.5 per cent, almost 50 per cent higher than the 1980 IMR for England and Wales. Even more alarming was the rate among Gypsies in East Anglia, where a 1983 report by Save the Children found a rate – admittedly for a smaller sample (265 births) – of 53.8 per 1000, which takes us back to the national rate that applied in 1945.

Contemporary health risks to children

> The scope for improving health lies outside the NHS. (*British Medical Journal*, 1991, p. 16)

It was argued at the beginning of this chapter that health standards are dependent not only on the provision of formal health care services but also, importantly, on a range of socioeconomic factors in society at large. It follows from this that children's present health needs and the policy implications of these can only be fully ascertained by examining at least the more immediate and significant of these factors. We have already surveyed the association between socioeconomic inequalities and health. In this final section of the chapter we develop this theme further by examining four major contemporary health risks to children.

Accidents to children

> Children are particularly vulnerable. Accidents are the commonest cause of death among children over the age of 5 and they cause one child in six to attend a hospital Accident and Emergency department every year. Road accidents account for about a quarter of all deaths among school-children and about two thirds of all accidental deaths in the same age group. (*Health of the Nation*, 1991b, p. 73)

In 1992, 661 infants and children aged over 28 days and under 15 years died as a result of a fatal accident. Approximately 50 per cent of these (310) were accounted for by road accidents, which cause a growing proportion of childhood deaths as children get older. Thus traffic accidents represent 20 per cent of the fatalities among children under the age of one, but 71 per cent among 10–14-year-olds. In the same year (1992) there were 39 341 road accidents involving injuries to children, 7434 of which involved serious injury (Department of Transport (DOT) (1993), figures supplied by the Royal Society for the Prevention of Accidents, RoSPA.

Most other accidents to children occur in and around the home. Figures based on children attending hospital accident and emergency units indicate that in 1992 there were one million such accidents to children under 15, of which some 40 000 were sufficiently serious to necessitate in-patient treatment. There is a wide range of causes of accidents in the home, the most lethal of which is fire. This particularly affects the 1–4 age group who are more likely to be in the home and less likely to be able to escape from flames. In 1992, fires accounted for 43 per cent of all fatal child accidents in the home (RoSPA (figures from OPCS), 1992). Falls are the most common type of non fatal accident. These accounted for 42 per cent of children's accidents in the home (approximately 450 000) in 1992, although fortunately falls generally result in relatively few fatalities (about 20 annually).

In terms of health care, it is manifest that accidents to children represent a heavy call on the resources available within the NHS. According to official estimates, traffic accidents in England cost £4.5 billion (Dept of Health, 1992, p. 102). Direct costs to the NHS of childhood accidents alone were estimated in 1992 at over £200 million.

This is therefore an important area for increased efficiency and savings. But the causes, and therefore effective prevention, lie outside the scope of the actual health services. The White Paper does make positive suggestions as to how the occurrence of accidents may be reduced, though 'the imposition of unnecessary regulations on business and individuals' is to be avoided (Dept of Health, 1992, p. 106).

However, an effective and comprehensive policy to reduce child accidents might well require a range of measures such as: a greater segregation of road traffic from main pedestrian routes; a national policy to develop networks of cycle tracks in urban areas; the avoidance of children living in high flats; and a major government initiative to reduce the use of temporary accommodation for the homeless. A government really committed to reducing child accidents might also introduce permanent 'summer time' and random breath tests, both measures long advocated by accident prevention pressure groups.

Children and smoking

> Every morning the tobacco industry wakes up with a problem. It has just killed 300 of its regular customers. If they are not replaced, the tobacco industry will die. Most of their new customers will be children. (Action on Smoking and Health (ASH), 1995)

Nowhere is the close dependence of children's health on that of their parents more devastatingly illustrated than in the case of tobacco smoking. The effects of parental smoking, and of maternal smoking in particular, damage a child's health from the moment of conception. Even after birth the effects of inhaling tobacco smoke in the home environment have an immediate and continuing harmful effect upon children's physiological functions. No wonder, then, that many of the responses to the government's 1991 consultative document, 'identified tobacco as the single most important cause of preventable ill health in the United Kingdom today' (Royal College of Physicians (RCP), 1992).

There are few if any rights of protection for children against the effects of adult smoking, nor against the promotional efforts of cigarette manufacturers to sell tobacco – ostensibly, of course, to people over the age of 16. This is in spite of the accumulation of substantial evidence as to the pernicious effects of smoking on children. For example, according to the RCP Report, *Smoking and the Young*, 'Over one-quarter of the risk of death due to the Sudden Infant Death Syndrome is attributable to maternal smoking (equivalent to 365 deaths per year in England and Wales)', while parental smoking 'is responsible for at least 17,000 admissions to hospital each year of children under the age of five' (1992, p. 9).

Children in fact face four major forms of tobacco-related health risk if one or both of their parents smoke: firstly their foetal health (or indeed their life) is endangered; secondly from birth onwards as conscripted 'passive smokers' they will suffer a variety of harmful effects during childhood; thirdly as they get older they are far more likely than children who have grown up in non-smoking homes to become active smokers themselves, and consequently to endure the relative unfitness and ill-health effects caused by smoking; and finally, their health as adults will be in considerable jeopardy throughout their probably foreshortened lives.

There has been a long-term decline in the incidence of smoking, so that whereas in 1972, 52 per cent of men and 41 per cent of women smoked, the respective figures for 1992 were 29 and 28 per cent (Central Statistical Office, 1995a, p. 127). However, these figures conceal more than they reveal. In the first place, from the point of view of children, a particularly unfortunate trend in the nation's smoking habits has been the disappearance of the previous gender difference, which has resulted in as many women as men now smoking. Furthermore, among the young, recent surveys consistently show a higher prevalence of smoking in young women, so that among 16–19-year-olds in 1990, 32 per cent of women were recorded as smokers compared to 28 per cent of men (General Household Survey (GHS), 1991, quoted in Power, 1995, p. 49). Even worse, evidence indicates that almost as many young people are starting to smoke as previously, and the highest proportion of smokers is in the 20–24 age group, with 37 per cent of women and 39 per cent of men in this age group being smokers.

There is a rapid habituation to smoking among children in early adolescence, especially around the ages of 14–15, so that by the age of 15, nearly one in four of the young have become regular smokers. On the basis of these figures it is calculated that as many as 450 children start smoking every day in Britain.

As part of its health strategy, John Major's Government set ambitious targets to reduce the prevalence of smoking among 11–15-year-olds 'by at least 33 per cent by 1994', and among pregnant women by a similar amount 'at the start of their pregnancy' by the year 2000 (Dept of Health, 1992, p. 20). The RCP report acknowledged the 'high government awareness of the role of preventative medicine', but concluded that, on current trends 'it is difficult to see how these targets are going to be met' (Royal College of Physicians, 1992, p. viii). The *British Medical Journal* expressed similar doubts as to the attainability of the government's targets unless a comprehensive and properly funded government-sponsored campaign were to be undertaken (Smith, 1991).

Unhappily, these assessments have proved to be only too accurate. Figures for 1994 from an OPCS survey reveal that, since 1992, among children in England aged 11–15, there has in fact been an increase of 2 per cent in the numbers of regular smokers – from 10 per cent in 1992 to 12 per cent. This most recent survey also confirmed that in England, Wales and Scotland, girls were more likely to smoke than boys. As the British Medical Association (BMA) commented:

> We now face a whole generation of new smokers . . . If these figures are not arrested immediately only a ban on tobacco advertising combined with more resources put into teenage smoking education will tackle this problem. (Quoted in the *Guardian*, October 18 1995)

Children's health problems related to smoking undoubtedly pose the most serious and pressing challenge of health prevention. Any major reduction in the prevalence of smoking among all age groups would, directly and indirectly, achieve major long term health improvements for children. With smoking, as in the case of accidents, the NHS – and the taxpayer – is called upon to meet health costs caused by factors largely beyond its control. Given the deleterious effects upon health of tobacco and the enormous human and economic costs involved, any government-sponsored initiatives could in the long run prove highly cost-effective.

Smoking entails the subordination of a child's right to health in favour of the putative rights of adult groups. Thus, over the issue of smoking, children's rights clash head-on with those of adults, and the present situation provides moreover a clear instance of where the liberty of some is the cause of direct harm to others. If those to whom the harm is done were not children, and if the habit of smoking had not for a long time been socially acceptable, then the denial of rights involved and the resultant abuse of child health would have long since been unacceptable.

As it is, in the present context, children's immediate and long-term health interests can only be enhanced by a concerted programme of action, as recently adopted in New Zealand, Canada and California.

Asthma

> Asthma is the most important chronic disease in childhood, being both common and at times very severe. Over a prior 12-month period about 15 per cent of children will report episodes of wheezing suggestive of asthma and about a quarter of these will have restricted activities due to the condition. (Botting, 1995, p. 123)

Asthma is not only the most common childhood respiratory disorder, it is also one of the few common treatable conditions that is increasing worldwide – from Finland to the highlands of New Guinea and New Zealand (Barnes and Newhouse, 1994, p. 13). Yet asthma is also one of the oldest reported illnesses, with references to the condition found in writings from ancient Egypt and classical Greece (the word itself is of Greek origin meaning 'gasping for breath' or 'panting'). The underlying physiological condition is inflammation of the air passages and it is this that produces the range of symptoms experienced by those who suffer from the condition. However, what actually triggers this inflammation in the first place is insufficiently understood, and, as in the case of traffic pollution, is the subject of continuing debate.

Asthma is most prevalent among children. Estimates vary according to how the condition is diagnosed, but as many as 30 per cent of children may exhibit asthma-type symptoms at some stage during their childhood, and as many as a million children are thought to be chronically affected to some degree. The illness can be classified according to the degree of severity – 'mild', 'moderate' or 'severe'. Thus the effects of asthma on children's everyday lives will vary considerably according to how severely they are affected. About half of all children with asthma experience only 'infrequent episodes of cough and mild wheezing', but the other half suffer from more frequent and more severe episodes for many years, and of these some 5–10 per cent have continuing respiratory symptoms and need constant supervision (Fletcher, 1991, p. 118). Children with infrequent and mild asthma often largely outgrow their symptoms but those displaying moderate and severe symptoms are less likely to do so.

The causes of asthma are an area of current debate. Certainly the tendency to develop allergies, including allergic asthma, often runs in families. But there is considerable doubt over the exact nature and the extent of the influence of heredity in explaining the incidence of the disease. So because the prevalence of asthma is fairly evenly distributed throughout the country and across various lifestyles and ethnicities, current medical thinking therefore is that it is factors in the environment which 'are important in determining whether an individual develops asthma, although the allergic tendency makes it somewhat more likely' (Barnes and Newhouse, 1994, p. 127). These factors include air pollution and diet as well as certain domestic allergens such as house dust mites and tobacco smoke (Anderson *et al.*, 1995, p. 125).

Smoking, in particular, aggravates asthma, and asthmatic symptoms are twice as common among children whose parents smoke (Royal College of Physicians, 1992, p. 9). It is thought that women who smoke during pregnancy increase the risk of a susceptibility to allergic diseases in their children. Passive smoking too during early childhood, especially when it is the mother who smokes, may also increase the risk of a child developing the illness (Barnes and Newhouse, 1994, p. 11).

With possible climatic changes leading to longer and hotter summers in the UK, there is growing concern over the effects of air pollution caused by traffic fumes containing nitrogen dioxide and minute particles from diesel engine emissions (particulates). Greater concentrations of ozone, too, are generated by the action of sunlight, and lingering emissions of sulphur dioxide from coal-burning power stations may also be present in the urban atmosphere. Hot and calm weather conditions, moreover, tend to trap polluted air in and over our cities, even at street level. Although none of these pollutants on its own is thought to normally exist in the atmosphere in sufficient concentrations to trigger increased attacks, it is thought possible that there may be complex chemical reactions between them, which would explain the apparent heightened incidence of asthma associated with atmospheric pollution (ibid., p. 10).

Certain foodstuffs, such as nuts and shellfish, also act as triggers for the onset of asthma. It is now also recognised that certain food and drink additives such as tartrazine and monosodium glutamate can worsen asthma (ibid., p. 130). Again, as with traffic pollution, these substances are so widely used by the food industry that they are difficult to avoid.

The apparent increase in childhood asthma raises several issues of social policy. As the most important cause of illness in children, it can certainly be a disabling condition for many unless properly assessed and managed. Certainly, the average school class may have 2–3 asthmatic children who are likely to suffer some absence and who may find it difficult to participate in some school activities. Schools therefore need to be in close touch with the parents of asthmatic children, and supervision in schools of younger children's medication may also be necessary.

There are also important health care considerations. The treatment of asthma represents a heavy expense on NHS budgets – something of the order of £400 million according to the government's Green Paper (Dept of Health, 1991b, p. 99). General practitioners treat 87 per cent of attacks, but there are on average s⁓ ⁓e 155 children admitted to hospital every day because of the condit and several children die annually as a result of acute attack deaths under the age of 15, and 49 deaths of young people aged 19 were recorded in 1988). The National Asthma Campaign others argue that many asthma deaths are avoidable. Early a careful diagnosis is important for the avoidance of any permane⁓ damage to the respiratory system and for the effective management of the condition, especially among those falling into the moderate and severe categories of sufferers.

The increasing pressures upon medical staff, both in hospitals and in general practice surgeries, cannot help improve the medical care available to asthmatics, so clearly the successful combating of asthma does require the proper funding of our health care services. More government action to improve public transport and reduce atmospheric pollution caused by urban traffic congestion also appears to be necessary.

Children's diets

> An adequate and balanced diet is essential for children's growth and health. (Woodroffe *et al.*, 1993, p. 167)

In contrast to certain other spheres of child health there appears to be at least something to celebrate in connection with the diet of British children. Specific nationwide evidence on child nutrition from dietary surveys undertaken during the 1980s found British school children to be taller and heavier than ever before (Power, 1995, p. 44). In addition, the British national diet would appear to have improved in nutritional quality since the 1970s (Dept of Health, 1991b, p. 108).

Nevertheless in spite of such indications of progress, the content and nutritional balance of the British diet, especially for many children, is far from satisfactory. We have already discussed in Chapter 3 the extent of child poverty and there is ample evidence to demonstrate that the nutritional quality of many poor children's diets is seriously deficient (see, for example, Cooper, 1994; Dobson *et al.*, 1994; Dowler and Calvert, 1995; NCH Action for Children, 1995). However, contemporary dietary inadequacies pose both short-term and long-term health risks to *all* children. We therefore conclude this chapter with a brief review of the nutritional problems which affect children in the late 1990s.

Children's diets at home

In current health policy discussions the issue of diet is a recurrent theme, and specific dietary targets have been set as part of a wider official strategy to combat preventable diseases widely associated with premature death, and for which, according to the *British Medical Journal*, 'about 30% of attributable risk can probably be ascribed to diet' (Smith, 1991, p. 19). The objective of a significant reduction in coronary heart disease (CHD) and stroke is to be achieved partly by a reduction in food energy derived from 'saturated fatty acids', and from total fat from an average of 42 per cent to no more than 35 per cent (Dept of Health, 1992, p. 20). (In 1991, only 14 per cent of adults were estimated to be deriving no more than 35 per cent of their food energy requirements from total fats.)

Unfortunately, recent evidence from the Nutrition Task Force (NTF) suggests that the situation is deteriorating rather than improving. More people are becoming obese, while families are eating 'almost twice the amount of fatty and sugary foods recommended by the Department of Health's advisory body, COMA' (*Guardian*, 9 October 1995). Furthermore, given the allure for children of highly flavoured and sweet foods, and given the irresistible pressures of advertising on the impressionable young, the diets of many children at home may be even less satisfactory than information about adult eating habits would indicate. Available evidence on children's diets thus reveals that 'the main sources of energy intake of school children are bread, chips, milk, biscuits, meat products, cake and puddings' (Power, 1995, p. 4).

Nor are the diets of very young children any less inadequate. A recent official survey of the diets of children aged 1.5 to 4.5 years indicates widely unsatisfactory diets even among this very young age group. Most of the diets were found to contain a high level of 'junk foods' with too much fat and sugar (Dept of Health and Ministry of Agriculture, Fisheries and Food, 1995).

Future health implications

National debate over food has moved beyond the issue of scarcity to what is now much more in question: the *composition* of the food children eat. Expert opinion has become convinced that the British adult diet – and even more so children's – is nutritionally unbalanced. We have, then, a general situation where most children are growing up in homes in which too much energy is derived from foods with a high fat and sugar content. This situation bodes ill for future health standards in this country for two reasons: first, the eating habits learnt in childhood will shape the food tastes and diets of coming generations of parents, and second, unhealthy eating in early life is now thought to be a critical influence on people's health in adult life. Thus the future incidence of certain forms of disease is being determined by the eating patterns of today's children. No wonder, therefore, that the National Heart Forum has recently warned that 'rates of coronary heart disease would soar in the 21st century if childhood eating habits did not change' (*Guardian*, 3 November 1995).

If current medical thinking is correct, whereas with previous generations any physical symptoms caused by food deprivation and malnutrition were clearly apparent during childhood and adolescence, now the harm to children's health resulting from poor-quality diets will not become apparent until later in adulthood. Meanwhile the true long-term health risks caused by poor eating habits among children and young people are obscured by physical appearances, and by the abundance of choice in food and the seeming affluence of many homes.

Children's diets at school

The dietary problems of many children have been compounded in recent years by the changes in eating habits that have been taking place within the schools. The recent decline of school meals service in particular has had from the point of view of children's nutrition several unfortunate dietary consequences. We examine these and discuss the social policy issues which they raise in the remainder of the chapter.

The school meals service since 1945

As with the nation's health services, it was the Second World War which transformed the uncoordinated and fragmented provision of pre-war school meals into the service that has in more recent times been an integral part of the life of all British schools. Minimum nutritional standards were established in 1941 for school meals, and programmes for the rapid expansion of the service were inaugurated from 1940 onwards. This policy was taken further in 1944 when R. A. Butler included in the Education Act a clause making the provision of milk and meals a *statutory* duty upon all LEAs.

At the beginning of the war, school meals had been a largely charitable provision for the poor, with under 3 per cent of British schoolchildren receiving some kind of meal. At the cessation of hostilities in 1945, a nutritionally balanced school dinner was being provided for a third of Britain's children, and plans were well in hand to expand this further to provide for three-quarters of the school population.

The expansion of the service was continued after the war, but for austerity reasons school dinners never became, as intended, a free element within the family allowance scheme, although universal free school milk was introduced in 1946. But school dinners, at a modest charge which essentially covered the cost of the food, continued to grow in popularity and by 1970 some 70 per cent of schoolchildren were staying at school for a midday meal.

After the early 1970s sharply increased charges were imposed for school meals, especially under Conservative administrations. In 1972, the Secretary of State for Education and Science, Margaret Thatcher, removed the requirement on LEAs to provide free school milk to children aged over seven; and as one of the earliest measures of the first Thatcher government, the 1980 Education Act effectively repealed the 1944 school meals legislation so that, except for the minimal provision of meals for those children entitled to 'free school dinners', local authorities since 1980 have no longer been required to provide a comprehensive meals service available to all children; moreover, the nationally maintained nutritional standards were also abandoned as a further effect of the 1980 legislation.

The 'residualisation' of the school meals service

Local authorities at the time of writing, as in the 1930s, can do very much as they please, so there are now wide variations between LEAs in the scope and quality of school catering, and in pricing policies.

Widening prices have inevitably been accompanied by growing differences in local participation rates. A number of reasons are proposed for the national decline in participation rates, but there has been a consistent correlation between price levels and participation rates. Thus from the peak participation rate of 70 per cent achieved in 1970, the rate held steady at approximately 65 per cent until 1980. Since then it has declined to 43 per cent (1993 figures), with 35 per cent of pupils having packed lunches and the other 22 per cent making their own alternative arrangements (Central Statistical Office, 1994, p. 29).

Certain local authorities have ceased to offer a service at all in their primary schools (for example, Dorset, Lincolnshire, Hereford and Worcester, and Somerset), except for a residual provision for those children entitled to – and claiming – free meals. Indeed, many local authorities would seem to have so eroded the quality of the meals served in their schools that once again staying for school dinners is stigmatised, and the free children, as before the Second World War, are identifiable as a group of poor children in receipt of poor-quality public provision – a situation that, as Carol Noble (1987) suggests, quoting Le Gros Clark (1948), is all too reminiscent of the 1930s, when 'the social context of school meals, in the eyes of the parents, was that of the Poor Law and the relieving officer'.

The dietary content and nutritional value of school meals

If the eating habits during the school day of many of the 57 per cent of school children who have no prepared school meal leave much to be desired, those of the other 43 per cent of children who do take a prepared school meal are often just as unsatisfactory, if not more so. Indeed, considerable evidence has accumulated that the nutritional quality of the meals eaten in many schools has deteriorated, though of course there are some notable exceptions among individual LEAs.

An *Observer* survey in 1990, for example, into the eating habits of children in the privately-run cafeteria of a Merton (Surrey) comprehensive school, citing an earlier official report that schoolchildren were eating a diet 'dominated by chips, buns and pastries', also found that chips were the most popular item on the school menu, accounting for 23 per cent of sales; canned drinks, pizzas and biscuits were also found to be 'big sellers' (*Observer*, 27 May 1990).

Another survey of 844 children aged between 11 and 16, commissioned by Gardner Merchant, a contract caterer, indicated that for the 50 per cent of children who ate school meals, hamburgers, pizza, hot dogs and sausages were the children's favourite choices. (It is, of course particularly these products that have recently been targeted as containing bovine spongiform encephalopathy (BSE) infected beef.) The same survey revealed that 9 per cent of children had nothing to eat before going to school in the morning – the equivalent of nearly 300 000 children nationally, and one in six of the sample was found not to have a hot meal in the evening – equivalent to 528 000 children nationwide (*The Times*, 20 November 1991).

The 'packed lunch' alternative

The 1980 Education Act obliged local authorities to provide facilities where pupils could eat their own packed lunches and snacks. Increased prices following the Act provoked a marked rise in the numbers of children bringing their own food. Thus in many schools eating may be going on periodically, and often surreptitiously, throughout the day in classrooms, in common rooms and indeed everywhere in and around school premises. Given the length of the school day and the early hour at which many children leave home, especially those of secondary school age, it is no wonder that the eating habits of some children have become a process of grazing or snacking in school and on their way to and from school – hence, of course, the reliance of many for their energy requirements on fast food, chips, crisps, confectionery and highly-flavoured sweetened drinks.

A 1991 survey by a group of Women's Institute health workers in Lincolnshire, reported in the *Daily Telegraph* on 7 May 1991, found that packed lunches were unsatisfactory, so much so that the group were reportedly 'appalled by what they had seen'. One of the survey team, a local GP, suggested that there was a link between the junk lunches which some children were found to be eating and the increased incidence of iron deficiency anaemia and recurrent viral infections among 8- and 9-year-old children she was treating at her health centre.

Social policy implications

Fortunately, there is a brighter side to all this. Much of the evidence demonstrates that parents are concerned about the quality of their children's diet consumed in schools. However, as a recent *Which?* report on school eating habits wryly comments, 'we found dramatic differences between what many parents wanted and what the children in our study were eating'. Even so, over half the children in the junior schools and three-quarters in the secondaries stated that they were interested in eating healthily (*Which?*, September 1992, p. 502).

Where healthy eating policies have, in fact, been introduced, school meals are very popular indeed. Certainly, many local authorities do promote nutritional guidelines, but the national picture is one of considerable fragmentation and of wide variation in standards. It is also probable that, with the relegation of the 'food and nutrition' component in the 'Design and Technology' syllabus (formerly 'Home Economics') within the National Curriculum, that food education in both theory and practice is being thoroughly undermined in many schools. Indeed many children's educational performance may also be suffering in subtle ways because of the erosion of the scope and quality of school catering. Once again, so it would appear, school meals are part of the problem of children's diets, and no longer, as they may once have been, for all too brief a period of our welfare history, a means of improvement.

The most urgent policy requirement is for the reimposition of nutritional guidelines for school meals. This was proposed in an abortive Private Member's Bill in 1987 and has been the first and foremost recommendation of several expert reports. Belatedly, the government promised to publish 'voluntary nutritional guidelines' during 1996 (*Guardian*, 3 November 1995); but it is doubtful whether, without the imposition of *statutory* guidelines, that healthier eating habits and nutritionally improved meals can be ensured throughout the school system. Policies to reverse the commercialisation of school catering and the reintroduction of subsidies to make school meals better value for money – and of better nutritional value – may also be necessary to achieve any effective reversal of the decline of the service and to help promote the urgently needed improvements in children's eating habits.

Conclusion

Standards of child health have improved greatly since 1945, and these improvements are in important respects a result of advances in medical knowledge and the improved provision of health care through the NHS. However, although the child population is no longer weakened and reduced by barely treatable infectious diseases, it exhibits other debilitating and disabling illnesses which in certain instances may actually be increasing.

Furthermore, the current incidence of childhood mortality, low as this now is, and of morbidity, do not affect all groups of children to an equal extent. As we have seen, social and economic inequalities throughout the post-war period have continued to correlate closely with health inequalities. Unequal health risks thus devolve upon income inequalities and relative deprivation; and, as noted in Chapter 3, there is considerable evidence that the proportion of children growing up in some degree of poverty has increased markedly since 1979. Improvements in the health of many children can therefore only be achieved by a determined and co- ordinated policy assault on these widening inequalities.

The discussion of health care raises the question of the adequacy of provision for children in the late 1990s. A central problem of the recent NHS reforms is the danger of the fragmentation of the service and therefore the possibility of the emergence of growing area-based differences in the scope and standards of NHS health care. Experience so far suggests that GP fundholding has taken hold most effectively in the more affluent districts, a tendency which, if it were to become general, could very quickly lead to a two-tier health service in which poor families living in deprived neighbourhoods would be increasingly disadvantaged. Yet while certain risks clearly exist, there are some positive signs that benefits are beginning to emanate from the reforms, although it is perhaps too soon to draw any firm conclusions. What needs to be emphasised, however, is that children are almost entirely dependent upon the NHS. For this reason in particular a thriving and adequately funded public health service is critical for maintaining the health standards of the child population.

There is clearly considerable room for the prevention of ill-health and for raising the general standards of child health. But as our review of contemporary health risks to children illustrate, possibilities for improvement can only derive from a range of policies exterior to our presently constituted health services.

The strategy for health proposed in *The Health of the Nation* (Dept of Health, 1992) announced specific improvement targets and at the same time explicitly recognised that these could only be achieved by a broad-based assault on the underlying causes. This preventative approach was widely welcomed; but, as a number of critics have noted, policies aimed at effecting changes in life styles and consumption patterns that do not include direct government intervention to regulate and control the sources of health abuse are likely to fail.

Moreover, policies of economic deregulation and privatisation aimed at promoting unfettered commercial activity so as to generate increased national wealth – regardless of the social costs – are especially inappropriate where children are involved. Children have little protection as 'consumers' from the exploitative promotional activities of the powerful conglomerates that dominate the food, tobacco, drinks and confectionary industries. The food industry, for example, in 1994–5 spent £559 million on advertising, mainly on promoting confectionery, soft drinks and fast foods. The Health Education Authority in the same year spent £104 000 on nutritional education literature. McDonald's and other food retailers are now 'sponsoring' schools and providing reading books for young children, as well as other resources. But children are not consumers in any proper sense of the word since they have clearly neither the knowledge to make rational choices nor the ability to calculate the health risks involved. Unfortunately, commercial interests treat them as if they were. Thus present economic policies, based as they are on wish-fulfilment as to the benign effects of a supposedly free market economy, are making improvements in child health more difficult. Indeed, recent evidence on diet and smoking habits among the young – also on alcohol – indicates that some health risks to children and adolescents are in fact increasing. Any recorded improvements in adult health are therefore likely to be of limited duration if long-term damage to children's future health is steadily accumulating.

A successful strategy to achieve significant improvements in child health must, upon the evidence reviewed in this chapter, be based on a twofold approach. First, an effective assault on the causes of ill-health among children needs to address the glaring economic inequalities that exist between different social strata. This would involve major changes to present policies in housing, education and social security in particular. Second, in view of the obvious vulnerability and susceptibility of children to advertising, any comprehensive programme to improve children's long-term health must include direct government action to limit the promotional activities of the food, tobacco and drinks industries. As it is, children are afforded scant protection against these modern forms of exploitation, which in terms of their effects upon health are no different from the much decried abuses of children in nineteenth-century mines and factories. A social policy that pretends to defend children's proper interests should do no less.

Further reading

Allsop (1995) and Baggott (1994) provide detailed analyses of the NHS. Accounts of child health are found in Wooodroffe *et al.* (1993) and Botting (1995). Health inequalities are discussed in Townsend and Davidson (1992), in Whitehead (1992) and in Benzeval *et al.*(1995). The Major government's health strategy is set out in *The Health of the Nation* (Dept of Health, 1991 and 1992). A symposium of British Medical Journal articles in response to the initial Dept. of Health consultative document (1991a) has been edited by Richard Smith (1991). Barnes and Newhouse (1994), Donaldson (1994), and Lewis (1995) provide introductions to asthma. The Royal College of Physicians' (1992) *Smoking and the Young* is similarly valuable on tobacco smoking. Accidents are discussed in Botting (1995).

5

Housing Policy and Children

We will base all our work on the belief that all children and young people are entitled to a good start in life, to be protected, to have somewhere to live, to have enough money to live on, to be treated fairly and to be listened to. (*Children's Society*, 1996)

Introduction

Housing for children is critical, and the younger the child, the more important is the quality of the physical shelter and of the immediate environment generally. An infant's proper growth and development will partly depend on satisfactory housing. A family's home is, for example, the principal determinant of children's essential play opportunities throughout childhood. Children do not choose their housing conditions, and until a child goes to school the home provides the main, or only, physical setting for that child's development and for all his or her early relationships and social interaction.

Furthermore, housing conditions also affect children indirectly since a family's housing has a powerful effect on the well-being of a child's parents. Security, comfort, ease of management and warmth are important factors for facilitating effective parenting; conversely, overcrowding, poor conditions – indeed homelessness – are all circumstances that are likely to lessen the ability of parents to care for their children, and to threaten the stability of family life. Most adults can escape from the limitations of their living conditions by resorting, for example, to the pub or to the local public library. Mothers and children, however, necessarily spend a far greater proportion of time at home than do the majority of adolescents and other adults; and mothers and young children generally have far fewer choices as to where to spend their time.

Housing policy differs in important respects from the other main areas of social policy. There is no universal right to housing except for some categories of carefully filtered homeless persons (see below). Nor is there a nationally administered and provided housing service as with health and social security.

State housing policy throughout the twentieth century has consisted of a complicated pattern of interventions in the housing market in the form of controls, taxation policies and subsidies. As a consequence, housing policy has always been subjected to sharp changes of direction according to the fortunes of the wider economy and regardless of people's housing needs.

So how well have children been served by housing policy since 1945, and how satisfactorily are their housing needs being met at the close of the twentieth century? We examine these questions in the following sections.

Housing policy and progress 1945–79

The near total cessation of house construction during the First World War aggravated pre 1914 deficiencies, so by the end of the war in 1918 there was a worsening housing crisis. In response, Parliament, with the Bolshevik Revolution in Russia as a compelling warning and fearful of the potential threat of a mass army returning home, passed the Housing and Town Planning Act in 1919, and so ushered in the era of publicly provided rented housing – 'homes fit for heroes'.

Between the two world wars some four million new houses were built, including 1 112 000 government-subsidised council houses built by the local authorities and 430 000 subsidised houses built by private enterprise for owner-occupation. Extensive programmes of slum clearance were also undertaken. By 1939, therefore, the state had accepted responsibility for housing conditions generally, and for the supply of some new housing, either directly through local authorities or indirectly via subsidy for privately-built houses for owner-occupation.

Housing need at the end of the Second World War

Never had expectations been higher – nor the prospects of satisfying them more remote – than they were at the cessation of hostilities in

1945. Virtually no new houses had been built during the war, and in addition wartime destruction meant there had been some considerable depletion of the housing stock as it had existed in 1939. Twenty-one major cities had been attacked during the Blitz in 1940–1, and raids continued intermittently during the remainder of the war. By May 1945 nearly half a million homes had either been destroyed or made permanently uninhabitable, while over three million had been damaged – in all, two out of seven homes (Central Statistical Office, 1995b, p. 11).

As millions of men and women returned from war to rebuild their disrupted lives, so housing became one of the principal post-war political issues, which, in fact, it was to remain until the 1970s.

High-output policies and the rise of owner-occupation

With a rising birth rate after the war, the housing shortage remained acute; and popular demand for an ever-increasing supply of new homes was to dominate housing policy for the first twenty-five years after the war. Inevitably, policy was directed for almost the entire period at producing the largest quantity of new housing compatible with other welfare needs and within the bounds of economic possibility. There was, therefore, a broad political consensus over the desirability of maintaining a high level of house production. Disagreement may have existed over exactly how much could be achieved and by whom, but no one questioned the ultimate objective. Indeed both Labour and Conservative governments tended to steal each others' housing policy clothes; and elections came to hang on the credibility of the opposing party's much publicised target figure for house production. Thus what has been termed, 'the numbers game', became a critical aspect of the politics of housing in the 1950s and 1960s.

Under Labour, the production of permanent homes in the initial post-war years was dominated by the local authorities, but by the mid-1960s Labour had accepted the Conservatives' policy emphasis on building for owner-occupation, even though both Labour and Conservative administrations maintained substantial programmes of local-authority house construction throughout the period.

By the end of Labour's second post-war period in office in 1970, nearly 7 million new dwellings had been completed following the end of the Second World War, and a total of 900 000 slum houses had been demolished and 2.5 million people rehoused by 1968. Thus in 1971, although serious housing shortages remained in many areas, a small surplus of dwellings over households was recorded for the first time since the end of the war (Dept of the Environment, 1977, p. 10).

Labour lost the election in June 1970 but the bipartisan approach to housing policy was by and large continued during the 1970s. However, two policy developments were to foreshadow future housing policy under Margaret Thatcher. First, under the Heath administration (1970–4) local authorities were increasingly encouraged to sell off their council houses to sitting tenants; and second, Labour's 1974 Housing Act established housing associations as an important 'third arm' of social housing provision under the aegis of an expanded Housing Corporation.

Post-war housing policy and children

In many respects, children have been the main beneficiaries of post-war housing policies. But they may also have been more adversely affected than other groups by any policy failures of the period. There is, moreover, evidence to indicate that some of the improvements achieved between 1945 and 1979 have for many households with children more recently been reversed. In the following sections we examine three post-war developments which have directly affected many children – new towns; changes in house design; and high rise housing. And we conclude the chapter with a discussion of the effects upon children of housing policy changes introduced since 1979 and of the effects of homelessness.

The new towns

The modern concept of a planned environment that would combine the advantages of both the city and the countryside – while excluding the evils of each – was formulated by Ebenezer Howard in 1902 in his book, *Garden Cities of Tomorrow*. Howard and the Garden Cities Association (later the Town and Country Planning Association) established two such 'garden cities', at Letchworth and Welwyn in 1903 and 1920 respectively. However, it was the growing attraction of planning urban development as an antidote to the haphazard ribbon development of the 1920s and 1930s, as well as the unique circumstances created by the Second World War, which together, by the end of the war, made the creation of a ring of satellite 'new towns' around London appear in official circles a highly desirable strategy for containing urban sprawl.

Between 1946 and 1950, fourteen new towns were thus designated in the UK following the 1946 New Towns Act and the Town and Country Planning Acts of 1944 and 1947. Eight of these so-called Mark 1 new towns, including Stevenage, Basildon, Harlow and Crawley, were located around London, with two in Scotland and one in Wales. A further eighteen were established between 1950 and 1970, although some later ones entailed major expansions of existing towns, such as Peterborough and Warrington, rather than the building of new towns on greenfield sites as originally conceived – like the earlier Mark 2 towns of Milton Keynes and Telford. At the time of writing, there are thirty-two new towns containing a total population of 2.9 million (see Short, 1982; and Cherry, 1988).

There has been much criticism of the failure of the new towns to achieve the idealised objectives originally set for them – a balanced distribution of social classes and their harmonious integration. However, in more mundane matters, the new towns provided a wonderfully improved physical environment for hundreds of thousands of families: the separate zoning of residential areas and industrial and commercial locations; the provision of parks, playing fields and bright new schools; and the segregation of main traffic routes away from residential neighbourhoods, all made the new towns exceedingly attractive for young couples with children and for prospective parents.

New town industry for the most part required young, skilled workers, so the population that began to move into the new towns from the late 1940s onwards tended to be self-selecting. There was also, in the initial phase of new town development, a very youthful population. Thus, according to the 1966 sample Census, whereas under one in four of the population (23 per cent) of England and Wales were under the age of 15, the comparable figure for the Mark 1 new towns was almost one in three (32 per cent) (Schaffer, 1970, p. 189).

From the point of view of the quality of life for children in the new towns, it is worth drawing attention to two aspects. First, many parents welcomed the improved environment that a new town offered their children. Michael Young and Peter Willmott (1962), for example, in their classic study, *Family and Kinship in East London*, found that the majority of their informants thought the new green-field urban development of 'Greenleigh', built away from London, was 'a more suitable environment for children'. And Colin Ward, in his recent review of the new towns, suggests that:

> Children's happiness is determined by personal relations, not by places, but many New Town residents chose to move there precisely because they reckoned that the house, garden and nearby space for play would provide a better environment for child-rearing. I think they were right. (1993, p. 147)

The other related feature that undoubted improved the lot of many children – and their mothers – was the relatively high quality of the housing. Almost all of it is of modern construction and conforms to the improved standards and design features laid down for post-war housing. Thus, from a housing point of view, those families who have grown up in the new towns since the war have enjoyed greatly improved standards compared to those left to grow up in the decaying neighbourhoods of the old industrial centres.

Improved house design

The introduction of subsidised local-authority housing in 1919 resulted in immediate improvements in the interior space and design of working-class housing. Reduced subsidies and economic stringency, however, led to a marked retreat in the later 1920s and 1930s from the higher standards achieved immediately following the First World War.

A similar pattern has occurred since the end of the Second World War. The Dudley Report of 1944, which set the standards for post-war council housing, again incorporated major advances in space and amenities. To qualify for the new subsidies, a minimum interior space of 900 square feet, exclusive of stores, was fixed; the kitchen was to allow for cooking by either gas or electricity, instead of an open range, and was to be extended according to alternative plans as well as to be more generously fitted. Bathrooms were moved to the bedroom floor instead of being, as in earlier houses, chilly annexes

to the scullery with no hot water supply; and for families of five or
more, an upstairs and a downstairs WC were required (Burnett,
1985, p. 298–9). These houses, as Peter Malpass and Alan Murie
note, 'remain the most spacious council houses ever built, averaging
over 1000 square feet, compared to 800 square feet in 1939, and just
over 900 square feet in the 1950s' (1994, p. 75). Interestingly,
Malpass and Murie raise the question of why 'governments should
choose to build the best homes at the most difficult times', suggest-
ing that in similar circumstances at the end of each world war, 'The
quality of this housing reflected the political and economic power of
organised skilled labour' (1994, p. 69).

Post-war houses not only incorporated higher standards but there
was also an increased variation in both exterior style and layout and
interior design. Unfortunately, however, as economic pressures
mounted from the late 1940s onwards, these standards established
in the aftermath of the war were slowly eroded.

By the end of the 1950s steadily rising living standards prompted
an official review of 'the standards of design and equipment' of all
forms of new construction for domestic occupation. The recommendations contained in the ensuing report, *Homes for Today and
Tomorrow*, were dominated by two overriding considerations –
more space and better heating, reflecting a concern with the quality
of living which the physical conditions of a house facilitated (Dept of
the Environment, 1961). Its recommendations therefore – including
brighter and better-fitted kitchens, better electrical installations, and
improved facilities for heating all living areas – were all directed at
enabling people 'to express the fullness of their lives' (Burnett, 1985,
p. 307). These revised 'Parker Morris' standards were made man-
datory for public sector new town housing in 1967, and for all
council housing in 1969, but they have never applied, as was
originally intended, to houses in the private sector.

There can be no doubt that although standards of house design
have varied since the war, in general there have been substantial
advances. Compared to the conditions prevailing in the first decades
of the twentieth century, mothers (as the principal carers) and their
children have benefited greatly from the housing improvements
achieved since the Second World War. In the more spacious and
better-designed houses of the post-war era the possibilities for a
more varied and enriched domestic life for all members of the family
have been greatly enhanced.

High-rise flats

A post-war innovation in public-sector housing was the construction of tall blocks of flats of five or more storeys. Blocks of flats had always been part of local-authority provision, and with the post-war emphasis on increasing the production of new dwellings, local authorities were encouraged from the late 1940s onwards to include flats as part of 'mixed development' housing schemes. However it was during the 1950s that high-rise flat construction was to become a distinguishing feature of post-war British housing. The new subsidy regime introduced by the Conservatives in 1956 related subsidies to height with a rising scale, reaching a maximum of 3.4 times the basic house subsidy, which was given for blocks of twenty storeys or more. These changed subsidy arrangements initiated a boom in high-rise flat construction, which peaked in the mid-1960s and then declined rapidly in the early 1970s following the removal of the subsidies by Labour in 1967 and the Ronan Point disaster in 1968, when a gas explosion caused the collapse of the whole of one side of a high-rise block in Newham killing five people.

Patrick Dunleavy, in his comprehensive 1981 analysis of the high-rise boom, notes that as no proper statistics were collected before 1966 it is difficult to say exactly where such developments were located. The available evidence indicates that the construction of high-rise blocks was concentrated heavily in the conurbations especially in London, Liverpool, Glasgow, Leeds, Manchester, Sheffield and Newcastle-upon-Tyne.

In total between 1955 and 1975 nearly 440 000 high-rise flats were built, nine out of ten of them in 'inner urban areas'. It is suggested that the majority of the three million people displaced by slum clearance during these years were rehoused in mass housing estates, with a million and a half of these in high-rise flats.

At the height of the boom, high-rise flat construction represented a significant proportion of all local authority dwelling construction (26 per cent in 1966). Even so, as late as 1972, at the tail end of the boom, two-thirds of all local housing authorities reported they had no high-rise flats; and in relation to the total housing stock they represent no more than a small fraction – something over 2 per cent of all UK dwellings, or 15 per cent of all flats, but 25 per cent of all local-authority flats. However, far fewer have been sold under the 'right to buy' (RTB) policies than the much-preferred council houses, which means that high-rise flats are increasingly becoming a larger proportion of the remaining council stock.

High-rise blocks, however, have been one of the most troubled sectors of housing since their construction, and they have been associated with three main problems. First, the design faults of certain types of block, poor standards of construction, and the consequent maintenance problems, have together meant that we now have large numbers of dwellings that are prematurely obsolete, 'hard to let', and prohibitive to maintain in good order. In some instances, in fact, demolition after only thirty years of use has been the only solution. Second, there appears to have been little consultation with the communities involved as to the desirability of 'homes in the sky'. And, indeed, a common experience of high-rise living has been social isolation and the disintegration of the often vibrant community life which the tower blocks so brutally replaced. So as Patrick Dunleavy asks, why have public authorities 'produced distinctive forms of housing apparently at odds with majority preferences' (1981, p. 2)? He suggests that high-rise was a 'technological shortcut to social change (ibid., p. 53). While John Short argues that the true explanation for this imposition of a widely unpopular form of housing lies in a combination of factors:

> Suggested by architects, promoted by central government and pushed for by the big contractors, the high-rise blocks were touted as the solution to problems of land availability and as a panacea to modernizing the construction industry . . . The high-rise tower was a potent phallic symbol of municipal virility and aggression. (1982, p. 109)

A related and third problem has been the suitability of the households allocated to high-flats. From the earliest days it became clear that this form of accommodation was less suitable for families with young children. Survey evidence varied over time perhaps according to the degree of adaptability which the passage of time had itself made possible. Dislike however among families has always been strong; high-flats many asserted were 'not the right place to bring children up' (Burnett, 1985, p. 302).

A study undertaken in the Tyneside area by Elizabeth Gittus into the problems of high-rise living for mothers with children under five provides a detailed account of the disadvantages experienced. About half the mothers mentioned 'the lack of play opportunities, the strain of having to watch the children continually, or the adverse effects on the children's personality of their having to be kept indoors' (Gittus, 1976, p. 81). Mothers' heightened fears of accidents to their children were also considerably increased if they lived in high-rise flats, especially the hazards of balconies, windows and stairs. Not surprisingly, two-thirds of the mothers reported that they restricted their children's play activities because of the increased dangers.

Similarly, Pearl Jephcott's study, *Homes in High Flats*, found that large numbers of children in Glasgow were living in the new high-rise blocks which were replacing the slum tenements – in 1968 some 6700 children under the age of 14. The tenants themselves, she reports, 'were almost universally agreed that a high flat was not a good home for children, and that it made problems for mothers'. For younger children especially, she suggests that the restrictions imposed by the high-rise flat environment could well deprive them 'of that variety of stimuli on which intellectual development depends' (1971, pp. 140–1). Dunleavy sums up the evidence thus:

> The only point about high-rise on which there is now a sociological consensus is the markedly unfavourable effects of this form of accommodation for families with children . . . And the effects on children's mothers is equally serious. (1981, p. 96)

The provision of high-rise flats as part of the post-war drive to replace slum housing and raise housing standards has thus been a mixed blessing for children and their parents. On the one hand they have provided accommodation built to modern standards, but on the other, as an environment for child-rearing, they have been a continuing cause of parental anxiety and social disadvantage. Most unfortunately, with a deliberate decision not to replace the council houses sold off since 1979, current policies are resulting in many households dependent on social housing being restricted increasingly to high-rise housing as the only available choice. Already there are reports of a movement of families with young children back into the higher storeys of the tower blocks. Thus a report in the housing journal *Roof* (November/December 1992) noted that, 'Children are returning to blocks in large numbers', and that whereas in 1987 most councils said their lettings policies specifically excluded children from tower blocks or from the higher storeys of these, by 1992, however, authorities such as Birmingham, Rugby, Waltham Forest and Solihull 'have since found it necessary to reverse these policies' (Clarke, 1992, p. 9).

Housing policy since 1979

Recent Conservative administrations have maintained in theory the commitment, originally stated in their 1971 White Paper, to 'a decent home for every family at a price within their means'. What has been distinctive, however, about housing policy since 1979 is the primacy that has been afforded to private enterprise for the achievement of this goal, and the presumption that it can best be achieved within the single tenure of owner-occupation.

Policy measures have been consistent with this broad emphasis on private provision and individual ownership. Thus the specific objectives, as spelt out in the 1987 housing White Paper, have been to encourage owner-occupation, to minimalise the local-authority role in housing provision, to revitalise the privately-rented sector, and to target resources on the most acute problems (Atkinson and Durden, 1994, p. 183).

The essential legislative basis for current policies is contained in three Acts of Parliament: the 1980 Housing Act; the 1988 Housing Act; and the 1989 Local Government and Housing Act.

The 1980 Housing Act

A new departure from previous policy was the introduction of a 'right to buy' for sitting council tenants, with a sliding scale of discounts on the market value of the property according to length of tenure.

The 1988 Housing Act

By the time of the 1987 election, with some three-quarters of a million council houses having been sold since 1980, the process of relegating the role of the local authorities in providing rented housing could now, it was judged, be taken further. Attention was therefore switched after 1987 to more thorough going attempts to revive the private rented sector, and to transferring the main role for providing social housing from the local authorities to the voluntary sector.

Specific measures contained in the Act included ones designed to bring about the creeping deregulation of rent controls in the private rented sector, and to restrict the amount of public money going to housing associations by requiring them to raise an increasing proportion of their finance from the private sector (as much as 45 per cent in 1996).

The 1989 Local Government and Housing Act

This measure has since April 1990 allowed central government to restrict subsidies directly, and to impose its own rent regime on local housing authorities in line with notional market rents in the private rented sector.

As a result of these legislative changes and with the progressive reduction since 1990 of tax relief on mortgage interest payments (15p in the pound on a maximum mortgage of £30 000 since April 1995), the costs of housing are now more closely dependent on market criteria than at any time since 1939, and in some respects since before 1915.

The consequences for children of post-1979 housing policies

Increased home ownership – a decent home within the reach of every family?

Owner-occupation in Great Britain in 1993 accounted for 66 per cent of tenure, compared to 54 per cent in 1978. This tenure is composed of 9.7 million households with a mortgage and 5.7 million households who are outright owners (mainly among older age groups). Approximately half of this increase of 12 percentage points since 1979 has been as a result of the RTB policy; and the other half to private-sector construction and sales.

The growth of owner-occupation since 1979 has had two major consequences: first there has been a decline in choice between renting and owning; and second, a related increase has occurred in the number of households with relatively marginal incomes for sustaining the fluctuating costs of house purchase over the medium to long term, but who none the less have been persuaded into home ownership. With the shrinking availability of affordable good-quality public rented dwellings, together with the deregulation of the lending institutions and the penalty of higher rents, it was no wonder that so many people found themselves during the 1980s with little choice other than to buy. In any case by the mid-1980s two-thirds of all British dwellings were only available on the basis of purchase so, inevitably, the pressures to own have intensified. In this context it is all too easy to comprehend the extent to which many households entered into unsustainable financial commitments in order to get their feet on the first rung of the home ownership ladder. This raises the question of whether policies to promote owner-occupation have not resulted in many young families living in poorer-quality accommodation in the owner-occupied sector, especially in maisonettes, flats and cramped two-bedroomed terraced houses, than would hitherto have been allocated to less well-off households in the public sector.

Recent house purchase, moreover, has increasingly been based on two household incomes. For families, this means that women have either to delay starting a family or to return to work shortly after a child's birth; and hence, of course, the frantic search by many parents for some reliable form of child care. Either way, many parents, given also the current insecurities of the job market, are denied any real choice of how exactly they wish to care for their children during their early years because of the financial demands of home purchase.

What this also means of course is that those who were unlucky enough to have bought their homes in the latter half of the 1980s have committed themselves to heavy repayments even though house prices subsequently fell in the early 1990s. If these households consisted of young couples they are also now in the latter half of the 1990s those most likely to contain young children. There is therefore a strong prima-facie case that those households who have been worst affected by the hyper-inflation of the housing market in the 1980s and its subsequent collapse, are now composed disproportionately of families with young children.

Negative equity and repossessions

This conclusion is supported by accumulating evidence of the growing extent of financial difficulties experienced by many households in meeting their housing costs. In 1991, house prices began to fall and continued to do so until 1994, since when they have largely remained 'flat'. The result of falling prices has been that many of those who bought their homes towards the peak of the boom now find them often worth considerably less than the amount they had originally borrowed – a shortfall referred to as 'negative equity'. At the time of writing, a large number of owner-occupiers are trapped in their homes. Thus in early 1996, according to a survey by the Nationwide Building Society reported in the *Independent* (31 January 1996), up to 1.7 million households are in negative equity.

Compared to many other recent house purchasers, however, those households locked into negative equity can be considered among the more fortunate. Many tens of thousands who bought their homes during the 1980s have found in the recessionary 1990s that with reduced incomes they can no longer continue to pay their mortgages. Thus a further symptom of crisis in the housing market has been a rising tide of mortgage arrears and house repossessions. In the peak year, 1991, as many as 75 500 properties were 'taken into possession', and since then the number of annual repossessions has averaged some 50 000 homes. This means that for the years from 1990 to 1995 a total of 350 000 households, or well over three-quarters of a million people, many of them children, have lost their homes (Central Statistics Office, 1995a, p. 181).

Research findings published by the Department of the Environment (DoE) in 1995 reveal that all occupational groups have been affected by the current crisis in owner-occupation. 'Repossession,' the report emphasises, 'primarily hits families with young children.' Indeed, 'two-thirds of households that lost their homes,' the authors note, 'contained at least one dependent child aged 16 or younger, with almost three out of ten of them containing three or more dependent children' (Ford and Kempson, 1995, p. 30). Significantly, four out of ten repossessed households eventually end up in rented social housing, with a further 37 per cent renting privately. Only 8 per cent return to owner-occupation. Most damagingly, however, for children, the DoE study shows that 'the majority of cases moved into temporary accommodation immediately following the loss of their home. Often the location and/or facilities were problematic and in some cases there was overcrowding. Consequently, one in five of them had moved three or more times in less than two years, moving from one address to another' (ibid., p. 33).

By the mid-1990s it appears that the sheer overcrowding and physical housing deficiencies of an earlier era have merely been replaced for many families by the housing problems caused by the acute financial strains and anxieties in which a growing number now find themselves. And it is especially children who are being exposed to these new forms of housing stress. Undoubtedly, this situation has been brought about, at least in part, by an undue policy emphasis on owner-occupation regardless of other considerations.

Children in public sector housing

The term 'social housing' is now used officially to identify public-sector housing allocated at 'affordable' rents on a basis of need, and not solely according to the price mechanism. The sector consists of dwellings provided by local authorities, housing associations and co-operatives; and it is expected to provide homes for those households, as Clare Ungerson suggests, 'still unable to move into owner-occupation' (1994, p. 192).

Local-authority housing in Britain, which in 1978 represented 32 per cent of tenure had fallen by 1993 to 20 per cent, with total council dwellings stocks falling from 6.5 million dwellings to 4.7 million. Housing association properties have, conversely, increased numerically from approximately 450 000 units to 874 000 (4 per cent of tenure); and since 1990 their construction figures have substantially exceeded local-authority building programmes – 34 492 compared to 1768 respectively for 1993, which reflects the assumption by the housing associations of the main provider role for social housing. Increased building by housing associations has however only marginally offset the overall decline in the availability of affordable rented housing. Since 1979 in fact there has been a net loss of 1.4 million units of social housing, so that together council housing and housing association dwellings now accommodate no more than 24 per cent of households, compared to 34 per cent in 1979 (Newton, 1994).

The residualisation of social housing

Since 1979 this social sector generally has clearly become a more restricted and, as some might argue, an inferior form of tenure, so that a number of commentators speak of the 'residualisation' of council housing. However, this term needs to be used with some caution because local authorities still administer by far the largest stock of affordable rented housing, and as landlords they have an impressive record for the most effective use of this stock.

None the less, public-sector housing has become a more 'marginalised' or 'residualised' tenure because it has shrunk significantly in size since 1979 so that the choice of type of accommodation now available has become more restricted, and because the tenants concentrated in 'social housing' are increasingly the poor and socially disadvantaged. It is further argued that recent policies to promote owner-occupation and downgrade the traditional role of the local authorities have only served to create an image of 'a second-class sector of second-class people' (Balchin, 1995, p. 189).

The composition of the public-sector housing stock has changed gradually since the early 1980s. Thus whereas 36 per cent of council dwellings were semi-detached houses in 1979, only 28 per cent were in 1991, and, more significantly from the point of view of children, the proportions of smaller terraced houses and purpose-built flats had increased correspondingly. By 1991, the proportion of housing association properties provided in the form of either purpose-built flats or converted flats or rooms, had also grown – to nearly two-thirds of their homes. So with 35 per cent of council homes also being comprised of flats, clearly social housing has increasingly become a tenure of flats, which now represent some 40 per cent overall of the total stock in this sector.

In the same way that choice in social housing has narrowed, so too has the social profile of the tenants become less diverse. The income gap between those households dependent on social housing and other households has widened (see Page, 1993, p. 31). Typically, moreover, social housing tenants are 'economically inactive', many being pensioners, single mothers or unemployed. Thus by 1990, 61 per cent of heads of household with council tenancies were inactive compared to 42 per cent in 1981; while of new tenants moving into housing association properties as many as 75 per cent were not in any kind of work. The average weekly total household income, including that of a partner, of council tenants was £86.40 (at 1990 prices) in 1992, compared to an average income of £336.60 for home-owning households with a mortgage (Newton, 1994, p. 88).

The sale of council houses

The changing composition of the stock and of the tenants of local-authority housing is mirrored in the patterns of sales. Of course the sale of council houses is acknowledged as 'perhaps the most notable piece of policy' and one of which Conservative politicians are particularly proud because of the degree of electoral popularity attributed to it (Williams, 1992, p. 159). However, any analysis of the housing needs of children, and of how policy might best serve their interests, immediately raises serious doubts and criticisms concerning the long-term consequences of the RTB policy.

A striking feature of sales has been the remarkable consistency since the 1950s 'in terms of who buys and what properties have been sold'. Thus, according to Kerr (1989),

> purchasers were predominantly middle-aged, often with a grown-up family and including more than one wage earner. Manual skilled workers were over-represented among buyers and so, too, were white collar workers. (Quoted in Malpass and Murie, 1994, p. 301)

The purchase of semi-detached, three-bedroomed houses has been particularly popular, and flats correspondingly unpopular. Analysis of the pattern of sales, not surprisingly, indicates that former council houses have added importantly to the good-quality housing stock available in the owner-occupied sector; this seems to have been especially the case in the south of England and in rural areas (Malpass and Murie, 1994, p. 302). But such houses have, in consequence, been removed from the public-sector stock and are no longer available to families with children who are excluded from home ownership because of lack of means.

The consequences for children of a depleted public-sector

The loss since 1980 of a substantial proportion of the most spacious family homes in the public-sector means that poorer families now have a much more restricted choice and may never obtain a house at all. The RTB policy has thus effected a significant shift of housing resources towards older and better-off former council tenants and away from less-privileged households, who often have young children. For many households this has clearly resulted in an inversion of the relationship between housing need and the homes such households with children are actually occupying. Research conducted by Barnardo's, for example, on a Bristol council housing estate found a major problem of 'inadequate and inappropriate housing'. The majority of the children were cooped up in 'walk-up flats', although almost all their mothers had been brought up in houses with gardens and were in many cases desperate to move to a house. Yet, while many of the former council houses on the estate were found to be owned by middle-aged owners, many mothers with young children were living in flats (Gill, 1992, p. 12).

This study well illustrates the problems of bringing up children in inappropriate accommodation within a depleted public-sector. With a fifth of Bristol's council houses having been sold by 1989, fewer families were able to find an adequate home. Sadly, although many parents wanted to get away from the estate, in reality they were trapped, with no real prospects of improving their accommodation. So, as one mother forlornly commented: 'Considering the children are a lot older now, their need for a garden is gone . . . we needed a garden when they were babies' (ibid., p. 26).

The housing problems of less affluent households

The depletion of the social housing stock and generally increased housing costs in all tenures has widened housing inequalities between the majority who can afford to buy their own homes and those on lower incomes. Inevitably lower income groups have found access to good-quality housing becoming more difficult.

Sub-standard housing

By any yardstick there have been notable improvements in the overall quality of British housing since the 1960s. Measures of unfitness, lack of 'amenities', and of overcrowding were all shown by the 1991 English House Condition Survey to have fallen to an all-time low; and currently 84 per cent of English houses are now centrally heated, compared with only 57 per cent in 1981. However, problems do remain: there are still, for example, 1.5 million 'unfit' dwellings in Britain (7.6 per cent of the total stock) and an estimated £15 billion is required for urgent repairs; additionally, 20 per cent of houses have dampness problems (one in three of Scottish homes), and 6 per cent of households in Great Britain are living at a density of one or more people per room. There is also a shortfall of 400 000 dwellings required to match the number of households needing separate accommodation (Holtermann, 1995, p. 61).

The question thus arises as to how far children are affected by these continuing housing deficiencies and shortages. Evidence, unfortunately, does indicate that certain groups of children experience disproportionately bad housing conditions. We examine the housing plight of some of these groups below.

Single parents and housing

The allocation of housing according to ability to pay clearly disadvantages women, whose incomes generally – from whatever source – are on average substantially below those of men. But women are – with or without male partners – the principal carers of children. Thus at the heart of current policies there is a major contradiction: while women are at a financial disadvantage within a market-orientated housing system, more women are living independent lives and, in the case of 1.3 million single mothers, are carrying the prime responsibility for children. Large numbers of children have, therefore, through no fault of their own been correspondingly disadvantaged by growing housing inequalities.

The extent of poverty among single mothers has been well documented (see Chapter 3). If we relate these circumstances to an increasingly market-orientated housing system within which there is a diminishing resource of social housing, it is obvious that lone parents are likely to have serious housing difficulties. Thus, the analysis of households' housing circumstances as revealed in the 1991 Census, concluded that: 'Of all the household types distinguished by the census, it is the children of lone parent families who have seen the biggest deterioration in their housing situation' (Dorling, 1994).

Ethnic minority children

Children from minority-group backgrounds share with one-parent families many of the worst housing privations in contemporary Britain. Moreover, besides the similar high incidences of low incomes, benefit dependency and unemployment which they share with single parents, there are three additional circumstances that considerably aggravate the housing problems of black minorities. First, these communities are concentrated geographically in inner-city neighbourhoods, which often contain much of the poorest and least-preferred housing; second, there has been a continuing history of racial prejudice and discrimination which has handicapped access for black minorities to better-quality housing in all sectors; and third, the rather different demographic family structures of certain ethnic groups has contributed – partly because of the changed composition of the social housing stock – to additional housing stress within particular communities.

As was noted in Chapter 2, about half of the British black population lives in London. However, with higher house prices than in any other region, owner-occupation is an impossibility for most black households, the majority of whom are dependent on social housing (and much of this in the form of high-rise flats), or on private rented accommodation. London also has an older housing stock which is on aggregate in worse condition than elsewhere. Thus inner London has a higher proportion of unfit dwellings (16 per cent) than anywhere else in the UK, and the lowest proportion of 'good' housing (21 per cent). The 1992 London Housing Survey furthermore reported that the sales of council houses since 1980 has meant that the shrinking public housing sector is becoming 'less and less able to meet the needs of families', for the principal reason that one in three of local-authority three-bedroomed homes, and nearly four out of ten of those with four or more bedrooms, had been sold under the RTB policy.

Not surprisingly, the London Housing Survey found that a third of all children living in social housing in London are living in overcrowded conditions; and that as many as 150 000 children in all housing sectors are affected by overcrowding. Asian and Afro-Caribbean children, however, are twice as likely as White European children to be living in overcrowded conditions (NCH Action for Children, 1995, p. 76).

At a national level, children from the Bangladeshi and Pakistani communities are particularly badly affected, with 31 per cent of all households in these communities being one or more units below 'the bedroom standard', as against 12 per cent for all minority group households and 3 per cent for white households (Central Statistical Office, 1995a, p. 178).

The housing problems of all poor families

Many of the problems of single mothers and ethnic minorities are shared by all poor families, which besides these two groups include the unemployed, refugee and Traveller families, and families with members who are disabled or chronically sick. It is these groups, and especially those associated with social classes IV and V, who are generally among the poorest in the population and who are concentrated in the least satisfactory housing or in a depleted public-sector. Households with children, in particular, are thus more likely to experience overcrowding, the sharing of amenities in 'temporary' or multi-occupied accommodation, dampness and cold, the absence of play space, and childhoods impoverished by the insecurities and limitations of their physical environment, than nearly all other types of household in contemporary Britain.

Some evidence suggests that while housing conditions have been improving for the majority of the population, for some categories of children – such as those of lone mothers – they have actually been deteriorating (see Kumar, 1993, p. 130). The 1991 Census has subsequently revealed that 1.3 million children 'still live in households with more than one person per room, while 43,000 children under 16 live in households which lack exclusive access to a bath, shower or inside lavatory'. There remains also a substantial minority of sharing or 'hidden households', which in total contain 285 000 children – an increase of 9.4 per cent since 1981; and at the same time there has been an increase of 17 per cent in the number of households living in 'non-permanent accommodation' (such as mobile homes and caravans), so that 95 000 households containing 25 000 children under 16 now reside in this type of accommodation (Dorling, 1993).

The geographical segregation of the poor

Since the early 1970s we have been aware of problem estates and 'hard to let' properties – often flats. Many of the most notorious for their social problems have always contained unduly high proportions of children and young people. However, since the early 1980s local authorities have lost many of their better-off tenants and many of their best houses. Thus a conjunction of growing family poverty and the consequences of government housing policies have conspired to produce growing ghettos of poor households in many of the most disadvantaged neighbourhoods.

Department of the Environment surveys undertaken during the 1980s indicated that there were over 300 000 council dwellings on 'difficult-to-let' estates. Four-fifths of these were found in cities, with over a quarter of these (28 per cent) in Inner London alone. Reasons for the unpopularity of the estates included poor design, vandalism and crime, social stigma, their size, and the consequent anonymity and loss of social control. Specific social factors which appeared to contribute to the general malaise of such neighbourhoods were the concentrations of 'families with problems', 'high child density', and 'lack of play facilities'. Some of the surveyed estates contained double the proportions of children compared to the national average (45 per cent and 22 per cent, respectively), with an average child population for the surveyed estates of 33 per cent. The paradox of the vitality of children and the social difficulties on problem estates is eloquently stated by Anne Power:

> The estate, as a separated but unintegrated community, as a vast uncontrolled but boring no man's land, the estate as an environment often hostile to family living and to children's love of the outdoors and thirst for adventure, caused the loss of confidence by adults in their own community of children. Children became both the perpetrators and the victims. (Power, 1987, p. 155)

Since the mid-1980s there have been important government initiatives to improve the worst estates. However, the failure to replace the sold-off council houses and to build affordable new homes in anything like the numbers required has meant that the spatial concentration of the poorest households has continued inexorably.

The ghettoisation of many children and adolescents into housing developments characterised by high unemployment and widespread poverty is threatening to extend into the newer housing association estates. These are now building by far the largest share of social housing and, as David Page's (1993) report has shown, these new estates appear very much at risk of becoming the problem neighbourhoods of the future.

Poor families in the countryside

The sale of council housing has also had a similarly damaging, though different, impact on rural communities. The Archbishops' Commission on Rural Areas drew attention in 1990 to some of the social consequences of the sales policy in rural areas: 'In every large village many council houses are now sold, while in many small villages virtually all the stock has ceased to be available as rented accommodation . . . We feel strongly that there has not been proper recognition by the Government of the real value of council houses in rural areas as the major source of homes to rent for less well-off households' (Archbishops of Canterbury and York, 1990, p. 104).

Other reports about rural areas have also found that the loss of public housing since 1980 has contributed significantly to the slow disintegration of rural society in many parts of Britain. Far from the fantasy of maiden aunts cycling along country lanes and local worthies sipping real ale and watching cricket on the village green, rural reality is one of low-income families forced away to the council housing estates of the towns, and of village schools, post offices, churches and local bus services ceasing to function. Thus one commentator writes of 'The new rural clearances', and quotes a country vicar with a parish in rural Warwickshire as admitting that, 'every couple he had married in the last 15 years had been forced to leave the villages where they were brought up because of the shortage of affordable housing' (Platt, 1987, p. 24). Analysis of the sale of council homes in rural areas of Scotland similarly concludes: 'Many low income rural households may suffer as a result of this policy' (MacGregor *et al.*, 1987, p. 84).

Homelessness

'Homelessness' is a particularly difficult condition to define with any exactness. There are, in fact, degrees or states of homelessness, from the 'rooflessness' of the 'street homeless' to those who have accommodation that is so deficient that it fails to constitute a home as popularly conceived. Some commentators, to overcome such conceptual difficulties, have suggested that 'Homelessness in Britain is a manifestation of housing need in its most extreme form', an inclusive definition which would accommodate a broad spectrum of acute housing needs (Greve, 1990, p. 13). The crux of the matter is what constitutes a 'home'.

The present legislative position

The officially acknowledged amount of homelessness can only be understood by reference to the relevant legislation, since this lays down an official definition and identifies who is entitled to help. The legislative basis of present policy is contained in Part III of the 1985 Housing Act which consolidated the policy provisions for homelessness originally established by the 1977 Housing (Homeless Persons') Act.

You are 'homeless' if you have no legal right to occupy accommodation or are prevented from doing so for a good reason; and you are 'threatened with homelessness' if that right or ability to occupy is to be lost in the following 28 days (Housing Act, 1985, Part III, Section 58). In practical terms, this definition says little about the condition of the accommodation nor about the number of people living in it. Under the 1985 Act local authorities had a duty to secure permanent accommodation for households they accepted as homeless. Eligibility for acceptance depends on the household being in 'priority need' and not having made itself 'intentionally homeless' by deliberate choice or by knowingly acting in a way likely to forfeit the right to occupy their home. A household is also normally required to prove a 'local connection' with the particular local-authority to which it has applied.

Those defined as being in 'priority need' are: 'families with dependent children; pregnant women; people who are vulnerable because of old age, physical disability, mental illness or handicap, special reasons including young people "at risk" and victims of domestic violence; people made homeless by an emergency' (Burrows and Walentowicz, 1992, p. 5). The large majority of single people and couples without children are thus non-priority groups for whom local authorities have no statutory housing responsibility.

A new Housing Act became law in July 1996 and took effect in January 1997. This measure effectively dilutes the previous duty of the local councils to provide *permanent* housing for the homeless, to one of securing suitable accommodation for no longer than two years. For many homeless households this could well result in a permanently insecure and transitory existence, with families moving periodically from one insecure tenancy in the private sector to another. Given this change to the homelessness legislation, it really must be doubted whether the rights and needs of children have been adequately taken into account by the government.

How many homeless people are there?

Homelessness has occurred throughout the post-war period. However, the numbers of households accepted by local authorities as being homeless rose most dramatically during the 1980s, from 58 000 in 1978 to 117 900 in 1986, and peaking at 170 500 in 1991. Numbers averaged 150 000 for the years 1993–95 (GB figures from *Social Trends*, 1995 and 1996 editions). In total, therefore, since the early 1980s some 3.5 million people – half of them children – have become homeless.

The true number of homeless people is unknown. What the official figures do tell us is the number of households who *have applied* to their local councils, and the number of these who are subsequently accepted as homeless. Approximately half of all homeless applicants are, in fact, turned away by their local-authority as not meeting the required criteria. So, of 339 400 households who applied to their local councils during 1993, only 160 800 were accepted (CSO, 1995a, p. 184).

Half of those who lose their homes are children, and between 70 and 80 per cent of all households accepted as homeless each year consist either of families with dependent children (60–65 per cent) or pregnant women (12–14 per cent). Thus with an average of nearly 200 000 children a year since 1990 experiencing the loss of their home, homelessness has become a deplorably common experience for children. Moreover, contrary to the popular myths exploited by some politicians, analysis of these figures lends little support to the accusation that homeless families are using the legislation to jump up the housing waiting lists, or that those accepted as homeless consist disproportionately of young women who have purposely become pregnant in order to obtain comfortable accommodation provided at public expense. In fact, the majority of homeless families (59 per cent) housed by their local councils are already on council waiting lists; and while single mothers do represent a disproportionate number of the homeless – 40 per cent of all acceptances, the DoE's own reports show that the majority of these have experienced the breakdown of a marriage or other partnership, are in their mid- to late twenties, and that only a very small proportion are unmarried teenage girls (Greve, 1990, p. 9).

Placing the blame for homelessness on the irresponsible behaviour of the homeless themselves, to escape any moral responsibility for doing something about this problem, is in any case irrelevant in view of the fact that those who are in many respects the most vulnerable to harm from the experience of homelessness are children.

The unofficial homeless

Many people in grossly unsatisfactory housing conditions, including many young people, simply do not apply to be rehoused; or, if they do apply, they are turned down by their local authorities. Unofficial estimates of the 'hidden homeless' – often women, and of 'hidden households'– that is, those sharing with another household who would prefer not to be, and of all those in a variety of hostels, lodgings, or other forms of temporary and insecure accommodation, indicate that the true figure may be well over 1.5 million households in the late 1990s (Burrows and Walentowicz, 1992, p. 8).

The causes

The issue of the causes of homelessness is best approached at two levels: (i) the precipitating or 'immediate' causes; and (ii) the underlying structural ones. The former have been consistent over the years, so that the following figures of acceptances for 1994 give a fair indication of the relative importance of the various immediate causes: about a third became homeless 'because friends or relatives were no longer able or willing to accommodate them'; 21 per cent were due to 'a break up with their partner'; 10 per cent to mortgage default or rent arrears; and 35 per cent to the loss of tenancy in the private rented sector (Central Statistical Office, 1996, p. 187). The underlying causes, on the other hand, are to be found in a combination of structural changes in society and housing policies since the late 1970s. Thus John Greve, for example, identifies changes in the housing market, employment opportunities, wage levels, demographic change, and policies relating to social security and housing benefit. These, he argues, 'shape the context within which the immediate causes operate', and produce a situation in which 'people are unable to find or retain housing at rents or prices they can afford and with security of tenure' (Greve, 1990, p. 16).

Only at this deeper causal level is the trebling of homelessness since 1978 explicable. And in all this a policy mix of reducing public *investment* in housing, the selling of council houses, and the raising of housing costs to market levels, represents a major contributory cause. The current incidence of homelessness is thus the most visible symptom of recent policy failures and of the worsening problems of access for many groups.

The experience of becoming homeless

Under legislation at the time of writing, to become homeless entails in most instances involuntary changes of accommodation, and often of housing tenure and neighbourhood. An application results from a crisis situation which normally involves the immediate or impending loss of one's home and a failure to obtain any alternative, mainly because of financial circumstances. Present shortages of housing in the social sector, and the likelihood of being housed initially on acceptance in any kind of stop-gap temporary accommodation, are all too familiar to those in housing need. For the majority of the homeless, therefore, an application results from desperation and with some awareness of the likely unpleasant consequences.

The experience of homelessness can be broken down into three distinct phases: the initial loss or the threat of the loss of one's home; the transitory phase of moving into council accommodation (often temporary); and the final stage of being allocated a permanent tenancy, most often in a council or housing association property.

Children are necessarily involved at each stage of the trauma. In the first phase they will certainly be affected by the chronic anxieties of their parents, whatever their age, and by all the financial and emotional stresses that are likely to occur during the phase of a family losing its home.

The ensuing application to a local-authority results in either a refusal, in which case the household is left to struggle on unaided in any way it can, or in official acceptance. In the latter case, this entails the surrender of personal control over one's housing situation. Security of a kind is provided, but at the cost of forfeiting any choice over accommodation and its immediate physical surroundings. For a family this generally means its social networks of contacts and relationships are held in suspension; and a family's home, that basis of its very existence, becomes a matter for the discretion of the particular council's housing department.

The fortunes of homeless families during this second stage are inevitably highly variable and unpredictable, depending on local-authority practice and the size and availability of the social housing stock in the area. Until the recent past, several thousand homeless people were initially placed in bed and breakfast (B&B) accommodation; and many thousands more in various forms of 'temporary accommodation'. The second transitory stage of homelessness, which lasts from the time of initial acceptance until the allocation of a permanent tenancy, is thus the period of greatest uncertainty and inherent insecurity. Yet, in spite of a recent overall reduction in the numbers involved, in 1994 there was still a total of 52 400 households, mainly families, who were living at some stage during that year in either B&B or other temporary accommodation (Central Statistical Office, 1996, p. 187).

The transitory stage is clearly often an exceedingly harrowing time. Families can be moved several times, often with little prior warning, from one temporary home to another; standards are, moreover, often abysmally deficient, especially in the worst of the B&B, hostel and other 'short-life' accommodation. A critical factor is the length of time families are forced to remain in this kind of accommodation. In the late 1980s in high stress areas innumerable cases were reported of young mothers confined to cramped B&B hotel rooms for anything from six months to three years. Thankfully this situation has been much improved, although the practice still exists.

The third stage occurs when 'an offer' by the local council of a permanent tenancy has been accepted by the homeless family, who only then can escape the endemic insecurities of being homeless and begin to pick up the pieces of their disrupted lives. However there may be inherent difficulties at this stage also. With less choice in the public-sector, many councils make only 'one offer' to homeless families, often allocating them to the least popular estates and to inappropriate accommodation, hence, of course, the undue concentration in some neighbourhoods of poor households, and the increasing prevalence of families with young children residing in flats.

Official acceptance of a family as being homeless – up to the time of writing – has meant in the long run some hope of reasonably secure accommodation. But the route is fraught with stresses and uncertainties, and for many children these may be gravely traumatic, with lasting detrimental psychological and other effects. Furthermore, the 1996 Housing Act, even though amended to ensure that local authorities provide a safety net of temporary accommodation for two years rather than for one as originally proposed, threatens to remove the hope of long-term security and to condemn homeless families to the continuing insecurity of the second stage in the process of being rehoused.

The effects of homelessness on children

All adverse housing conditions are harmful in varying degrees to children. However, the experience of homelessness is especially damaging to children in four important respects: developmental retardation; psychological effects; the effects on children's physical health; and the educational consequences.

Developmental retardation

A repetitive theme in all the literature about the ways in which bad housing conditions affect children concerns the impact on children's normal development. Parents talk of lost potential, endless frustration, a denial of space for play – in short, the absence of a secure environment within which a child's normal developmental processes can proceed; indeed, the kind of environment which well-housed parents take for granted for their children. Over prolonged periods of housing deprivation, serious retardation is clearly probable, and damage may be done to a child's innate intellectual potentialities, to its speech patterns, its normal physical development and the acquisition of physical skills and competencies, and to its emotional development, from which the child may never recover. The worst situation is undoubtedly B&B, though other forms of temporary housing may scarcely represent any noteworthy improvement. The following account of the work of a Barnardo's project in south London among families in temporary accommodation vividly describes the problems:

In that small room, all their possessions are piled up around the beds. Floor space is minimal to the point of being non-existent. With dangerous corridors, no outdoor garden space and no money, parents find themselves stuck in their room for weeks with small children who crave movement and exploration. The scenario is painful, desperate and potentially explosive. (*Nursery World*, 7 March 1996)

We simply do not know what human potential continues to be lost day in, day out by our inability to ensure a better housing environment than this for all our children.

Psychological effects

Any psychological effects on children are intimately connected with the above developmental factors. But the worst housing conditions may also be a cause of much psychological disturbance. Again, we simply do not know the quantitative effects of high levels of parental stress, or perhaps the prolonged frustration, on normal developmental patterns. What is clear, of course, is that housing stresses, from whatever source, are conducive to temporary (and often permanent) relationship breakdown. The effects of parental tensions and conflicts, perhaps lived out within the confines of overcrowded hostels, are of course not fully known. But in the extreme case of domestic violence the disturbing psychological effects on children of any age are clearly likely to be very serious. It is not surprising, therefore, that a 1986 survey of children living in Bayswater hotels found that 40 per cent had possible behavioural problems (Stearn, 1986). Another London-based survey of inner-city residents revealed that 45 per cent of the homeless sample exhibited 'significant mental morbidity', compared with 18–20 per cent of the non-homeless. Reviewing this research, the Royal College of Physicians concluded that: 'The high prevalence of mental morbidity among people in temporary accommodation may be related to uncertainty about the future, poor housing conditions and overcrowding . . . The increased mental morbidity of parents is likely to have an adverse effect on their children's development' (1994, p. 43).

A study completed in 1996 by the Department of Psychiatry of Birmingham University, of 194 children aged from 2 to 16 living in hostels for homeless families, similarly found that nearly a third of the children (30 per cent) displayed signs of 'mental health problems of sufficient severity to require referral for treatment' (Vostanis *et al.*, 1996, p. 15). Only 3 per cent of the children in the sample were, however, in contact with the mental health services 'despite the high rates of mental disorders among this group' (ibid., p. 19).

The effects on children's physical health

The most enduring case for good housing is the ill-health effects of bad housing. To be homeless exposes children to severe health risks. For example, the unsuitable temporary housing in which many homeless families are lodged is associated with a high rate of serious accidents to children – falls, burns and scalds in particular. A lack of proper cooking facilities is also a major cause of the very poor diets on which a number of reports have shown homeless families to subsist (see Stearn, 1986; and Conway, 1988).

Bed and breakfast accommodation has a particularly deleterious effect on children's health. A joint report by the BMA and the Health Visitors Association, for instance, noted that homeless children showed 'a high incidence of depression, disturbed sleep, poor eating, overactivity, bedwetting and soiling, toilet training problems, temper tantrums and aggression' (Health Visitors Association, 1989, p. 12).

Respiratory illness is greatly aggravated by cold and dampness, especially that caused by condensation. Temporary accommodation of all kinds is often poorly heated and damp, as of course are also many flats and multi-occupied houses, thus housing-related respiratory illness is widely prevalent among children living in bad housing conditions.

Homeless families' health needs may be great but access to health care facilities for them is often very difficult. The take-up of immunisation, for example, is low, and many families find it difficult to register with local GPs, so that they are forced to make frequent use of local hospital casualty departments. Summing up the situation, the Royal College of Physicians (1994) concluded that: 'There is evidence of increased mental, physical and obstetric ill health compared with housed populations, and there are many clinical reports of increased ill health and behavioural problems, especially among the children' (p. 39).

The educational consequences

A strong association between bad housing and educational difficulties has been known to exist for some time. The longitudinal studies, for example, of J. W. B. Douglas (1964) and of Ronald Davie and his colleagues (1972), found that children living in overcrowded and defective housing conditions gained lower test scores, were severely retarded in reading, and displayed bad social adjustment. Generally, of course, educational achievement is linked to developmental maturation, so that in the light of the restricted development of many children growing up in poor housing conditions, some parallel educational handicap is highly predictable. The educational effects of homelessness should therefore be viewed not as the only, but rather as the worst of the educational disadvantages caused by bad housing.

The ill-effects of homelessness on children's education, however, is beginning to be more widely recognised. Thus a survey by the schools' inspectorate (HMI) of children living in temporary accommodation carried out in 1989 in twenty-eight primary and secondary schools in London, Manchester, Blackpool and Great Yarmouth revealed a considerable range of difficulties faced not only by pupils but by the schools and their staff. Lack of sleep, for example, made these children 'tired, listless and unable to concentrate'; homeless children were also found to be 'irregular attenders', and more likely to be late; and because of poor diets they were reported as having an increased risk of illness (DES, 1990a).

A more extensive survey undertaken by the Health and Education Research Unit of the Institute of Education of London University on behalf of Shelter has since confirmed and extended many of these findings. If anything, in fact, in the new competitive climate in schools resulting from the 1988 Education Reform Act (see Chapter 7), the situation is now worse in a number of respects (Power *et al.*, 1995).

With the delegation of expenditure budgets to individual schools, the LEAs have lost control over the greater part of their educational expenditure. Thus LEAs are reported as finding it difficult to make any additional provision for coping with the problems presented by large numbers of homeless children, who inevitably incur additional administrative costs because of the frequent transfers involved. The schools too face a range of serious problems. Some schools lose income, for example, because of unpredictable fluctuations in the numbers of homeless children enrolled. Again, some LEAs were reported to have entered into lengthy dispute over who should fund the education of homeless children who had been moved across LEA boundaries – a common occurrence in London especially following the abolition of the Inner London Education Authority (ILEA). Indeed, the report cites instances of 'special needs' children in fact excluded from school because the LEAs involved could not agree as to who should fund the place (Power *et al.*, 1995, p. 43).

The survey also revealed that the policy of open enrolment disadvantaged homeless children. Thus, because their families were often moved into a neighbourhood only temporarily, the popular schools were often full; and alternatives could involve complicated (and expensive) travelling arrangements which in most cases LEAs were unwilling or unable to finance. There is some suggestion, too, that with schools' reputations being increasingly dependent on their pupils' test results, many schools are reluctant to accept homeless children, who are likely to perform badly in tests. Not surprisingly, many homeless children were found to miss school altogether for weeks or months on end while in temporary accommodation. And even where parents can find schools willing to accept their children, the same school may not have places in each of the particular year groups and may not therefore be willing to accept all the children in a family. In these circumstances, any idea of parental choice must be meaningless for homeless parents.

The research also demonstrated the many practical problems facing homeless children – the loss of friendships; the difficulties of constantly having to readjust to new schools and of maintaining continuity in the curriculum; and the difficulties of completing assignments and doing homework with nowhere to do it other than in a shared room. Homeless children, moreover, even when they have found a school willing to accept them, still find it difficult to participate fully in school life. They tend to be stigmatised and treated as 'outsiders', so their relationships with their peers and with teachers are often difficult.

Small wonder then, given these disadvantages, that the survey found that of the seventy-one headteachers involved in the survey, 86 per cent 'reported that homelessness had an impact upon pupils' academic progress', and three-quarters of the sample reported that both attendance rates and pupil behaviour were affected (ibid., p. 47).

Conclusion

So how well have children been served by post-war housing policies? The record, of course, is mixed. There is no doubt that great improvements have been achieved: over half of British homes have been built since 1945, and the majority of families have enjoyed housing amenities, home comforts and security which many of their parents and grandparents would have thought inconceivable before the Second World War. At the same time, though, it is also clear that British housing problems have not been wholly solved, and considerable numbers of children remain among the worst affected.

For the first thirty years after 1945 the state assumed responsibility for the assessment of national housing needs and for the satisfaction of these in so far as economic and other circumstances allowed. However, housing policy since 1979 has involved a growing reliance on the market as the best means of meeting housing needs. Allied to this has been an unflagging commitment to the expansion of home ownership as the normal and preferred tenure. This dual policy emphasis has entailed the abandonment of the earlier post-war social priorities which underlay the broad policy consensus of the period. We have moved, as Clare Ungerson argues, from a housing politics focused on 'need' to one dominated by 'ownership' (1994, p. 213).

Unfortunately, faith in market forces and in the advantages of home ownership have not solved Britain's continuing housing problems. In place of the early post-war emphasis on investment in housing, government policy since 1979 has increasingly left supply to the market; but at the same time the state has become entangled in complicated strategies for the promotion of owner-occupation. However, construction levels since 1979 have fluctuated at levels substantially below those achieved in the previous thirty years. In addition, the owner-occupied market is only slowly emerging from crisis, while the incidence of homelessness has reached epidemic proportions since the mid-1980s.

In no other policy area can recent governments have paid so little heed to the consequences of their policy decisions for children. The interests of the young would appear to have been sacrificed to the ideological zealotry of the New Right of the Conservative Party. And the sacrifice seems all set to continue. Thus the voluntary bodies working with the homeless are unanimous in their opinion that the changes contained in the 1996 Housing Act will seriously damage the housing prospects of many homeless children and further erode their already limited housing rights.

Of course, the housing market may emerge from its state of stagnation and this would certainly reduce the damaging effects of negative equity for many. However the increased job insecurity of the 1990s may be less easily dispersed, so that unless the economy picks up rapidly in the late 1990s the stresses on some families in owner-occupation would seem likely to remain. With some 50 000 council dwellings, moreover, still being sold annually, and with the 1996 Act promising to further promote the sale of housing association properties, it is highly improbable that present shortages of social housing will ease in the near future.

Children's lives are demeaned and distorted – sometimes perhaps beyond repair – by bad housing conditions; and often their health may be seriously undermined and their educational opportunities unnecessarily restricted and impoverished. There is therefore a strong case for arguing that any measures to improve the housing circumstances of less well-off families would achieve more for children's welfare than any other social policy reforms.

Further reading

Malpass and Murie (1994) and Balchin (1995) provide detailed accounts of post-war housing policy. Greve (1990) and Burrows and Walentowicz (1992) are good starting points on homelessness. Pascall (1986) and Sexty (1990) discuss women's housing needs. Accounts of the health effects of bad housing can be found in Conway (1988), Kumar (1993), and Lowry (1991).

6

Early Childhood Education and Care

> Early childhood is valid in itself, and is part of life, not simply a preparation for work, or for the next stage of education. (Early Years Curriculum Group, 1989, p. 3)

Introduction

Our purpose in heading this chapter with the quotation above is twofold. First, it demonstrates that, in contrast to other aspects of social policy relating to children, the field of early years education has at its core a strong ethos of child-centredness. Indeed, the nursery education movement, based on the ideas of Froebel, Montessori and others, has always stressed the principle of respect for the child as an individual (Bruce, 1987). To this extent, then, the nursery education tradition is, in our view, very close in its essential philosophy to the UN Convention on the Rights of the Child, and to the approach taken in this book.

The second reason for starting with this quotation is that it establishes a benchmark against which to evaluate UK policy in the period since 1945. It has been suggested that early-childhood policy in the UK over the past thirty years has experienced 'many false dawns, each to be followed by disappointment' (Jackson, 1993, p. 64).

However, when viewed from the perspective of the child and measured against the principle of respect for early childhood as a valid stage of development in its own right, it is arguable that UK policy has been almost uniformly negative. Indeed, we would go so far as to suggest that no other aspect of the post-1945 UK welfare state has failed children so badly as its policy on early years education and care. If children in general are afforded a low status within UK social policy, this is particularly so in the first stage of their life.

The low status of early childhood

This starts with the language used to describe young children in the UK. The most common terms are 'under-fives' or 'under-eights' both of which, as Gillian Alexander has pointed out, signal 'not yet old enough' (Alexander, 1995). Similarly, we would argue, the use of the other frequently used epithet 'pre-school' is equally negative as a description of the early years stage. At best, the term defines the early years by reference to what is to come. At worst it implies that this stage is merely a preparation for school. Perhaps most dismissive of all, though, is the term 'rising fives' to describe 4-year-old children admitted early to primary school. It is as though all those of working age were to be categorised as 'pre-retirement' or 'rising dead'!

The use of any shorthand term to encompass children from 0–5 years is problematic and runs the risk of ignoring the vast difference between, say, a 1-year-old and a 4-year-old. This is not the same as the difference between a 31-year-old and a 34-year-old, or even an 11-year-old and 14-year-old. The developmental changes during the first few years are so vast that one epithet cannot adequately cover this stage in an individual's life.

Having said this, we would accept that there are times when a shorthand term is useful. The more serious objection to the terminology that pervades current thinking about early childhood is the fact that it is defined not in terms of what it is, but rather what it will become. Very young children, in our view, should not be regarded as 'pre', 'under' or 'rising' anything. It implies a negative or 'deficit' view of early childhood which is incompatible with an approach that values young children as individuals in their own right.

Nor would this matter so much if it was simply a question of language. It is very apparent, however – particularly when in comparison with other European countries, for example – that early childhood hardly exists as a separate phase in terms of UK policy (see David, 1993). One reflection of this is the fact that children enter formal schooling at a relatively early age. The official starting date is at the beginning of the term following the child's fifth birthday, but in practice, as we shall see, many children are admitted considerably earlier. So much so that the majority of 4-year-old children in the UK are in primary-school classes. This compares with a policy of starting at 6 or 7 in most other comparable countries.

It is important to bear this in mind when discussing early years education. The issue is frequently confused in the UK and often deliberately so, not least in government circles, by failing to distinguish between young children in specialised early years provision and those in primary schools. The UK record on provision of education for four-year-olds looks very much worse in comparison with the rest of Europe if we confine the discussion to nursery education alone.

We shall discuss UK policy on admission to school in more detail later in the chapter. It is worth adding at this stage, though, that when the age of 5 was first established as the date for starting school in the 1870 Education Act, it was, as Martin Woodhead (1989) has shown, essentially an arbitrary decision. Certainly the parliamentary debates made little, if any, reference to any child-centred, and still less educational, rationale for this decision. Indeed, existing educational theory, as, for example, in the work of Froebel and Owen, would have pointed to the age of 6 as being more appropriate.

However, the evidence suggests that it was adult concerns that tipped the balance towards an earlier start. Two arguments in particular seemed to hold sway. The first was that of parents faced with losing the child-care services of older children who were now to be within compulsory education. In these circumstances, parents had a strong interest in sending their younger children to school at the same time. The second was voiced by employers, who felt that the sooner children started school the sooner they could finish and be available to work.

Perhaps even more remarkable than the arbitrary nature of the initial decision is the fact that policy on the age of starting school was confirmed by the 1944 Education Act and has continued since then with virtually no scrutiny or reference to the needs of children. Indeed, the only serious challenge to this policy came from the Treasury during the 1950s, at a time when the education budget was under severe strain in the face of rising birth rates (Timmins, 1995, p. 198). Yet this decision to set the age of 5 as the school entry age, which appears to have been treated as an administrative detail or afterthought, has exercised a profound effect in restricting the concept of early childhood in the UK.

The education care division

This is exacerbated when we turn to the other end of the early childhood stage. Policy on early childhood in the UK has been based, as we shall discuss later, on a distinction between 'care' and 'education'. Within this framework, the very youngest children (0–2) are deemed to be in need of 'care' rather than education. Furthermore, while education has throughout the twentieth century been accepted as a legitimate, if under-resourced, field of government responsibility, the same cannot be said of 'care'. This has been regarded as a private, family responsibility (see Chapter 1), with the state confined to the limited role of providing for a small number of children who are considered to be 'at risk' or 'in need'.

Broadly speaking, then, children in the UK are seen as the exclusive responsibility of their parents up to the age of 2, and eligible for primary education from the age of 4. This means that in terms of public policy, early childhood barely exists as a stage in its own right. This stage is, in effect, restricted to the 3-year-olds. This contrasts sharply with the position in most other European countries, where children start school later and the years 0–6 constitute a more clearly-defined early childhood stage of development.

Early years day care and adult interests

If UK policy on services for young children has been shaped by the lack of a clearly defined and positive concept of early childhood, it has also suffered from its excessive focus on adult concerns and interests. The Commission on Social Justice (CSJ) has suggested that 'under fives provision is good for children, good for parents and good for the economy and society' (Commission on Social Justice, 1994, p. 123). The truth is, however, that despite the fact that children head this list of potential beneficiaries, both the CSJ itself and the wider debate about early childhood services in the UK have been largely preoccupied with the needs of the economy and society, or with those of parents. This has been particularly so in the case of day care. Gillian Pugh has made the point that 'the history of day nurseries reflects a response to social and economic factors rather than a coherent approach to services for under fives' (Pugh, 1989, p. 143).

She goes on to cite the example of the expansion of day nurseries during the Second World War, when women were needed in the factories, followed by their closure when post-war policy emphasised the role of women within the home. The scale and speed of the expansion had been spectacular, with the number of nurseries in England and Wales increasing from just 14 in October 1940 to 1345 by July 1943. After the war, the closure programme, though less swift, was no less determined. Within a year, the number had fallen to 914, and within ten years less than half were still open (Cohen, 1988, p. 2). Thus at a time when there was an unprecedented increase in the level of social provision in the UK, early years day care stands out as one service that was cut back radically. More recently, concern over the shrinking proportion of the population of working age – the 'demographic time bomb' – has provoked increased interest in the provision of day care services in order to release more women for the labour market (Cohen, 1990).

The provision of day care has also been seen by women as an equal opportunities issue. The demand for universal day care has been one of the central aims of the women's movement throughout its existence. Within the European Union child care has been firmly located within this framework. The European Childcare Network was established in the mid-1980s as part of the European Community's Action Programme on the Promotion of Equal Opportunities for Women.

Of course, it is true that none of these adult concerns is necessarily incompatible with the interests of children, though automatic congruence should not be assumed. However, the point is that the debate rarely starts from the needs of young children. It is easy to forget, in much of the literature on day care, that it is the children who are the real 'consumers' of the service, and not their parents.

'Investing' in young children

If an adult focus has characterised debates about day care in the UK, then the same is true of early years education. In spite of the strongly child-centred tradition within nursery education, policy in the UK has been driven mainly by a more instrumental philosophy based on 'investment'. Evidence from comparative studies, such as that of Tricia David, would suggest that in practice the nursery tradition has never enjoyed as much influence on UK education policy as elsewhere in Europe. The Plowden Report in 1967 was perhaps the high point of child-centredness in official attitudes in the UK. However, as we shall see, the impact of this report on policy was limited and brief. For the most part, in debates surrounding early years education we find an emphasis that is far removed from that of the child-centred nursery tradition.

This is clearly illustrated by the growing number of official and semi-official reports of the late 1980s and early 1990s calling for an expansion of early years education (prominent examples include: Commission on Social Justice, 1994; Royal Society of Arts, 1994; National Commission on Education, 1993; and House of Commons Select Committee on Education, 1989). The dominant theme throughout these reports is 'investment', and nursery education is repeatedly evaluated in terms of its potential contribution to future economic and social development. The following extracts give the flavour:

> Only lifelong learning can win us the prize of economic success . . . we learn more and develop faster in our first five years than at any other time in our lives. If we want to be serious about investing in people, we must start at the beginning. (Commission on Social Justice, 1994, p. 122)

> the best indicator of the capacity of the economy tomorrow is the quality of our children today. (Ibid., p. 311)

> Along with health care and parental education, investment in good early learning for all its children is arguably the best investment a nation can make. (Royal Society of Arts, 1994, p. 9)

It is arguable that to view early years education as an 'investment' is not only antithetical to the nursery education tradition and at odds with the UN Convention's emphasis on respect for the child, but it has also led to policy developments that are detrimental to the development of young children. We shall return to this discussion later in the chapter. For now, we would simply reiterate that although early years education and care can clearly embody a wide range of values and serve a variety of policy objectives, UK policy has not placed the child at the centre of its concerns.

The pattern of provision: choice or lottery?

The lack of any coherent rationale, let alone a child-centred one, has resulted in a pattern of provision of early childhood services that is complex and confusing. A 4-year-old child, for example, might find itself for all or part of the day in one or more of a number of settings. These would include day nurseries, playgroups, childminders, nursery schools or classes, or reception classes in primary schools (and this does not include those who are cared for in their own homes by parents, relatives, nannies or au pairs). The position is further confused by the fact that each form of provision outside the home might be in the private, voluntary or public sectors.

Moreover, each service differs in terms of its hours, costs and the training background of its staff, to say nothing of its philosophy and aims. Some are classified as 'day care' and are the responsibility of local authority social services departments and the Department of Health; and others as 'education' and come within the province of the Department for Education and Employment.

Looked at from the point of young children, the division between 'education' and 'care' makes little or no sense. The needs of a 3-year-old are the same whether s/he is in a nursery class, a playgroup or with a childminder. There is no pedagogic or child development rationale underlying the care/education divide. Rather it reflects and reinforces differences that owe more 'to history and the professional jealousies of providers than to the needs of children and their families' (Pugh, 1992, p. 10).

It may also be the case, as Tricia David has suggested, that governments have used the division between 'care' and 'education' with their different philosophies and patterns of service, to create a polarisation between parents who want and need to work on the one hand, for whom full day care is a necessity, and those, on the other hand, who stay at home and are content with part-time 'education' provision (David, 1993, p. 155). The effect of this has been to channel much of the debate about early years provision into a discussion about the needs of parents, or more specifically, working mothers.

Yet apart from a relatively small number of innovative attempts to combine day care and nursery education in one centre (for a fuller discussion of 'co-ordination' of services see Pugh, 1988), and despite the fact that the Rumbold Committee set up to consider the future of nursery education in the late 1980s, concluded that everyone who works with young children should be termed an 'educator' (Dept of Education and Science, 1990), the division continues to hinder the development of early childhood services in the UK.

Of course it may be suggested that what all this reflects is a healthy diversity of choice which is to the benefit of children. Ministers have frequently put this forward as a central principle of policy (see, for example, *Hansard*, 22 March 1988). The reality is, however, that for most families there is little or no choice. As the Rumbold Committee concluded, 'access to services is still largely determined by where a child lives, when his or her birthday is, whether the parents have access to information about services, and whether they can afford fees where there is no public provision' (Dept of Education and Science, 1990, pp. 27–8).

It is an indication of the low level of public provision that relatives are by far the most commonly used form of day care. The government's 1990 Survey of Day Care Services for Children in England revealed that of the 78 per cent of children who were regularly looked after by someone other than their mother, over half were receiving all or most of their care from the father, grandparents or other relatives (Dept of Health, 1991a).

It should also be stressed that any discussion of early childhood services which confines itself to the picture in the UK as a whole is profoundly misleading. Local diversity in the level and form of service provision is a feature of UK social policy generally. But in no other area is it as acute as in early childhood services (see, for example, Moss, 1991; and Pugh, 1988). To give an indication of the wide variation in levels of provision in 1990: nursery education provision ranged from nil in Gloucestershire to 194 places per 1000 children aged under 5 in Hounslow, while day nursery places varied from nil in Rotherham and Barnsley to 58 per 1000 under fives in Islington, and childminders from 13 per 1000 under fives in Knowsley, compared to 126 per 1000 in Brent (Moss, 1991).

The striking feature of these comparative figures is not only the degree of variation but the fact that they do not follow any simple urban/rural dichotomy. Nor do they reflect variations in the levels of need. Comparable inner city areas have widely divergent patterns of provision. What they do indicate, as Moss points out, is the 'reluctance of successive Governments to set and enforce either national targets for levels of provision, or in the case of day care, national standards for supervision and support' (ibid., pp. 89–90).

If access to early childhood services varies from region to region, and local authority to local authority, there is also evidence of social class and ethnic inequalities. In their research based on the national longitudinal study of child health and education, A. Osborn and J. Milbank (1987) found substantial contrasts between social classes in their use of early years services. Whereas only 10 per cent of children with fathers in a professional occupation (social class I) had no experience of early years services, the comparable figure among children with unskilled or unemployed fathers (social class V) was 44 per cent. When more sophisticated indices of families' socio-economic position were used the relative inequality in use of early years services was even greater (ibid., pp. 76–7).

This has come about because although the children from families at the bottom end of the socioeconomic scale made greater use of the local-authority-provided services, particularly day nurseries, this was not enough to compensate for the greater disparity in favour of children from the better-off families in the private and voluntary sectors. Playgroups, in particular, were largely the preserve of the children of professional families. A similar conclusion emerges from a national study of playgroups carried out by the Thomas Coram Research Unit at the end of the 1980s (Dept of Health, 1990).

Data on ethnic variations in the usage of early years services is poor. For example, the study by P. Moss and C. Owen (which uses General Household Survey data for 1979 and 1986 to estimate use of early years provision) is inconclusive on this question because of the small numbers of ethnic minority children in the sample data (Moss and Owen, 1990). Osborn and Milbank devote only a short section of their report to this issue: they conclude that, as with social class differences, children from ethnic minority families are over-represented in local authority day nurseries, but this is more than outweighed by their under-representation in other forms of provision. Overall, their data suggested that as many as 46 per cent of children from Asian families and 35 per cent of those from Afro-Caribbean families had no early years experience, compared to a corresponding figure of 28 per cent for children from white families (ibid., p. 83). A similar picture emerges from other small scale local studies (Commission for Racial Equality, 1989, p. 16).

Overall, then, there is evidence that access to early years provision is not equally available to all. Moreover, it may seem surprising that many of the children who are most in need of early childhood services are those who are least likely to have access to them. However, this may be less surprising when we consider the heavy reliance in the UK on the private and voluntary sectors, and the high cost of much provision. As Gillian Pugh has suggested, 'a policy that leaves service development to market forces tends to disadvantage those who are already disadvantaged' (Pugh, 1992, p. 13).

The mixed economy of provision

If the idea that the range of provision in the UK offers diversity and choice for young children and their families is of dubious validity, it is worth stressing that this 'mixed economy' approach to early years services is not by any means unique to the UK. Where policy in Britain does differ from that of most other comparable countries, as Peter Moss has pointed out, is in 'the low level of public sector involvement in either providing or funding services' (Moss, 1991, p. 87). In this respect, government policy was established in the immediate post-1945 period and has been consistent ever since.

A Ministry of Health Circular in 1945 stated the position as follows:

> Ministers are of the opinion that, under normal peacetime conditions, the right policy to pursue would be positively to discourage mothers of children under 2 from going out to work; to make provision for children between 2 and 5 by way of nursery schools and classes; and to regard day nurseries as supplements to meet the special needs of children whose mothers are constrained by individual circumstances to go out to work or whose home circumstances are unsatisfactory from the health point of view or whose mothers are incapable for some good reason of under-taking the full care of their children. (Ministry of Health, 1945)

By and large, and with only minor changes in emphasis, this has regularly been reaffirmed as official policy and remains the position in the late 1990s. The 1989 Children Act, for example, which has often been seen as a significant step forward in terms of children's welfare, confines local authorities' duty to provide day care to those children who are deemed to be 'in need'. Although the Act does also extend to local authorities the discretionary power to provide day care for children who are not 'in need', the main emphasis is very much on the residual role of day care as laid out in the 1945 circular.

One change in emphasis in the 1980s and 1990s which should be noted is that the stress on discouraging women with young children from working has been dropped in favour of an emphasis on individual choice. Officially, government policy started to adopt a neutral stance on a mother's right to work. This meant that responsibility for the care of children remained firmly with the family or, more specifically, the mother. The following comment by Edwina Currie is typical of many statements by ministers during the 1980s;

> Our view is that it is for parents that go out to work to decide how best to care for their children. If they want to or need help in this they should make the appropriate arrangements and meet the costs. (*Hansard*, 12 July 1988)

If government policy on day care has remained remarkably consistent during the period since 1945, this is no less true in the case of early years education. The difference is that there is at least an acceptance that nursery education is a legitimate responsibility of government, albeit one that has low priority in terms of resources. The tone was set in the 1950s. For although the 1944 Education Act imposed a duty on local authorities 'to have regard to the need' for securing nursery education, the post-war 'baby boom' and the commitment to raise the school leaving age (to 15) meant that provision for the early years was starved of resources for over twenty years. Indeed, so stagnant was activity on this front that the Ministry of Education ceased to report on nursery education in its annual reports until the middle of the 1960s (Tizard *et al.*, 1976, p. 73).

The Plowden Report (1967) followed by the 1972 White Paper *Education: A Framework for Expansion* gave rise briefly to a more positive commitment to nursery education. The latter set a target of expansion to provide places for 50 per cent of 3-year-olds and 90 per cent of 4-year-olds by the end of the decade. It is perhaps worth noting that whereas the 1945 Ministry of Health circular had included children aged 2 among those for whom nursery education would be appropriate, this group now no longer figured in official targets. In practice, although the Plowden Report did give a boost to the number of nursery education places, financial constraints continued to mean that nursery education was a low priority for local authority spending. This was formalised in the 1980 Education Act, which reduced the local authorities' duty to provide nursery education to a permissive power, thus making it an even more discretionary service.

In Table 6.1 we can trace the effects of this policy framework on the development of both care and education services during the postwar period. Not surprisingly, the most substantial growth has been in services that are low cost and/or in the private sector. Two services that are both low cost and mainly private are childminding and playgroups. The latter, in particular, is very characteristic of the UK approach to early years services in the post-1945 period. Beginning in the 1960s as a stop-gap self-help response to the lack of nursery education provision, it grew rapidly to become the major early years provision – albeit offering only very limited part-time attendance for most children.

Table 6.1   Places in early years' education and care facilities in the United Kingdom, 1951–1992/3 (000s)

	1951	1961	1971	1981	1992/3
Nursery schools (F/T)	22	21	20	22	15
" " (P/T)	–	3	–	67	70
Primary schools (F/T)	148	181	263	281	376
" " (P/T)	–	3	38	167	329
Non-Maintained Schools (F/T)	–	–	19	19	29
" " " (P/T)	–	–	14	12	21
Special schools (F/T and P/T)	–	–	2	5	7
Local authority day nurseries	40	22	23	32	28
Local authority playgroups	–	–	–	5	3
Registered day nurseries	10	18	296	23	127
Registered playgroups	–	–	–	433	475
Childminders	3.5	14	90	110	352

Source: *Social Trends 25* (1995); Tizard *et al.* (1976).

Playgroups have occupied an ambivalent role as providers of early years education in the UK, as Tricia David indicates (David, 1993, pp. 137–8). Initially the playgroup movement saw one of its roles as campaigning for an expansion of nursery education. By the 1970s, however, there is evidence that it saw this as a threat to its own existence and began to stress the distinctiveness and importance of its own contribution to early years education. Much of this derived from what David terms its 'powerful and transforming effect on the lives of many women involved in running groups' rather than its work with children. Whether or not the playgroup movement has hindered the development of nursery education in the UK, as Sonia Jackson (1993) has claimed, is a moot point. Certainly, playgroups came to be used by governments as a flexible and cheap substitute for nursery education in many parts of the country. It is hard to believe that there would not have been much more pressure for local authority provision without this safety valve.

We should perhaps add that during 1995, in line with the increasingly instrumental and formal emphasis in early years education, which we discuss more fully later in this chapter, the Pre-School Playgroup Association, the umbrella organisation of the playgroup movement, changed its name to the Pre-School Learning Alliance and dropped the term 'playgroup' in favour of 'pre-school centre'.

Another safety valve, particularly for mothers working outside the home, has been provided by childminding. As with playgroups, this aspect of provision has been favoured by governments because it provides a low-cost, flexible service (Dept of Health and Social Security/Dept of Education and Science, 1978). It has also been supported because it offers least challenge to the idea that children are a private, family responsibility. By leaving it to mothers to arrange for their children to be looked after by a substitute 'mother', with only minimal state support and regulation, UK policy has tended to reinforce the dominant ideology.

Because of its largely private nature, we know rather less about childminding than is healthy for a society that purports to be concerned about children. It was not until the 1948 Nurseries' and Childminders' Regulations Act, that the state involved itself in childminding at all. This Act laid down a set of minimum standards to be applied to anyone caring for other people's children in their own homes for reward. The responsibility for the regulatory role fell to local authorities and has remained poorly resourced, with the result that few authorities go much beyond the enforcement of basic health and safety requirements.

We cannot even say with certainty how many children are cared for by childminders in the UK at any one time; the number of registered childminders is only a proportion of the total. Moss has estimated that by the late 1980s probably 80 per cent of minders were registered, although the precise figure is somewhat speculative (Moss, 1987). Some of the recorded growth in childminding in the post-war period has undoubtedly been caused by a shift from illegal to registered childminding. However, there has also been a real increase in childminding stimulated by the growth in the number of mothers employed outside the home. Although it clearly plays an important role in the care and education of young children, particularly those under the age of 3, it is fair to say that the history of childminding in the UK suggests that it is more accurately seen as a service for working parents than for children.

The final point to note in relation to Table 6.1 is the extent to which early admission to primary school has developed as a supplement, or even an alternative, to nursery education. Indeed, as we have already noted, the two forms of provision are frequently discussed as though they were one and the same. The reality is that, in educational terms, they are very different (Woodhead, 1989). We shall examine in a later section the impact of this policy on the quality of early years education. In terms of the overall quantity of provision, however, the number of early admissions to reception classes has for much of the post-war period grown as fast or faster than places in nursery provision *per se*. Indeed, for 4-year-olds, admission to primary school has become the norm.

Peter Moss has estimated that less than 20 per cent of children under the age of 5 in the UK benefit from any form of public funding. This includes those in maintained nursery schools and classes, primary schools, and local authority day nurseries, together with a small amount of subsidy for some playgroups and an even smaller number of local-authority-sponsored places with childminders (Moss, 1991). Moreover, since the 1980s, the proportion of children in those services which receive some public funding has been growing more slowly (and in some cases, such as day nurseries, has been declining) compared to those in the private sector.

The quality of provision

If the state's involvement in the provision of early years services in the UK has been very limited since 1945, then its role in regulating and supporting the quality of provision has not been much greater. Since 1948, local authorities have been charged with the responsibility of regulating the main forms of day care provision. However, when services are largely privately provided with little or no public subsidy, there are severe limits on the standards that can be imposed by a regulatory body without pushing up prices beyond the means of many families.

In this context, there is an implicit tension between the aim of establishing standards designed to ensure good-quality care for children and that of preserving parents' ability to purchase the services in the first place. The 1948 Nurseries' and Childminders' Regulations Act clearly leant towards the latter stance. It required local authorities to impose only minimal standards, and even these, as Elfer and Beasley (1991) have shown, proved hard to implement. The result is that the quality of day care provision ranges widely. Furthermore, although there is a shortage of large-scale studies of day-care quality, reviews of the research that does exist (for example, Melhuish, 1991; and Clark, 1988) suggest that some elements of day care have proved to be seriously inadequate.

The 1989 Children Act was widely hailed as a significant step towards improved regulation of day care and the promotion of the welfare of young children. Certainly, it does extend local authorities' responsibilities and broaden the standards they are expected to apply in their inspection and registration of day care. However, the same conflict with keeping costs down applies, and a subsequent circular (Dept of Health, 1/93) stresses the need for flexibility. It urges local authorities not to impose standards that are 'unrealistically high to the point that they inhibit expansion' (ibid., para. 3).

Any idea that the 1989 Act was intended to empower local authorities to impose standards that would truly recognise the rights of children was soon to be thrown into question. The London Borough of Sutton was challenged in the courts by a childminder who had been deregistered for smacking a child in her care, contrary to the council's policy. The childminder argued that she was acting in accordance with the parents' instructions. In the event, the local authority lost the legal battle in 1994, and the government subsequently added its voice in support of the childminder. The Sutton case clearly underlines the fact that the regulatory role of the state continues to be a minimal one in relation to day care.

Moreover, the duty to inspect and register day care provision is essentially a negative and reactive one. Local authorities are also empowered (though not required) under the Children Act 1989 to promote quality day care in a more positive fashion, through the provision of training and support services. However, all the evidence suggests that local authority support for the two main forms of day care provision, childminders (Ferri and Birchall, 1986) and playgroups (Statham, 1990) is extremely patchy and rarely adequate. Despite some impressive work in developing and disseminating quality standards by voluntary agencies such as the National Children's Bureau and the National Childminding Association, the overall commitment of resources to training and support of day care workers in the UK has remained woefully inadequate throughout the post-war period.

Furthermore, without public subsidy it is inevitable that affordable day care can only exist where the pay and conditions of its workforce are poor. This in turn contributes to a high level of turnover and instability of provision – a feature which has emerged consistently from research on both childminding and day nurseries (Moss, 1991). Indeed, it is not unreasonable to conclude from the evidence that the heavy reliance on the market in the provision of day care, if it does not in fact preclude good-quality care for young children, certainly makes it improbable.

When we turn to early years education, there is certainly a clearer and stronger acceptance of the state's responsibility for regulating standards. One reflection of this is the fact that, in contrast to day care, there have been a number of official inquiries into early years education, such as the Plowden (1967) and Rumbold (Dept of Education and Science, 1990) reports. Also, within the education sector, the inspectoral and advisory role of central and local government has been much more prominent. Throughout most of the post-war period, Her Majesty's Inspectors (HMIs) and local education authority advisers have played an important part in promoting and monitoring the quality of early years education. However, following the shift to a more market-based approach to educational standards initiated by the 1988 Education Act, this has changed, and Her Majesty's Inspectorate has been disbanded, in favour of a new agency, OFSTED (the Office for Standards in Education). This has a narrower and more specific brief, to provide inspection reports that can be used by parents to guide their choice of schools.

When it comes to staff qualifications and training, we find a similar disparity between early years education and care. Although concern has been expressed about the fact that early years teachers are not necessarily trained specifically for work in nursery education, their general teaching qualification marks them out from most other early years workers. Pay and conditions, together with opportunities for in-service training, are also much better in the education sector.

Nevertheless, despite these positive indicators in relation to the quality of early years education, the overall emphasis throughout the post-war period on low-cost provision of the service has meant that quality has been compromised. The most obvious indicator of this has been the extent to which 4-year-olds have found themselves in primary schools rather than in a nursery setting. Numerous academic studies and official reports have drawn attention to the inappropriate nature of much primary provision for 4-year-old children (see, for example, Bennett and Kell, 1989; Dept of Education and Science, 1989 and 1990). The House of Commons Education Select Committee summed up the position well in 1986:

> The teachers are seldom experienced or trained for children of these younger ages; they commonly have no ancillary help of the kind that a nursery gives; they may have up to 34 or even more children in a class and with an age span from three or four to six or even older; they must give a considerable amount of their time and attention to the development of literacy and mathematical skills in the older children; they rarely have sufficient equipment or the space needed by the younger children. (House of Commons, 1986, para. 5.41)

Rarely has early admission to primary school been advocated on educational or child-centred grounds. Rather, it has provided policy-makers with a pragmatic and politically expedient response to the shortage of early years education and day care places. From the point of view of parents too, early admission to school has a number of attractions. Not least of these is that, unlike most of the alternatives, a school place is free. Also, the fact that a place in a reception class is more likely to be full-time than a place in a nursery school or class means that it is more convenient for working parents.

It may also be the case that, despite the research evidence to the contrary, many parents believe there are educational advantages in children starting 'proper' school as early as possible. Tricia David has suggested that young children in the UK have been affected by a widespread 'Gadarene rush to formalize' that has gathered pace within education in the 1980s (David, 1993, p. 161). The most obvious manifestation of this was the introduction of the National Curriculum and Standard Assessment Tests (SATs) in the Education Act 1988. Although these changes do not apply directly to nursery education, they do inevitably have enormous consequences for the early years.

For a start, as primary schools are being required to publish their test results for 7-year-olds in competitive league tables, there has understandably been a move towards 'baseline testing' of 4-year-olds when they enter school. Perhaps more significant, however, is the challenge posed to the traditional ethos of nursery education by the instrumental emphasis of the National Curriculum. It has been suggested that the two approaches are not simply different but 'mirror images, exact opposites in every respect' (Blenkin and Kelly, 1994, p. 40). While the nursery tradition, as we have seen, celebrates the child as a child rather than a future adult, and is thus focused strongly around play, the emphasis of the National Curriculum is very much on the acquisition of skills as a preparation for the world of work.

There is little doubt that since the 1980s there has been a growing emphasis generally in UK education policy on more instrumental aims and a shift to more traditional approaches. This is reflected specifically in early years education, where increasingly quality is equated with success in preparing children for entry to formal schooling. The traditional values of the nursery movement may not find it easy to survive within this climate.

Nursery vouchers

The nursery voucher scheme is potentially one of the most signifi-cant developments in early years policy in recent times. Introduced initially on an experimental basis in four local education authorities in 1996, it was extended nationwide in April 1997. The principle of subsidising consumers (or more accurately, their parents) rather than providers of early years services is a radical departure in the UK. The scheme involves the payment of a voucher worth £1100 for every 4-year-old, to be used to pay for 'nursery education' provided by an approved supplier. It is clearly intended to strengthen still further the philosophy that early years provision is a commodity to be purchased by parents within a competitive market. The assumption is that market forces will bring about an improvement in both the quantity and quality of services on offer.

It is difficult at this stage to assess precisely the impact that nursery vouchers will have on early years provision. Not only has the pilot scheme yet to be fully evaluated, but the Labour party is committed to abandoning the policy. The 1997 national distribution of vouchers may thus prove to be a one-off event. There are, however, some early indications from the pilot project that are worth picking up because they emphasise inherent weaknesses in UK early years provision. Although these problems have been both emphasised and exacerbated by vouchers, they will persist even if vouchers are scrapped.

The first point to note is that vouchers appear, in the pilot areas, to have emphasised the fragmentation of early years provision and to militate against a coherent and integrated approach to planning and delivering services. *The Times Educational Supplement* (TES) referred to a 'free for all' in the pilot authorities as providers scrambled to attract vouchers (*TES*, 25 October 1996). Particular tensions emerged between local-authority-maintained schools and the private and voluntary nursery schools. Local authorities, moreover, have been accused of changing their admission policies for reception classes in order to increase the number of voucher-carrying 4-year-olds. In one of the pilot authorities, Norfolk, this led to the closure of three pre-schools within the first six months of the voucher scheme (*TES*, 1 November 1996).

This leads to the second issue highlighted by the voucher experiment. Perhaps the most striking feature of nursery vouchers in the pilot areas was that they had very little to do with nursery education at all. The majority of the vouchers went to children who were attending local-authority or grant-maintained primary schools – around 67 per cent in Wandsworth, for example (ibid.). The term 'nursery voucher' is a complete misnomer. The fact is, as we have already emphasised, that UK policy on early years education is based on early admission to school rather than on a distinctive nursery education approach. There can be little doubt that this will be exacerbated by nursery vouchers, given the financial incentive to schools to maximise their income.

Ironically, then, there is a distinct danger that vouchers will further undermine nursery education. This point was made by the Audit Commission, which drew attention to the danger for 3-year-olds and younger who would be left in nurseries that are increasingly likely to lose 4-year-olds and their voucher income to schools (Audit Commission, 1996, p. 83). Despite the Labour Party's commitment to abolishing vouchers, it shows no inclination to tackle the trend towards early admission of 4-year-olds to school, and there is no indication in its policy paper, *Early Excellence* (Labour Party, 1996), that a Labour government would shift the balance back in favour of nursery education.

Day care for school-age children

So far our discussion has confined itself to services for children in the pre-school years. One important area of provision, which has been largely neglected in the UK, is care for older children outside school hours. There is no statutory obligation on local authorities to provide day care after school or during holidays, and the evidence suggests that few do so. The Children Act 1989 does require local authorities to provide services for 'children in need', as we have seen, and this would include after-school care. However, response has been limited by financial constraints.

A survey by Kids Club Network in 1989 indicated that there were after-school places available for only about 0.2 per cent of primary school children, and holiday schemes for 0.3 per cent. Most of these are concentrated in a few urban areas – over a third of them are in Greater London (Kids Club Network, 1990). The result is that an estimated one in five children between the ages of 5 and 10 is left at home alone during school holidays, and one in six returns to an empty house at the end of the school day (Kids Club Network, quoted in Leach, 1994).

Towards child-friendly employment agencies

The needs of children for day care, whether in their early years or when they are at school, have not been a high priority in the UK. Policy has been based on the assumption that this is essentially a private, family responsibility. However, it is arguable that day care is not the only, or perhaps the optimal, response to the needs of children whose parents are in paid employment. It may also be that more flexible and child-friendly employment policy is required. This is not a matter over which individual parents generally have much control or choice. Trade unions and collective bargaining may be more influential, but are likely to lead to inequitable outcomes between different industries or individual employers.

The UK has fought shy of introducing legislation designed to enable parents to combine paid employment with their child care responsibilities. Beveridge's assumption that women would remain at home dominated policy for many years after the Second World War. It was not until 1975, on the eve of entry to the EEC, that the UK introduced limited employment protection rights to women on maternity. It is important to stress that this is not the same as statutory maternity leave, and many women are not covered by these provisions. There is also no statutory paternity leave and the UK has consistently blocked attempts by the European Union to legislate in this area.

By the mid-1990s most countries within the European Union have some form of parental or family leave which allows for more extensive time off when children are very young, together with statutory leave to care for sick children. Although there is still considerable variation in the generosity of these schemes and none yet matches the level of support for parents available in Sweden (see Leach, 1994), the European Union is moving forward without the UK. The policy of the government in the UK since 1979 has been to leave it to individual employers to make such provisions, on the basis that any legislation would interfere with the market economy. However, as Penelope Leach has pointed out, when 'societies' attention, energy and excitement are focused on the market place . . . whole segments of society are sidelined' (ibid., p. 4). Such has been the fate of young children.

Conclusion

There is little doubt that early years education and care have begun to enjoy increasing prominence on the UK policy agenda in recent years. Changes in women's employment patterns together with mounting concerns over educational standards have focused attention on the quantity and quality of early years provision. When the Audit Commission reviewed the position in England and Wales in 1996, it stated: 'There is a consensus that education provision for under fives is beneficial' (Audit Commission, 1996, p. 7).

If this is true, then it is a state of affairs that has not always characterised post-war policy. Nor is it, arguably, yet reflected in current legislation. The provision of early years education and care, as we have seen, is not a statutory obligation on local authorities, except for a relatively small group of children 'in need'. The level of public funding for early years services in the UK remains comparatively very low, and provision patchy.

Moreover, any optimism that the current consensus will provide a new deal for young children must be tempered by the fact that the debate has, we have suggested, been far from child-centred. Whether on the needs of working parents or the requirements of the economy for a skilled workforce, the emphasis of the debate has, in the main, been dominated by adult concerns. The drift has been away from nursery education towards early admission to primary school; away from 'play' and towards 'basic skills'. The challenge facing early years provision into the twenty-first century will not only be to expand the number of places available but also, in the words of the Audit Commission, 'to begin with children's needs without any pre-set views about ways of meeting them' (ibid., p. 46).

Further reading

Pugh (1992) offers a useful and wide-ranging collection of articles relating to the early years. For a good historical account covering 1945–75, see Tizard *et al.* (1976). Cohen (1988 and 1990), and Moss and Melhuish (1991) provide a good overview of early years provision and a wealth of data, while David (1990) is a lively critique of contemporary policy.

7

Primary Education

What a wise and good parent would desire for his own children, that a nation must desire for all children. (Report of the Consultative Committee on Primary Education, 1931; quoted in Maclure, 1979, p. 191)

Introduction

An account of education policy for children necessitates drawing a somewhat crude distinction between primary and secondary education, since in broad terms primary schools educate 'children', while secondary schools educate 'adolescents'. In practice, of course, this division is blurred because, first, many pupils at the point of transfer from primary to secondary school at the age of 11 are still children rather than adolescents; and, second, maintained 'middle schools' and preparatory schools in the independent sector educate pupils up to the age of 12 or 13. The stage of education identified here as 'primary' thus refers broadly to the educational experience variously provided for children aged between 4 and 13 years of age in formally designated infant and junior schools or departments (collectively known as 'primary schools'), as well as in middle schools and private preparatory schools.

Any distinction drawn between primary and secondary education can also be misleading, because some at least of the pedagogic practice in the early stages of education is shaped by the entry criteria and curricular requirements of the secondary schools. Some reference to secondary education is for this reason unavoidable in any meaningful analysis of the primary stage.

Education policy, unlike a number of other areas of social policy, is specifically designed for children. In effect it is social policy for children (and adolescents). But as our discussion of early years education policy – or lack of it – has illustrated, rather than children's needs being placed at the forefront of education policy considerations, a variety of adult concerns and perspectives determine the policy outcomes. What is critical in this is who decides how, and for what purposes, schools are provided. And from what perspectives and motives adults reach such decisions.

To write specifically about 'British' primary education presents a further problem. The concept of a 'national' system of education is in certain respects inappropriate as a description of the organisation of schooling in the United Kingdom because of internal national differences, the great diversity of types of school, and the ages at which pupils attend these. Moreover, an influential and prestigious private system of education, currently educating some 7 per cent of British children, coexists alongside the maintained state system. There are significant differences between these two sectors. However, important educational and administrative variations also exist within the state sector because of the complexity of its historical development. Inevitably the structure of British educational provision is thus diverse and 'extraordinarily complex'.

The pattern of schooling, moreover, within the maintained sector has since 1979 become more varied. Thus some children who attend the primary sector may now transfer at eleven to a 'city technology college' (CTC) or to a 'city college for the technology of the arts' (CCTA). As a further alternative, under the 1980 'Assisted Places Scheme' (APS), which is currently being further expanded, parents may apply for their child to be admitted (with fees set according to a prescribed income scale) to a recommended independent school on the completion of their primary school education.

The complexity of the institutional structure of the school system is mirrored by an increasingly complicated administrative structure. Under a provision of the 1988 Education Reform Act (ERA), for example, schools may choose 'to opt out' of LEA control and be run wholly by their governing body. There are now over a thousand such self-governing 'grant-maintained schools' (GMS), funded directly by the Department for Education and Employment (DfEE) through 'funding agencies' set up under the 1993 Education Act.

Thus, although the state has by law a duty – unlike for the early years – of making appropriate educational provision for children between the ages of 5 and 16, children's education in Britain can none the less be a highly variable experience.

So, allowing for such educational complexities, how has education policy for the primary years developed since the end of the Second World War? And how satisfactory is the situation in the late 1990s? We now address these questions.

The establishment of primary education

Before the 1988 Education Reform Act (ERA) it was war that had been the most effective catalyst of twentieth-century educational reform. War may not have been the only locomotive of educational history but the circumstances created by war have certainly been a decisive influence. All the definitive measures that determined the shape of British education before 1988 coincided with major military conflicts: 1902, 1918, and 1944. The exact nature of the effects of war on social policy is a widely debated issue, but with regard to the history of British education, it is difficult to dispute Richard Titmuss's contention that, 'the growing scale and intensity of war has stimulated a growing concern about the quantity and quality of the population' (Titmuss, 1958, p. 78). Nowhere has this concern been more apparent than in education policy.

The origins of post-war primary education

It was inter-war developments in the theory and practice of education, reflected in a series of official reports from expert committees, which laid the basis for the 1944 Education Act and subsequent developments in primary education.

The influential 1926 Board of Education Hadow Report on 'The Education of the Adolescent' thus argued forcefully that education should be provided in stages related to age and to children's developing capacities. 'Primary education,' the report stressed, 'should be regarded as ending at about the age of 11 +. At that age a second stage . . . should begin' (quoted in Maclure, 1979, p. 182).

Nor are these developments merely a matter of arcane history. What is worth pointing out especially with regard to contemporary debates over the national curriculum and compulsory testing, is that it was the Hadow Report and subsequent inter-war reports that advocated a distinctive primary school curriculum with an emphasis on activity-based methods rather than on the discredited rote learning of an earlier era.

The 1944 Education Act

The need then for a distinctive stage of common education for children up to the age of 11 had already been accepted before the outbreak of the Second World War. But it was the wartime 1944 Education Act that was to provide the legislative framework for the effective implementation of this and other important proposals. As if straight from the Hadow Report, the 1944 Act stated:

> The statutory system of public education shall be organised in three progressive stages to be known as primary education, secondary education, and further education. (Education Act, 1944, Part II.7; extract taken from Maclure, 1979, p. 224)

Whatever subsequent criticisms have been made of the 1944 Act and of the ways in which it was implemented, it has provided an enduring basis throughout the post-war years for a significant expansion of education at all levels. At the time too it was seen as a major advance over the past – a new beginning. Indeed, Winston Churchill, when the Act became law, telegraphed his congratulations to R. A. Butler, the then President of the Board of Education, assuring him that he had 'added a notable Act to the Statute Book and won a lasting place in the history of British education' (Lord Butler, 1971, p. 122).

For the first time all children were given the right – at least in theory – to secondary education, while as a concomitant the 1944 Act afforded primary education the promise of becoming a separate and pedagogically distinct phase of educational experience and development. More generally, the Act established a lasting compromise between the voluntary (church) and the LEA-maintained sectors and it represented, in Professor Lawton's words, 'a dramatic change in attitude'. 'The fundamental change,' Lawton argues, 'was that two traditions – secondary and elementary – *could* now become one tradition: the principle of equality of opportunity was established even if the realisation was still extremely difficult' (Lawton, 1975, p. 3).

The post-1944 challenge

Public expenditure on the education service was to grow faster during the 1950s and 1960s than expenditure on any other of the social services, so much so that between 1951 and 1975 it increased as a proportion of total public expenditure from 6.8 per cent to 12.5 per cent, and from 3.5 per cent of GDP in 1957/58 to 5.5 per cent in 1967/8 (Lawson and Silver, 1973, p. 464). Two factors, however, meant that the achievement of improved and uniform standards in primary schools in particular was exceedingly difficult. In the first place there was the huge backlog of sub-standard schools inherited in 1944, a problem compounded in the cities by bomb damage – one in five of all schools had either been destroyed or damaged. In the second place, there was the post-war 'baby boom' which meant that in most years up to 1975 more primary school places had to be provided year by year.

The elementary school legacy

A large proportion of the former elementary schools were lamentably inadequate when they were relabelled 'primary schools' after the 1944 Act – a measure more of hope than of certainty, and one which added not a single new classroom. Particularly unsatisfactory were rural schools and voluntary schools. Moreover, the content of elementary education, as well as the infrastructure, was similarly deficient. The main uses of elementary education were, declared Sir Richard Livingstone in 1944, 'to enable a minority to proceed to further education, and the rest to read the cheap press'. The curriculum, he added, had become 'a mass of uncoordinated subjects, a chaos instead of a cosmos' (quoted in Lawson and Silver, 1973, p. 416). With an acute shortage of qualified teachers and excessively large classes, the task of providing an improved quality of education at the primary level, or indeed at any level, was an immensely daunting one facing the incoming Labour government in 1945.

Demographic change and primary education

The post-war rise in the birth rate occurred in two cycles – the first in fact starting from 1943 and lasting until the mid-1950s, and the second from the late 1950s until 1970. As a result of these trends, between 1941 and 1971 the total UK population under the age of 15 increased from 10.1 to 13.4 million (Central Statistics Office, 1974, p. 75). This surge in the child population first inundated the primary schools. Thus between 1946 and 1955, some 900 000 additional primary school places had to be found; and from the early 1960s a second wave followed, so that again, between 1961 and 1973, the size of the 5–10 year age group grew dramatically from 4.5 to 5.6 million.

Progress and problems in primary education from the 1940s to the 1970s

Priority however during the first two decades after the war was given (necessarily, perhaps, in view of the raising of the school leaving age from 14 to 15 in 1947) to secondary and higher education. Only during the 1960s was greater priority afforded to primary schools. Even so, the pre-war innovations in primary education had become more widely accepted during these years. Thus group work and activity methods, and new methods of teaching children to read and develop their writing skills were being introduced slowly; while new equipment and materials for mathematics, for movement and physical education, and even for foreign-language teaching, were increasingly finding their way into the schools. Primary school design, too, which allowed for libraries, and for drama and music activities, and provided reading and workshop bays, and in the infant schools and departments space and facilities for constructive play, became internationally renowned and showpieces for foreign visitors. The cramped, overcrowded formal classroom with rows of desks was slowly giving way to open-plan school design.

But while such changes were slowly permeating primary schools, they were not happening everywhere. Moreover, resources remained a critical problem throughout almost the whole period. Class size, for example in almost 10 per cent of all primary classes remained obstinately at more than forty until the late 1960s; and large numbers of primary school buildings remained wholly inadequate – 16 514 primary schools in fact had one or more specified serious defects according to the Department of Education's own 1962 survey (Plowden Report, 1967, pp. 390–2).

Children and their primary schools – the Plowden Report (1967)

The Plowden Report strongly endorsed the development of a child-centred approach to primary education, arguing the case for what has been termed an educational philosophy of 'controlled progressivism' on the basis of developmental psychology – including the work of Piaget (Lawson and Silver, 1973, p. 453). The report made a wide range of recommendations for the general improvement of primary education, including an immediate phased programme of nursery education 'for all children whose parents wish it' (ibid., pp. 460–82). However, the most far-reaching recommendations concerned the prioritising of educational policy in the primary sector towards underprivileged children in the most deprived areas; and hence was born the concept of educational priority areas (EPAs), inner city areas which at that time lacked investment, contained the poorest housing, and were increasingly the districts within which the expanding 'immigrant' population was growing up. From 1968 the Labour government under Harold Wilson began to implement these EPA recommendations, including the provision of additional staff and extra money.

Selection at 11+

One problem which cast a long shadow over primary education especially in the junior years, was the issue of secondary school selection. The intentions of the legislators in 1944 had been to provide the basis for a 'tripartite' system of secondary education with three types of secondary school – grammar, technical, and secondary modern, each of which was seen as being appropriate for differing intellectual attributes and vocationally-related learning predispositions. Each form of secondary education was to enjoy 'parity of esteem', and the proposed test at 11+ was viewed as being purely diagnostic and essentially a device for channelling children in the right direction. Of course there was a nice coincidence between the types of secondary school available – though in woefully inadequate premises and quantities – and the supposed existence of three distinguishable types of ability. In practice, these policy intentions were largely subverted. Secondary technical schools, except in isolated instances, never got off the ground, while the 'new' secondary modern schools were often still sited in old 'all-age' elementary schools or in other highly unsatisfactory premises. The latter, moreover, for the most part made no provision for their pupils to take public examinations, thus effectively denying them access to sixth-form study, higher education, and professional occupations. Only the grammar schools offered improved educational prospects and provided avenues for obtaining recognised education credentials and thereby entry into the most desirable forms of employment.

Not surprisingly, parents, especially informed middle-class ones, keenly sought grammar school entry for their offspring. Primary schools thus came under considerable pressure to prepare their pupils for success in the 11+ examination, and the reputation of primary schools in general came to depend very much on how many of their pupils passed the 11+ examination. Inevitably, this examination acquired a significance out of all proportion to its real diagnostic value. From the early 1950s evidence began to accumulate as to its harmful educational effects, and its demoralising impact on the majority of children who failed, as well as on the secondary schools they subsequently attended. Nationally only 20 per cent of children passed 11+ selection to attend a selective grammar school; it thus became increasingly unpopular with a growing number of parents whose aspirations for their children were often depressingly circumscribed by the obstacle of the 11+. Comprehensive schools were proving successful in a number of local authority areas (both Labour- and Conservative-controlled); secondary modern schools were developing GCE and other public examination courses, so obviating one of the original justifications for the tripartite system; and all the time there was mounting evidence of the sheer inequity and inefficiency of selection at 11+.

The failure of selection and the demise of the 'tripartite' system of secondary education

In the 1990s selection is again in favour. This involves, as ever, the allocation of pupils to different secondary schools, regardless of parental (or child) preference, on the basis of some form of assessment. It may thus be worth summarising in this context some of the main criticisms of 11+ selection *per se* within the post-war 'tripartite' system.

Between the late 1950s and the early 1970s tripartism was abandoned almost everywhere. Lowe (1993) suggests the reasons for this collapse were essentially practical, in that the system neither offered equality of opportunity nor garnered children's intellectual abilities in sufficient quantity. Official reports revealed an all-too-premature loss of many of the most able children from the schools because of 'early leaving'; and that selection, far from accurately directing children according to intellectual potential, merely served to fit them into a pre-existing pattern of local secondary schools, which had been largely determined by historical accident.

By the mid-1960s, 11 + selection was shown to be inaccurate – and therefore manifestly unjust, distorted by too many 'extraneous factors', and involving marked social class biases (Sanderson, 1987, p. 55).

The Plowden Report reviewing the evidence, concluded that even when 11 + selection was based on the best-available testing procedures, at the age of sixteen 20 per cent of children were likely to be shown to have been 'misplaced' (Plowden Report, 1967, p. 154). Selection too was proving to be a geographical lottery, since the number of selective grammar school places varied widely both regionally as well as between and within differing LEA areas. Thus in 1959 the south-west of England was providing selective grammar school places for 35 per cent of its child population, while major cities such as Nottingham offered places for as few as 10 per cent. The number of places for girls was also lower in some LEA areas and there was an in-built bias against summer-born children, since, with the exam taken nationally in February, the ages of children taking it ranged from 10.6 to 11.5 years. Pervading the whole procedure was a persistent social class bias. Pressures on the primary schools led to streaming by ability at an early age, which gave considerable advantage to well-disciplined, articulate middle-class children. The tests themselves, and especially where teachers' reports and interviews were part of the assessment procedures, again were shown to favour middle-class children. If post-war education was intended to provide equality of opportunity and to develop the pool of national talent, the tripartite system was clearly shown to be failing badly.

Irresistibly, the momentum to abolish the 11 + examination gathered pace. Thus within a year of Labour's narrow election victory in 1964, Anthony Crosland, the new Minister of Education, issued Circular 10/65 which set out six alternative forms of comprehensive reorganisation from which LEAs could choose – with ministerial approval – to transform secondary education within their local area into a fully non-selective comprehensive system.

The end of selection which Circular 10/65 foreshadowed was widely welcomed in the primary sector. More thought could be given to the curriculum and to the educational needs of all children, and there would no longer be the stigmatising effects on particular schools nor on so many children.

The process of going comprehensive had already started in the early 1960s with support from successive Conservative ministers, notably Sir David Eccles and Sir Edward Boyle. By 1970, therefore, 30 per cent of secondary pupils in the maintained sector were already attending comprehensive schools, and between 1970 and 1974 with Margaret Thatcher as Secretary of State for Education in the Heath government, more grammar schools were to change their status than in any previous period, so that by 1974 this figure had risen to 62 per cent.

Compared to 1944 the situation in state education had by 1979 been transformed at every level. In the primary sector, given the desperate needs following the war and the year-by-year increases in pupil numbers until the mid-1970s, the improvements achieved between 1945 and 1979 can in many respects be seen as remarkable.

Educational attainments in terms of performance and participation in post-15 examinations (post-16 from 1972) improved markedly throughout the period, with increasing numbers taking GCE 'O' and 'A' Level courses. Moreover, in the two decades following the abandonment of 11 + selection, secondary school attainment as measured by success in public examinations improved significantly (Simon, 1985, p. 220). Such evidence certainly suggests that the quality of primary education, as the basis for all subsequent educational progress, had by the end of the 1970s improved substantially since the dark days of 1945.

Educational change 1979–96

Commentators on the extent of educational change since 1979 agree that British education has been 'transformed', especially since the 1988 Education Reform Act. Thus as Sally Tomlinson writes, 'over the past decade we have been living through the most comprehensive reworking of the education system since the 1940s' (1994, p. 1). And Stephen Ball comments: 'education is no longer a backwater of policy. It is now in the mainstream of the political ideology and policies of Thatcherism' (1990, p. 43).

The New Right's critique of post-war education

The political Right's critique of post-war development in education goes back at least to the first 'Black Paper', published in 1969, which, against a background of student unrest, averred that state education had 'disintegrated in chaos' and that the only solution was to return to 'pre-comprehensive, pre-progressive forms and methods'. The speech of Labour Prime Minister, James Callaghan, at Ruskin College in 1976, which raised the question of the presumed inability of the education system to meet the nation's needs for technological skills, is also viewed as having given powerful encouragement and added legitimacy to the mounting criticism of education policy by the New Right.

The Conservative criticisms of education perceived education professions as powerful vested interests pursuing their own ulterior motives; the LEAs were similarly seen as the 'producers' of education, subject to 'Left' political control and enjoying a near monopoly over the supply of education to the consumers – parents and their children. The solution to this educational malaise was seen to lie in the introduction of a market in education in the form of 'vouchers'; in this way, sovereignty would be restored to the consumers who, it was assumed, would exert their preferences for the traditional forms and methods of education; and at the same time the producers' monopoly would be broken.

Sir Keith Joseph, one of the intellectual pillars of neo- liberal conservative thought – and an important influence on Margaret Thatcher, was Minister of Education between 1981 and 1985. But in spite of his own conviction concerning the desirability of subjecting the education service to market disciplines in the form of vouchers, the opposition within the department and the sheer complexity, even impracticality, of such a policy, deterred him from attempting its introduction. It was to be his successor, Kenneth Baker, who, while excluding vouchers *per se*, persuaded the Prime Minister and the cabinet in the run-up to the 1987 election to accept a set of educational reforms that incorporated many of the ideas and proposals of the New Right. Following the Conservative election victory these were presented to Parliament as the Great Education Reform Bill (GERBIL), which duly became the 1988 Education Reform Act (ERA).

The 1988 Education Reform Act

Parental choice has since 1979 been one of the 'fundamentals of Conservative education policy', but it was the 1988 Education Reform Act that took this policy much further and brought market mechanisms to bear not only on the organisation and administration of the system, but to the very heart of the educational process – classroom teaching and learning. A quasi-market among schools was introduced by enabling both primary and secondary schools to opt out of LEA control on the basis of a majority vote by parents, and by the introduction of the local management of schools (LMS) whereby in LEA controlled schools 75 per cent of the expenditure would be determined within the school by its governing body. The governing bodies of opted-out schools would have control over the whole of the school's budget, which is paid directly by the DfEE via the Schools Funding Agency (SFA).

With the implementation of the 1988 Act from 29 July 1988 the education service thus began, in theory, to operate according to market criteria. Parents notionally had a free choice of schools to which to send their children; and as consumers they could base their choice on publicly available information including a range of performance indicators for each school. Schools would be rewarded financially according to the number of children on the roll. Thus successful, attractive schools would flourish, while the bad schools would atrophy and possibly even close. Moreover, the existence of a healthy private sector and an expanded independent state sector, consisting of the new City Technology Colleges and the opted out grant-maintained schools, is viewed as providing an increasingly diversified market of schools. As a number of commentators have remarked, this new dispensation manifests the essential features of a voucher system but without the vouchers.

As regards the primary schools, important consequences have resulted from the above reforms. The new 'National Curriculum' has become a statutory requirement in all maintained schools for children of compulsory school age (though not in the independent sector). Primary schools are legally entitled to opt out of LEA control, though by the end of 1995 only 260 had done so. The large majority of primary schools (over 18 000) thus remain under the management of their LEAs. However, under LMS provisions, primary school governing bodies and their heads now have major management responsibilities. We discuss some of the implications of the above reforms for children in the primary years in the following sections.

The primary school curriculum

The introduction of a subject-based curriculum at infant and junior school ages reverses a long-established approach to curriculum content in British primary schools. The new curriculum is organised in four 'key stages'. Thus Key Stages 1 and 2 of the National Curriculum now prescribe a standard teaching content for both infant and junior-aged children, respectively. This consists of three core subjects: mathematics, English and science; and six other foundation subjects: technology, history, geography, art, music and physical education. There are attainment targets for assessing progress in each subject and these are tested at the end of Key Stage 1 for infants at the age of 7; and at the completion of Key Stage 2 for juniors at the age of 11. Schools are increasingly obliged to publish the results of these tests, and hence provide what is seen by the Act's architects as crucial consumer information.

In the initial phase of implementation there can be no doubt that the new curriculum was overloaded and virtually impossible to deliver in its entirety. Accounts of its effects on primary schools indicate often almost impossible workloads for class teachers, enormous volumes of paperwork, and less time for actual teaching. Thus Angela Anning, writing about implementation at the infant level (Key Stage 1), speaks of 'six turbulent years' and asks, 'what was the purpose of this uncontrollable chaos?' (1995, p. 2). The answer to this question given by a number of commentators is that the National Curriculum represents a renewed emphasis on the instrumental or occupational functions of education. Furthermore, A. V. Kelly (1994), in his critique of the National Curriculum, suggests that, given the speed and the disregard of professional expertise involved in its conception and implementation, children are being subjected to ill-researched experimentation and may well therefore be missing other important educational experiences.

Few would dispute the need for continual curriculum monitoring and evaluation, nor deny that there have been – and remain – curriculum problems for primary schools. But what has drawn the most criticism is the extent of the curriculum changes and the rapidity with which these have been implemented. So, as Ted Wragg comments,

> One of Kenneth Baker's worst legacies was the most complex national curriculum and testing programme in Europe. We moved from extreme permissiveness to extreme prescription within a year. (1995, p. 111)

Since its original implementation, the Dearing Review (Dearing, 1993) has recognised 'the over-complexity and overload' of the whole curriculum and the testing procedures; and a number of simplifications have been introduced since September 1995.

However, some educationalists are also highly critical of the designation of the National Curriculum in terms of specific subjects throughout the primary stage – nine, in fact, with the single addition of a modern foreign language at the age of 11. Subject classifications, as conceptually useful though culturally variable conventions, are certainly important for the categorisation of knowledge in the adult world; but as such they are likely to be conceptually meaningless, even confusing to young children. Kelly's review of our present state of understanding of children's intellectual development suggests that the subject approach contained in the National Curriculum for the primary years is inappropriate and likely to restrict and distort young children's learning processes: 'For the model of learning which emerges from the 1988 Act itself and from all its supporting documentation,' Kelly suggests, 'is a factory-farming model of learning in which each child, like a battery hen, is to assimilate as much as possible of the food offered to it' (1994, p. 94).

Other analyses of Conservative educational reform also conclude that it can best be understood as a return to a broad strategy, albeit one that contains many inherent contradictions and inconsistencies, to effect a tightening of the connection between schooling and work. Thus Peter Taylor-Gooby and Stephen Ball both write of 'the new vocationalism' in education. What these commentators emphasise is that such reform is no progressive development building on the past, but rather a considered strategy to align schooling more closely with the changing needs of the economy; and as such it represents a return to earlier modes of educational provision in which children are treated as investment goods and the production of the appropriately trained school leaver is its chief justification and purpose.

Primary education at its best prior to 1988 was concerned to some degree with what education *is* rather than what it is *for*. By contrast, the focus of the National Curriculum is on what children will have been equipped to become when they leave school. The primary school curriculum is thus again subordinate to the vocational imperatives of the secondary stage. Kelly sums up the position thus:

> the pre-eminent tradition is now the 'preparatory' stage rather than the developmental (Blyth, 1965), that which again sees the experiences of pupils in the primary phase in relation to what these are preparing for rather than in terms of any intrinsic, or developmental, value they might have. (Kelly, 1994, p. 47)

Seen from this perspective recent reform may represent to some extent for children of primary school age the subordination of their intellectual capacities and interests to relatively remote occupational considerations.

Standards and classroom methods in primary education

A persistent criticism of post-war education policy has concerned standards. In particular it is widely asserted that children are failing to attain sufficiently high standards in what are viewed as the 'basics': namely, reading, writing and mathematics, and more, recently science.

It is these criticisms that have provided a major justification for recent reforms. At the primary level, however, there has been relatively little evidence on which to substantiate such criticism. What of course has long been a feature of school attainment in Britain has been the long tail of low performance. Thus the apparent poor performance of British children in any international comparison is caused to a large extent by the relatively low attainment of children of average or below-average ability. In its review of standards in primary schools, the then DES's *'discussion paper'* (Dept of Education and Science, 1992), while cautioning against any simplistic interpretation of international comparisons of standards, acknowledges that there is 'an extended tail of distribution which pulls the average down' (p. 16).

Surveying standards generally in primary schools, the DES's 1992 review, referring to the annual surveys of the 'Assessment of Performance Unit' undertaken between 1978 and 1988, reports that

> the major conclusion for English and mathematics is that, though standards remained much the same in most aspects of these two core subjects, there was some improvement in reading but there was also a worrying deterioration in important aspects of numeracy. (p. 13)

However, work undertaken in 1991 by the National Foundation for Educational Research (NFER) into reading standards among 7 and 8-year-olds found that between 1987 and 1991 'there was a statistically significant fall of 2.5 standard points . . . roughly equivalent to a decline of three to five months in reading age' (Dept of Education and Science, 1992, p. 14).

The first results from the new National Curriculum assessment tests have also been mixed. Results for 7-year-olds show a higher level of achievement in science than had been anticipated, but lower in mathematics, with the results for English being 'broadly as expected'. Particular concern has arisen over the standards achieved by 11-year-olds at the completion of the junior stage. HMI inspections, for example, have shown that standards in Key Stage 1 are generally better than for Key Stage 2. However, the first results of the national tests for 11-year-olds only became available in January 1996. These have been widely heralded as indicating a falling away of standards in English and maths between the ages of 7 and 11 (though not in science). So, as the *Times Educational Supplement* noted: 'The results will be seen to confirm worries about standards in junior schools' (26 January 1996).

Official explanations for the disappointing levels of achievement at the primary stage identify teacher incompetence and inappropriate classroom methods. Thus, according to the Chief Inspector of Schools, the fault partly lies in poor teaching. 'Many schools,' he emphasises, 'need to tackle urgently mediocre and poor standards by reviewing the quality and consistency of teaching in order to set and achieve higher targets' (*The Times*, 6 February 1996). Blame apparently can also be laid at the door of the so-called 'progressive' classroom methods employed in primary schools: 'We are now confident about what constitutes good teaching practice . . . Inspectors evidence shows that whole-class teaching – which is well suited to the efficient communication of new knowledge and understanding – figures significantly in seven-tenths of lessons judged to be good' (*Daily Telegraph*, 6 February 1996).

Unfortunately, there are several objections to this kind of simplistic interpretation, and in any case we should be cautious about too ready an acceptance of the validity of the various test results: the choice of criteria alone raises difficult cultural as well as racial and gender issues. Moreover, as Michael Bonnett argues, even the definition of what appears to be the simple skill of reading conflates the range of competencies involved (1994, pp. 18–19).

In the first place, there never has been a clear demarcation between what are perceived as tried and trusted 'traditional' methods and supposedly untried 'progressive' ones. The government's review of primary education by the so-called 'three wise men' emphasised this point when it stated:

> The commonly held belief that primary schools, after 1967, were swept by a tide of progressivism is untrue. HMI in 1978, for example, reported that only 5 per cent of classrooms exhibited wholeheartedly 'exploratory' characteristics and that didactic teaching was still practised in three-quarters of them. The reality then was rather more complex. (Dept of Education and Science, 1992, p. 9)

The conclusion reached by this report was that topic work and subject teaching were often inadequate, but that standards could best be ensured by a more selective and flexible use of the whole range of 'organisational strategies' including whole-class teaching, group work and individual teaching.

A second objection is that the timing is so out of order. The recent surge in pupils achieving 'A' Level passes and going on to higher education (a rise from 12 per cent of the age group in 1979, to 15 per cent in 1988, and 30 per cent in 1993), includes a majority of young people who were educated in primary schools between the early 1970s and the mid-1980s – the height, so many would have us believe, of the so-called 'progressive' era.

A third objection to the government's analysis of the failings of primary schools is that this takes no account of the effects of the reforms on either the children or their teachers. The Dearing Review, for example, was launched hurriedly, one suspects as a measure of crisis management, to slim down the curriculum and to simplify testing arrangements. Its subsequent recommendations were duly accepted by the government and so a more flexible, streamlined version has been implemented since September 1995. But this is the second major change within five years, and it appears to have been urgently necessary. So all we may be measuring as regards inadequate standards in today's primary schools are the educational consequences of the disruptiveness, the dislocation to previous learning patterns, and the increased stress levels among pupils and teachers alike.

A further objection concerns the adverse effects on children's learning ability and their levels of attainment resulting from socio-economic circumstances outside school. The deleterious effects of increasing child poverty, for example, should not be underestimated as a cause of low attainment. Kumar's (1993) summary of the effects of material deprivation indicates that children from materially deprived homes tend to do less well educationally.

Finally, the material circumstances of the schools in which standards are assessed are often grossly unsatisfactory: too few teachers, overcrowded classrooms, poorly maintained and sometimes unsuitable buildings, as well as a lack of resources for sufficient books that currently affects one in seven primary schools; and consider on top of this the recent implementation of complex reforms. Indeed, we would be fortunate not to find falling standards in such circumstances.

A wider choice for parents?

Choice in markets is presented in individualistic terms for parents (though not for children). It is individual parents who as consumers are making rational choices as to which schools they perceive are the best, while individual schools themselves compete to attract pupils and maximise their incomes. Inevitably, there are winners and losers. Moreover, this individualisation of the education market may serve to deflect attention away from patterns of inequality of access and attainment between social groups. Unfortunately, however, as Smith and Noble comment, 'to ignore the problem is not to make it go away' (1995, p. 27).

The principle of 'open enrolment' – that is, the absence of restriction on parents' rights to choose a place for their child in a school of their choice, was written into the 1988 Education Reform Act and is contained in 'The Updated Parent's Charter' (1994). The consequences, however, of the combined policies of opting out and open enrolment have produced considerable difficulties for parents and have made any rational planning quite impossible in many local authority areas. The Parent's Charter's statement concerning 'Your rights' is thus heavily qualified, with the second half negating the first,

> you now have a right to a place in the school you want unless all the places at the school have been given to pupils who have a stronger claim to a place at that school. (Dept for Education, 1994, pp. 9–10)

Given, then, that a quarter of secondary schools have now opted out, and that these schools can select up to 15 per cent of their intakes, and given, too, the financial incentives for schools to admit more promising pupils and exclude the least promising, the scene is all set for an increasing denial to many parents of their choice of school.

Open enrolment was introduced in Scotland before the implementation of the 1988 ERA in England and Wales, so Scottish experience may provide some indication of the wider national effects. Alder and Raab (1988), for example, in their study of parental choice in Dundee and Edinburgh, found that 'most of the schools which lost numbers were situated in the least prosperous housing estates schemes while most of the schools which gained substantial numbers were located in mixed inner-city areas' (Alder and Raab quoted in Ball, 1990, p. 67). Teresa Smith and Michael Noble, commenting on these Scottish studies, note

> that choice, operating largely, though not entirely, along social class lines, has the effect of reinforcing already existing social and educational divisions . . . Parental choice poses a serious challenge to equality of educational opportunity and has led to the re-emergence of a two-tier system, with a minority of 'rump' schools catering for the most disadvantaged areas of the big cities. (1995, pp. 60–1)

Evidence on GM school intakes also throws considerable doubt on any idea of widened parental choice. Very few GM schools in fact serve what might be defined as disadvantaged areas – only 18 out of 225 opted-out schools covered in one survey of 55 LEAs (quoted in Smith and Noble, 1995, p. 63). Other evidence indicates that, where selection exists, 'increased first choice realisation by parents of 'successful' candidates is matched by increasing rates of disappointment by those who fail the entrance examinations' (Power *et al.*, 1994, p. 30).

To encourage schools to opt out of LEA jurisdiction, the direct funding by the DfEE of GM schools has been more generous than for those which have remained under LEA control. Thus for 1993–4, while £85.7 million was allocated by the DfEE to GM schools for capital expenditure, £575.2 million was allocated for capital expenditure to the other 96 per cent of schools still controlled by their LEAs. The GM schools', therefore, while representing only 4 per cent of all schools in England, absorbed nearly 15 per cent of the capital investment for that year. Indeed, as C. Chitty suggests, 'The most compelling reason for a school to opt out is probably financial' (Chitty, 1992, p. 68).

Again, studies of the APS and the new CTCs provide scant evidence that there is any real widening of parental choice. In spite of the intentions behind the scheme – to enable children from low-income families to gain the advantages of private education – very few children with working-class parents have taken up assisted places. The limited research undertaken about the CTCs also fails to find any noted widening of choice.

Educational provision in Britain is increasingly becoming a patchwork of localised arrangements, with variable and uncertain choices facing parents at all stages of their children's schooling: 'Choice,' conclude Smith and Noble, 'even in mainstream schooling, is shown to be paper-thin when there is pressure on popular schools – except for the most articulate and persistent parents' (1995, p. 71).

In this increasingly competitive environment, primary schools are coming under a variety of renewed pressures. Their financial security will increasingly depend as much on the quality of their intakes as the quantity; and their reputations will come to depend increasingly on the academic attainments of their pupils in tests taken at the ages of 7 and 11. In those areas, moreover, where there is growing selectivity, pressures on primary schools to achieve high entry levels into the most attractive selective schools seem likely to intensify.

In the changed conditions of the 1990s, what we may now therefore be witnessing is a return of all the worst features of 11 + selection. Indeed current research is already beginning to echo earlier post-war evidence. Thus analysis by the Leeds University School of Education of the 1992 test results for children at the completion of Key Stage 1, found that summer-born children were behind in English, maths and science, while winter-born children did consistently better; moreover, children from high-status neighbourhoods did significantly better in maths and English (though less so in science) than children from low-status neighbourhoods (Smith and Noble, 1995, pp. 121–2).

Disadvantaged children

If a lower tier of secondary schools has begun to emerge, so too will a downgraded, lower-status stratum of primary schools. At the time of writing not only are primary schools pressed by the new competitive ethos, but many are also facing an increase in numbers in the economic context of a freeze on additional resources. Therefore, primary schools may well wish to avoid recruiting categories of disadvantaged children who have additional educational needs, so such children will increasingly be excluded from the most popular and successful schools.

Many poor children do achieve commensurately with their abilities while at school, and the effects of poverty are only one of the factors that influences children's overall levels of attainment. However, in view of the sharp increases in child poverty since the early 1980s it is difficult not to conclude that recent educational reforms will only damage further the educational opportunities of a growing number of poor children.

Few children from poor homes are likely to be seen as attractive recruits to schools scouting for intellectual talent. Nor are their parents – often unemployed, or single parents, or of ethnic minority background – likely to be able to provide additional sources of financial or professional support for their children's schools. And they are also more likely to live in inner-city and other 'deprived' urban areas, a circumstance which makes it easy and natural for schools in these districts to become ghettoes of educational failure. Of course the progress pupils make at school is a critical measure of 'school effectiveness', but, as Peter Mortimer and his colleagues' (1983) study of London junior schools showed, whereas school factors are most important in explaining different rates of progress, it is social factors that remain a major element 'in explaining both where children start and where they end up' (quoted in Smith and Noble, 1995, p. 27).

As we have seen, 9 per cent of our child population come from ethnic minority homes, and a large proportion of these are concentrated in a limited number of inner-city areas. While many groups of these children achieve well up to the average levels of attainment for all children, the picture is varied, and some groups, especially if their language at home is other than English, may present any school with particular needs or behavioural problems. There is, for example, increasing concern both at the growing numbers of pupils 'excluded' from school – 14 000 was estimated in 1996 – and at the unduly high proportion of black pupils included in this number.

Other minorities are also likely to be less than attractive as pupils for schools caught up in a competitive market for resources and survival. Traveller children, the children of refugees, and disabled children, are again categories of children with potentially additional cost implications for schools, and who represent at entry doubtful prospects for high attainment and the enhancement of school league tables.

Disabled children and children with special educational needs

In the present climate of financial constraint, these children pose a particular threat. A 'statemented' child is one who has been identified as being in need of certain appropriate special educational provision which the LEA or GM school has agreed to provide. However, with the implementation of LMS since 1990 the proportion of funding now allowed to LEAs for discretionary expenditure on their schools has been reduced to a fraction of what it once was. Many LEAs are therefore coming under increasing financial pressure, either not to agree a 'statement' in the first place, or to withdraw the designation from a child who has previously been statemented – which, of course, absolves the authority from continuing to make any additional provision. Schools similarly are under pressure either to exclude special educational needs (SEN) pupils or to minimise additional provision.

Such market forces already appear to be working to the disadvantage of disabled children. Research by the Centre for Educational Studies of King's College, London, between 1991 and 1994, of a sample of primary and secondary schools, found the schools 'increasingly keen to attract enrolments from "motivated" parents and "able" children who are likely to enhance their relative position in local systems of competition' (Ball *et al.*, 1994, p. 17).

What this change of emphasis was found to mean in practice was an increase in setting and streaming by ability, and a shift in resources

> away from students with special needs and learning difficulties. Well established and proven systems of SEN teaching in schools are being dismantled or much reduced in size. Resources are being directed more towards those students who are most likely to perform well in tests and examinations. (Ball *et al.*, 1994, p. 17)

Schools, moreover, that had previously attracted large numbers of statemented students were trying, according to this study, 'to reorient their recruitment efforts to attract different sorts of students' (ibid., p. 18).

Nor is the problem of special needs children a minor one. According to the 1978 Warnock Report about 20 per cent of children are likely to fall into this category at some stage of their education. Yet the 1988 ERA devoted 'one short paragraph' to the issue of SEN children; and even though subsequent follow-up advice from the then DES in 1989 does explain how the requirements of the National Curriculum may be modified for this group of children, there is considerable doubt by many that the requirements of the National Curriculum are in any way appropriate for many of the disabled pupils attending ordinary schools (Kelly, 1994, pp. 20–1).

Resources for primary education

In terms of per capita funding, primary-school children have always been the poor relations of the education system. According to the DfEE's own figures for 1993–4 total average educational expenditure per pupil in English schools was of the order of £1518 per primary pupil (£1727 for the under-fives); and £2144 per secondary pupil. The fees paid per child in 1992–3 for private day schools, by way of contrast, averaged £5170, and for a boarding school £9400. In addition, as has already been noted, very few primary schools have so far 'opted out'. Consequently, the more generous funding devoted to GM schools and the CTCs has been largely absorbed to date by secondary schools. Similarly, the public subsidy contributed to the private sector via the Assisted Places Scheme has also gone to fund secondary education places.

The introduction of LMS, as in the case of SEN work, is resulting in a redistribution of resources. Previous to LMS, the LEAs, with full control of their educational budgets, were able to safeguard the needs of disadvantaged pupils in schools in deprived neighbour-hoods; and in fact this is allowed for in the DfEE formulas in use at the time of writing for the financing of local government expenditure by the inclusion of an 'Additional Educational Needs' (AEN) budget. However, under LMS, local authorities are now required to pass on to the individual schools the lion's share of their entire education budget (approximately 83 per cent in 1993–4). Smith and Noble thus calculate 'that under LMS there is very little variation in the overall budget of schools on the basis of social disadvantage . . . schools in the most disadvantaged areas receive perhaps 5 per cent more funding per pupil than the bulk of schools in similar types of LEA' (1995, p. 49). Clearly, the Plowden principle of additional resources for additional need has, in practice, largely been super-seded.

Primary schools with large proportions of poor or otherwise underprivileged children have also been losing out in other ways with regard to resources. Because of the restrictions on school budgets, many extracurricular activities such as music lessons, swimming classes and field trips, have come to depend on financial support by parents. This process, described as a subtle form of privatisation, has meant that poor children are doubly handicapped: in the first place, their parents are much less likely than other parents to be able to afford such educational extras; and second, the parent body as a whole will be far less able to contribute a substantial subsidy to support these and other school activities.

Many primary schools benefit from a considerable capitation income contributed annually by parents. An NFER survey undertaken in 1990, for example, reported that primary schools raised £13 per pupil from sources other than LEA funding. But this varied considerably between individual schools and different areas of the country. Of the NFER's sample of primary schools, twenty-eight were found to raise only £1 per pupil. Schools in county towns and rural areas were raising more than twice as much as inner-city schools – £18.84 compared to £7.43; and schools in the south of England were raising on average £14.41 per pupil, while schools in Wales raised a more modest £8.29. Perhaps most significantly, the survey revealed that almost 80 per cent of their sample of primary schools, 'were spending funds raised by parents on essentials for learning' (quoted in Smith and Noble, 1995, pp. 53–4).

Inadequate maintenance and insufficient investment in recent years means that many school premises are deteriorating, and very large sums are necessary to bring all schools up to minimum acceptable standards (£4 billion at current prices). The National Union of Teachers' 1994 *Crumbling Schools* survey of 6500 schools (representing 27 per cent of all schools in England and Wales) revealed that 50 per cent of this sample of schools reported problems with roofs and ceilings, and rotting or non-opening windows; and in 'over one-quarter of the schools sampled a part of the building had been closed because its poor condition constituted a danger to pupils and/or staff' (National Union of Teachers, 1994, p. 5). Not surprisingly, some 43 per cent of the schools reported that the poor state of repair adversely affected staff morale. The discrepancy between the annual level of capital investment per child attending maintained schools and those in independent schools serves to underline these deficiencies – £100 and £468 per pupil, respectively (1992–3 figures).

The question of resources for primary schools is critical in several respects: 'The problem of shortage of subject expertise is now an acute one in primary education,' commented the 'three wise men' in their 1992 report. And they also questioned the significantly less generous funding for 10 to 11-year-olds in primary schools compared to 11 to 12-year-olds in secondary schools (Dept of Education and Science, 1992, p. 2). Yet curbs on public expenditure mean additional resources for primary schools are now even less likely. There is also some indication that the plight of less-privileged children attending primary schools in deprived neighbourhoods may be worsening as the newly-imposed market criteria increasingly determine the distribution of resources within and between schools.

And yet it is the educational opportunities of these children that most need enlarging if the government is really serious about raising educational standards.

Independent schools

The levels of tuition fees and capital investment suggest that for the most part independent schools remain well resourced and largely immune to the current stringencies on expenditure in the maintained sector.

Figures from ISIS (Independent Schools Information Service) (1995) indicate that in 1994 a total of 586 965 pupils were attending 2431 independent schools in England, Wales and Scotland. For England, this represented 7.2 per cent of the total school population (compared to 5.8 per cent in 1979). Included in this total are 60 000 children aged 2–4 attending either part-time or full-time nursery school; 200 000 pupils aged 5–10; and approximately 125 000 aged 11–13. 'Children' under 13 thus represent over half of all independent school pupils. Of the total number of pupils of all ages, boys represent 53 per cent and girls 47 per cent; and well over half (57 per cent) attend mixed-sex schools.

All private schools must register with the DfEE or with the appropriate government office in Wales, Scotland and Northern Ireland. They can be inspected and subsequently requested to conform to certain requirements for continued registration.

Policies since 1979 have strengthened the position of the independent sector within the British education system in a number of respects. Reduced levels of taxation, for example, on higher-income groups, and widening income inequalities, have obviously made the financial costs of private education far more affordable for some. The introduction of the APS under which some 30 000 pupils are attending independent schools has also contributed a large additional subsidy – £78 million for 1992–3 – on top of other long-standing state subsidies such as the tax advantages of charitable status. Financial constraints in the maintained sector have also made the better independent schools, with their enhanced range of facilities, increasingly attractive. Again, the exemption of the independent sector from the constraints of the National Curriculum may also have made private schooling especially attractive in the 1990s – although most preparatory schools say that, in practice, they 'have followed National Curriculum developments very closely' (ISIS, 1995).

It is officially asserted that class size is by no means the most important factor in determining children's attainment. However, with increased administrative burdens, rising class size, and an over-stretched teaching force in state schools, a critical attraction of independent school education must surely be the far more favourable pupil–teacher ratios; and these are particularly marked at the primary stage. Thus official figures for the UK for 1992–3 give a ratio of one teacher to 21.9 pupils in public-sector primary schools (Central Statistical Office, 1995a, p. 49), and more than 26 per cent of pupils in England are now in classes of 31 or more children. The comparable figure for the teacher–pupil ratio in independent schools is 1 to 10.3.

During and after the Second World War the existence of an exclusive and privileged private sector of education was seen as being problematic for its social divisiveness, its restrictive effects on the mobilisation of wider reserves of national talent, and because of the obstacle it presented to the establishment of any real equality of educational opportunity. Ways of achieving a closer integration of the state and private sectors of education were investigated by the Fleming Committee (1942–4) and by the Public Schools Commission between 1965 and 1970. Neither enquiry, however, resulted in substantial policy changes, although the latter did lead in 1974 to the ending of 'direct grant' status, so that the selective direct grant schools either became independent or entered the maintained system as voluntary schools (for extracts from these reports see Maclure, 1979).

Since 1979, however, official attitudes have altered significantly. From the perspective of the New Right – far from being seen as a problem – independent schools are viewed as a wholly commendable form of market diversification, and therefore an important extension of the educational choices available.

The Assisted Places Scheme, as well as the exemption of private schools from the rigours of the National Curriculum and from compulsory testing, and the greater emphasis on formal subject teaching in the early years in the preparatory schools, are all aspects of policy which indicate very clearly that, for recent Conservative governments, private education provides a model for state schools to emulate.

Whatever the merits or otherwise of the education provided within the more orthodox private schools, the old problems remain. They continue to be highly exclusive – indeed, to educate one child exclusively in private schools, a minimum investment of £100 000 is required sooner or later. This means that children attending private schools remain a very select category, well insulated from the educational milieux in which the majority of Britain's children are being educated. Unfortunately, too, private schools continue to afford disproportionate educational opportunities. They educate one in fifteen of children overall, but nearly one in five of those aged over 16; and they supply over one in four of university students, including nearly half of those attending Oxford and Cambridge.

Certainly, already at the primary level there is a privileged enclave of private education. So while the better-off can purchase proper nursery education, parents who cannot afford the fees are dependent either on self-help or on the fragmentary availability of a patchwork of diverse state provision. At other ages in the primary years, the glaring disparity in pupil–teacher ratios and class sizes between independent and maintained schools confers considerable advantages on the former, and makes any comparisons with the teaching methods adopted and the standards attained in the two sectors of rather limited relevance, or even misleading.

Conclusion

Since 1988, Conservative governments have launched themselves on the wholesale reform of state education. At the primary stage we have identified several inherent problems and disquieting possible consequences. Furthermore, education policy appears to contain serious contradictions. Administratively, for example, the English and Welsh system is making planning more difficult, and is fragmenting into a diversity of locally-specific markets; yet a National Curriculum and a more rigid system of inspection have been imposed, presumably to provide some kind of national coherence to a system that is increasingly being pulled apart by the winds of market competition. A stated purpose of the reform programme remains the raising of standards, yet constraints on public expenditure, rising class sizes, poorly maintained buildings, and growing economic insecurity for many teachers, all provide an educational climate ill matched to achieve this objective. And again, on the one hand there is an inspectorate admonishing teachers to raise their expectations of underprivileged children, yet on the other an extended tail of unpopular schools appears to be becoming institutionalised; and, simultaneously, the new testing regime is making anticipated failure all too apparent to precisely these children.

Educational reforms since 1979 are affecting children in the primary years adversely in three respects. Firstly, the scapegoating of education as a cause of Britain's economic difficulties – rather than the 'short-termism' of the City of London and our poor levels of investment – means that ill-considered reforms have been imposed on children and their teachers in the name of economic improvement. Secondly, the implicit vocationalism of the reforms means that a prime objective of children's learning is to meet future occupational needs, rather than that this should be of itself intrinsically worthwhile. And thirdly, the reintroduction of selection and generally increased competitive pressures on children and parents alike, in conjunction with changes in school funding and a determination by the government to provide schooling as cheaply as possible, mean that large minorities of children are facing widening educational inequalities and diminishing opportunities.

It is difficult to conclude that recent reforms are improving the quality of the educational experience for children. On the contrary, teachers report that children are becoming increasingly 'stressed', and parents more anxious. Moreover, the record of the past warns that any re-creation of an extended hierarchy of elitism and inequality is unlikely to result in social, or indeed economic, improvement.

Further reading

Policy synopses since 1945 are found in Rodney Lowe (1993) and Timmins (1995). Roy Lowe (1988) and Simon (1991) provide detailed post-war histories. Ball (1990), Chitty (1992), Kelly (1994) and Tomlinson (1994) variously discuss post-1979 reform. Analyses of the National Curriculum are provided in Anning (1995), Kelly (1994) and Alexander (1992). Smith and Noble (1995) examine current educational inequalities.

8

Child Welfare and Protection

Any act of commission or omission which deprives children of equal rights and liberties and/or interferes with their optimal development. (Gil, 1975)

Introduction

As a definition of child abuse, the quotation above accords with both the spirit of the United Nations Convention on the Rights of the Child and with our own approach within this book. In that respect we have seen in other chapters the extent to which UK social policy can be said to contribute to the neglect and abuse of children at a societal level.

However, official definitions of the problem of child abuse and neglect have tended to be drawn much more narrowly in the UK, as elsewhere. In this chapter, therefore, we shall be examining the role of social policy in protecting and supporting children within their families, together with the provision made for the care of children who live temporarily or permanently away from their family of origin. The principal responsibility for providing these services lies with local authority social services departments, although a number of long-established voluntary organisations such as the NSPCC also play a prominent part. It should be stressed that this is an area of policy where the legal and administrative framework differs within the UK. Our account will focus mainly on the position in England and Wales. Scotland and Northern Ireland each have their own separate systems. Although these are different in a number of important respects from England and Wales, the overall picture is broadly the same.

It is arguable that child-care policy provides a more subtle barometer of the status of children than does any other aspect of

196

social policy, for not only does it raise the issues that are common to other services such as health, housing and social security, concerning the responsibility of the state to provide for its youngest citizens, it also poses questions about the respective rights of parents and children within the family. It is by no means surprising then that child-care policy has produced some of the most controversial and emotionally charged issues involving children in recent times – the events in Cleveland and the Orkneys being just two examples (Dept of Health and Social Security, 1988; Scottish Office, 1992).

The 'liberal compromise'

In his speech commending the Children Act 1989 to the House of Commons, David Mellor – then Minister of State at the Department of Health – claimed:

> We hope and believe it will bring a better balance to the law – a better balance not just between the rights and responsibilities of individuals and agencies, but most notably, between the need to protect children and the need to enable parents to challenge intervention in the upbringing of their children. (*Hansard*, col. 1107, 27 April 1989)

The history of post-1945 child-care policy, as we shall see, has witnessed a number of shifts in the delicate balance between the need to protect children and concern to uphold the rights of parents. These have been reflected in changes in child-care legislation and policy. Lorraine Fox Harding (1991) provides a useful overview of the various perspectives that have influenced UK child-care policy over time. Although it is true that there are distinct variations in perception about the role of the state in protecting children – Fox Harding identifies four perspectives ranging from *laissez-faire* to children's liberation – it is nevertheless important to stress that, throughout its history and whatever its current emphasis, child-care policy in the UK has always operated within a broader political context which is inimical to state intervention in the family. We referred in Chapter 1 to the 'liberal dilemma'. This emerges in particularly acute form when it comes to the issue of child protection. On the one hand, children are seen as the responsibility of families who, in turn, are entitled to autonomy and privacy in their child-rearing role. On the other hand, it is accepted that the state has a duty to protect children from abuse and neglect within the family since 'the parent/child relationship is an unequal contract which children do not enter freely' (Dingwall *et al.*, 1983, p. 220).

The resultant 'liberal compromise', as Dingwall and colleagues argue, is to devise a legal and policy framework which 'allows the state to intervene into the family but which does not convert all families into clients of the state' (Hendrick, 1994, p. 283). This is the basis on which child-care policy operates in the UK. It does not aspire to being a universal service. For a brief period in the 1970s, following the report of the Seebohm (England and Wales) and Kilbrandon (Scotland) Committees, the role of social services was viewed much more expansively. Seebohm described the social services as reaching out 'far beyond the discovery and rescue of social casualties, enabling the greatest possible number of individuals to act reciprocally giving and receiving service for the well being of the whole community' (Seebohm, 1968, para.2).

The idea that child-care services should become universally available and as much a part of the social fabric as health or education provision was a novel and short-lived proposal. In practice, social services never did become part of people's lives in this way, and child-care, in particular, has subsequently become much more narrowly focused on 'social casualties'. The vast majority of children and families have no contact with the child-care system – they receive no services and fall outside its surveillance. In contrast to a number of other countries, England and Wales make no attempt to regulate the treatment of children in all families by legislating, for example, on corporal punishment. This is regarded as a private family matter. Parents are allowed to smack their children, and survey evidence reveals that over 80 per cent choose to do so (Newson and Newson, 1969 and 1989).

Child-care legislation, for all its emphasis on the welfare of the child, does not appear to offer any means for children to restrain parents from exercising 'reasonable' corporal punishment. Indeed, as the Sutton case illustrated (see Chapter 6), parents' right to smack children can be delegated to childminders. In this respect, children in the UK receive less support from the legal system than do their counterparts in countries such as Sweden and Norway. The threshold for social services intervention in families is pitched at a high level in the UK.

This is exemplified by the Children Act 1989. This Act is the most recent and most comprehensive contribution to child-care legislation in the UK, and like a number of its predecessors has been hailed as a 'children's charter'. Yet its limited scope, in so far as it fails to touch the lives of the majority of children, can be illustrated by two of its key sections. The first comes in Part III of the Act, which details the responsibility of local authorities to provide services for children in their area. Under its terms, local authorities have a duty to safeguard and promote the welfare of children who are 'in need', and to provide a range of services to enable them to be brought up within their families wherever possible (s. 17).

On the face of it, this might appear to suggest a broad responsibility for a substantial proportion of the child population. The evidence of our chapters on poverty and housing in particular indicates a high level of need among children. The Act defines a child in need as one who 'is unlikely to achieve or maintain or to have the opportunity to achieve or maintain a reasonable standard of health or development . . . or whose health or development is likely to be significantly impaired or further impaired . . . or is disabled' (s.17). Terms such as 'reasonable' and 'significant' are not defined, and are clearly open to a wide range of interpretation. Nevertheless there is a wealth of evidence which demonstrates the adverse affects of poverty and poor housing, for example, on children's health and development (Townsend and Davidson, 1992).

A case can clearly be made out for local authorities to interpret their duty to the 'child in need' not in terms of the pathology of the individual child or family, but rather in structural terms, encompassing in some areas whole communities. In practice, however, the evidence is that local authorities have been constrained by inadequate resources and by the dominant ideology of individualism to equate children 'in need' with those at risk of 'abuse'. Indeed, it appears that increasingly children have to be formally recorded on the child protection register in order to be classed as being 'in need' (see Colton *et al.*, 1995; Waterhouse and McGhee, 1996). Given the current narrow emphasis on child protection, most children never come in contact with the child-care system. It is also the case that the majority of those who do are filtered out at an early stage in the process without any action being taken or services offered (Dept of Health, 1995, p. 28).

This brings us to the second aspect of the 1989 Act which reveals the narrow focus of child-care policy. For a child to be subject to care proceedings under the 1989 Act, s/he must be suffering, or likely to suffer, 'significant harm' (s. 31). Again, the meaning of this term is not specific. It is true that awareness of certain forms of harm, such as sexual abuse, is now stronger than it was even in the 1970s. However, in other areas such as neglect (both physical and emotional), the threshold for intervention may be higher now than in the past. The evidence suggests that 'high risk' is defined principally in terms of serious physical and sexual abuse. In many inner city areas in particular, child deprivation and hardship is so endemic and so much the norm that it will not attract the attention or resources of the child-care system. Parton (1995) has described the 'neglect of neglect' as an issue in child-care policy since the 1980s.

If the child-care services only touch a small minority of children and families, they are also highly selective in their impact. This is highlighted most vividly in Bebbington and Miles' (1989) study of children admitted to care in the 1980s. They contrasted two typical children aged 5–9:

Child A	*Child B*
No dependence on social security benefits	Household in receipt of Income Support
Two-parent family	Single-adult household
Three or fewer children in family	Four or more children
White	Mixed ethnic origin
Owner-occupied home	Privately-rented home
More rooms than people	One or more persons per room

The chance of Child A entering care, Bebbington and Miles estimated, was 1 in 7000, whereas that of Child B was as high as 1 in 10.

Child-care policy and practice in the UK has always been focused, for the most part, on a small proportion of the poorest and most vulnerable families. Nick Frost has suggested that it cannot simply be understood in terms of the protection of children. Child-care policy, he suggests, 'in an environment of inequality and marginalisation becomes a process of judging and disciplining households defined as outside the mainstream' (Frost, 1990). Dingwall and colleagues similarly suggest that the increase in concern about child protection since the 1960s is 'better seen as a rather narrowly based concern about social disorder . . . its objects are not children as victims of mistreatment but mistreated children as threats to civil order' (Dingwall *et al.*, 1983, p. 220).

An age of optimism, 1945–70

The history of child-care policy since 1945 can be divided into a number of distinct phases. The first phase, beginning with the 1948 Children Act, lasted until the mid-1970s and was characterised by enormous optimism – even euphoria – at times. Accounts of this period have tended to portray it as one of significant advance in the welfare of the child. Jean Packman, for example, entitled her study of child-care policy during the thirty years following the Second World War *The Child's Generation* (Packman, 1975). The 1948 Act which established the framework for policy throughout this phase has been described as 'a decisive break in the political perception of the community's duties towards children and, therefore, of its concept of children's rights' (Eekelaar and Dingwall, 1990, p. 6). In similar vein, Jean Heywood refers to the 1948 Act's imposition on local authorities of a duty to exercise their powers to 'further the best interests' of the child as 'a clause, perhaps unmatched for its humanity in all our legislation' (Heywood, 1959, p. 158).

If there was a general feeling of change and renewal surrounding the welfare reforms of the 1940s, this comes through particularly strongly in contemporary accounts of those working in the childcare field. The sense of anticipation and excitement is palpable. Take, for example, the following purple passage from John Stroud's recollections of his early experiences:

> There was a tremendous crusading atmosphere about the new service . . . We were going to tear down the mouldering bastions. We were going to replace or re-educate the squat and brutal custodians. I had a dream of myself letting up a blind so that sunshine flooded into a darkened room as I turned, with a frank and friendly smile, to the little upturned faces within. (Stroud, 1960)

In truth, the main thrust of the 1948 Act was more prosaic and centred largely on administrative reforms. Whereas child welfare before the war had been the responsibility of the Poor Law Guardians, local education authorities and a number of children's voluntary organisations, this system was replaced in 1948 by newly created Children's Departments in local authorities staffed by trained workers. Certainly, this brought with it a new ethos on the welfare of children to replace the Poor Law emphasis on 'less eligibility'. However, the 1948 Act was focused principally on improving the conditions of children who came into local authority care rather than on preventing them coming into care in the first place.

This was soon to change. Partly through the optimism and crusading zeal of the new child-care workforce, and partly through a realisation that it could be cheaper to keep children at home, the emphasis gradually shifted to prevention. Equally, when this failed and children were admitted to care, the aim was to return them to their families as soon as possible. Legislative support for this came with the 1963 Children and Young Persons Act. The essence of this Act was contained in Section 1, which stated:

> It shall be the duty of every local authority to make available such advice, guidance and assistance as may promote the welfare of children by diminishing the need to receive children into care or keep them in care.

The same section goes on to indicate that local authority support for families might include, though only exceptionally, financial assistance. If the legislation is somewhat cautious, a glance at the Ingleby Report which preceded it will show that the spirit of the times was still relatively generous. Ingleby had stated that 'Everything within reason must be done to ensure not only that children are not neglected but that they get the best upbringing possible' (Home Office, 1960, para. 8). It should be noted that the main emphasis in child-care from 1948 through to the early 1970s was on neglect rather than abuse. Increasingly, however, this was also linked to delinquency, so that 'prevention' came to be seen as an issue of law and order as much as one of child welfare. This was perhaps reinforced by the fact that the government department with responsibility for child-care at this time was the Home Office. It may also be the case that the new emphasis on 'prevention' served to shift the focus away from the child towards the family as a whole.

This trend towards a family-centred rather than a child-centred approach was cemented by the reorganisation of social services in 1971 which brought with it the abolition of Children's Departments and the creation of new generic (that is, non specialist) social services departments. Whatever the merits or otherwise of this reorganisation, it was just the first in a series of organisational changes which, as Jean Packman (1993) has pointed out, has carried on unabated ever since, to the extent that 'it should now be regarded as endemic – a chronic condition without hope of cure'.

The 1970s: the permanency philosophy

The establishment of the new social services departments marks the beginning of the second phase in post-war child-care policy. This lasted until the mid-1980s and is characterised by a loss of optimism and a shift away from prevention as a strategy for tackling the needs of the neglected child. A number of factors led to this disillusion-ment. First, there was growing evidence that the emphasis on trying to reunite children with their families meant that children were spending longer in care. Particularly influential was a study by Rowe and Lambert (1973). This suggested that there was a large number of children 'drifting' in care, for whom rehabilitation was unlikely and who might therefore be better placed with new families. A new emphasis echoing the trend in the USA suggested that 'permanency' was best achieved for children by placing them in adoptive or long-term foster families.

However, the factor that perhaps did most to shake confidence in the policy of prevention and rehabilitation was the death, in 1973, of Maria Colwell at the hands of her stepfather after having been returned home from a period in care. It is a sad fact that children have achieved their greatest prominence in UK social policy in the last quarter of the twentieth century when they have been killed within their own families. Such cases have exerted an enormous, and even perhaps disproportionate, impact on child-care legislation and policy during this period – a point we examine below. The Maria Colwell inquiry was one such example, contributing as it did to the 1975 Children Act. This Act marked a significant shift in emphasis away from a child's links with his or her natural family in favour of adoption and fostering. Most controversially, it introduced a new power for local authorities to take over parental rights (and the parents to lose them) on no other grounds than the fact that the child had been in care for three years. Critics at the time, such as Holman (1976), argued that this meant that parents could lose their children through no fault of their own and that this would unjustly penalise poor families. The Act can also be construed as marking a substantial shift in emphasis from parental rights to the welfare of children.

The contemporary dominance of child protection

By the mid-1980s the picture was again changing and Britain was to enter a new phase in child-care policy. The dominant influence throughout this period was a series of headline-grabbing child-abuse inquiry reports such as those involving Jasmine Beckford (1985), Tyra Henry and Kimberley Carlile (both 1987), and the sexual abuse cases in Cleveland (1988). The inquiry into Maria Colwell's death was the first for thirty years in the UK but during the 1980s such reports came thick and fast. It is hard to believe, therefore, that in the interval between 1945 and 1973 the problem had disappeared. The reasons for the sudden re-emergence of physical abuse as an issue, first in the USA and later in the UK, have been well documented by Parton (1985). Suffice it to say here that both the 'rediscovery' of physical abuse and the new awareness of sexual abuse in the 1980s is more likely to reflect changing professional perceptions and a different political context rather than any real change in the experiences of children.

What is clear is that during the 1980s, there was a notable shift away from neglect towards physical and sexual abuse as the main concern of the child-care service. Alongside this came a growing body of research evidence which indicated that for very many children the experience of being in care was a sorry one. Much of this research was summarised in two official reports (Dept of Health and Social Services, 1985; Dept of Health, 1991). The picture that emerges is of poor planning and bad social work practice leading to insecure and unstable placements for children in care. Even worse, examples began to emerge of children being physically and sexually abused while in residential care (Levy and Kahan, 1991).

The upshot of all this was that the scope of child-care work narrowed considerably during the 1980s. The optimism of the 1950s and 1960s had well and truly gone, and with it any sense that local authorities could offer a broad range of support for children and families. The Jasmine Beckford inquiry had concluded that hers was a 'predictable and preventable' death. As a consequence, and influenced by the work of Cyril Greenland (1986) – an expert witness at that inquiry, the emphasis in child-care switched to developing fail-safe procedures for monitoring 'high risk' children. From being a child welfare service with a broad and ill-defined remit, albeit reaching a relatively small proportion of the child population, local authority child-care became essentially a child protection service concentrated on an even smaller number of cases at the 'heavy end' of the spectrum of risk. We shall discuss the implications of this shift later in the chapter.

The Children Act 1989

The final phase comes with the Children Act 1989 (this is closely paralleled in Scotland by the Children [Scotland] Act 1995 and in Northern Ireland by the Children [Northern Ireland] Order 1995). The 1989 Act has been described as 'one of the most radical and far reaching reforms of the private and public laws affecting children' (Bainham, 1990). There is no disputing its far-reaching nature, as evidenced by the fact that it repealed no fewer than 55 earlier Acts, in whole or in part. Whether it is truly radical is another matter. Certainly, it rewrites the language of child-care policy, replacing concepts such as 'prevention' with the more positive one of 'partnership', and parental 'rights' with 'responsibilities'. It imposes a number of new duties on local authorities and has been hailed by Packman and Jordan (1991) as harking back to the pre-Thatcherite era of the 1960s and 1970s.

On the other hand, the main purpose of the 1989 Act is clearly to forge a new set of balances between parents, children and the state. In this respect it could be said to be essentially conservative in its core principles. Because, although it does make the child's welfare 'the paramount consideration' to be taken into account, it makes it clear that this is best served by non-intervention in the family in most cases. As has been suggested, the bias is 'towards letting families/parents sort out their own disputes and difficulties' (Fox Harding, 1996, p. 165). Although the Act does provide a framework which would allow for progressive child welfare policies – Packman and Jordan (1991) use the terms 'communitarian or collectivist' – this is entirely dependent on the political context. As we have already seen, the Act was implemented in 1991 against a background of resource constraints and an ideology of individualism.

In at least one respect the 1989 Act, and indeed the whole of post-1945 child-care policy, is commonly regarded as radical. This is in the extent to which it places the child centre stage. Not only is the child's welfare paramount, there is also an obligation to 'have regard to the ascertainable wishes and feelings of the child (considered in the light of his age and understanding)'. To this end, the involvement of guardians *ad litem*, court-appointed social workers specifically to represent a child's interest, was extended. The fact that children were to have their own advocate in court proceedings served to strengthen and underline the idea of children as individuals in their own right with interests which might be quite separate from those of their parents.

In addition, the 1989 Act (section 26) imposed a new duty on local authorities to establish complaints procedures for children and young people who are accommodated. It also gave the child the power to take a number of legal actions on his or her own behalf – for example, to challenge the decision of a local authority to seek an Emergency Protection Order or Child Assessment Order. Rather more controversially, children have also gained the right, albeit in limited circumstances, to seek a Contact or Residence Order, determining where they should live and with whom they should have contact. This gave rise to tabloid press references to children 'divorcing' their parents.

If the 1989 Act is seen as marking a significant shift towards 'listening to children', there is perhaps an irony in that the legislation itself was framed without involving or consulting children or young people. Leaving this aside, the UK government, in its first report to the UN Committee set up to monitor the implementation of the Convention on the Rights of the Child, clearly sees the Children Act 1989 as its flagship of children's rights:

> It accords very closely with the principles in the Convention. In particular it shares with the Convention two overarching principles

namely that the best interests of the child should be the first consideration and the voice of the child should be heard. (UK First Report to UN
Committee on the Rights of the Child, para.1.6)

Indeed, in one respect at least, as Freeman has pointed out, the
1989 Act could be said to go further than the UN Convention in its
commitment to children's welfare. For while Article 3 of the
Convention declares that 'the best interests of the child shall be *a
primary* consideration', the 1989 Act elevates children's welfare to
the paramount position (Freeman, 1995, p. 71). Whereas, however,
the UN Convention applies to all aspects of policy relating to
children, the scope of the Children Act 1989 is, as we have shown,
much more narrowly confined. Nevertheless there is a marked
contrast in the UK between the child-centred emphasis of the 1989
Act and the absence of any recognition of children's rights within
other services such as education (Sinclair, 1996).

However, if we need to temper our enthusiasm for the child-
centred nature of child-care policy because of its limited scope and
application, then we also need to bear in mind that child-care
practice may not always live up to the ideals enshrined in law and
policy. When the Butler-Sloss Report (1988) on events in Cleveland
drew attention to the fact that 'the child is a person and not an
object of concern', it was providing a reminder to professionals
which has needed to be frequently repeated throughout the history
of child-care.

A more recent study by Farmer and Owen (1995) of consumer
views about the child protection process concluded that 'children
gained from being protected but felt they were not properly
informed or consulted about what was happening, and felt a loss
of control over what actually happened to them'.

Other commentators (Lyon and Parton, 1995; King and Trowell,
1992) have drawn attention to the increasingly legalistic nature of
the child protection system in England and Wales. The emphasis is
on establishing 'legal truth' in an adversarial setting. It is backward
looking in the sense that its concern is to elicit who did what to
whom, and when. Despite a number of attempts to make its
procedures child-friendly, it is a process that is inherently alien to
children and renders them powerless. There is a striking contrast
between this approach and that adopted in some other European
countries (for example, the Netherlands) where the emphasis is

much less on the legal facts and more on children's future ther-
apeutic needs. While closer to home, the Scottish system of Children's Panels offers a more child-centred model (for a brief
discussion of the Dutch, French and Scottish alternatives, see King
and Trowell, 1992).

Children in care accommodation

As we have seen, the emphasis in UK child-care policy for most of
the post-war period has been predominantly on keeping children
within their families. Despite this, a number of children do spend all
or part of their childhood living away from their birth family. We
shall now consider the experiences of this group of children. But first
we should note the change in terminology brought about by the
Children Act 1989. Previously, children living away from home were
designated as being 'in care'. This was either a voluntary process or
as a result of a court order. The 1989 Act replaced 'care' with the
more neutral and possibly less stigmatising term 'accommodation'.
Children are now 'looked after' or 'accommodated' again on a
voluntary basis or as a result of a legal care order. In both cases
parents retain parental responsibility which they share with the local
authority as long as the child is accommodated.

The numbers of children in care/accommodation

In 1949 there were just over 55 000 children in care in England and
Wales. Subsequently the numbers rose steadily, peaking at over
100 000 in the late 1970s. Since then, the trend has been one of
steadily falling numbers. This has continued since the 1989 Act, to
the extent that the most recent figure is below 55 000 children in
accommodation. Partly this reflects the demographic changes outlined in Chapter 2. It is not simply a question of falling numbers of
children, however – the proportion of the child population entering
care/accommodation has also been declining.

Quite what this indicates is not absolutely clear. On the surface it
may be seen as a positive outcome of preventive work with children
and families. This reflects a predominantly negative view of care/
accommodation as a service which should only be used only *in
extremis*. While this may indeed represent the reality of the care

experience for many children, as we shall see, it is not immediately apparent that the reduction in the number of children who are accommodated has been accompanied by an upsurge in the level of support for children in their own homes. If care/accommodation is viewed more positively, in line with the philosophy of the Children Act 1989, as a resource which can be available to families as part of a shared responsibility or partnership arrangement for the care of children, then declining admissions do not necessarily constitute success.

Length of time in care/accommodation

The annual figure on the number of children in care/accommodation gives a snapshot picture taken on 31 March; it does not measure the total number of children who pass through the system during the course of the year. In fact, rates of entry into care have tended to be much more stable over the entire post-war period than have the numbers in care at any one time. The variation in the latter has more to do with the rate of discharge and length of time in care than the numbers of children entering the system.

For young children in particular, periods in accommodation tend to be short – a matter of weeks or months rather than years. The Department of Health summary of research on child-care placements in the 1980s revealed that whereas a third of children left care within a month and 50 per cent within six months, after that the rate of discharge slowed to a trickle.

The annual statistics are therefore weighted towards the cohort of children who are in long-term accommodation. These tend to be older. For example, of the 55 000 children in accommodation in 1992, only 17 per cent were aged under 5, and 61 per cent were aged over 10 (and almost 25 per cent were aged over 16).

Black children and the care system

Although there is no national data and poor local authority monitoring of the ethnic background of children entering care, research evidence such as that of Barn (1993) and Rowe *et al.* (1989) indicates that black children have tended to be over-represented in care/accommodation. The precise pattern of this over-representation is less clear. There is general agreement that children from an Asian background are under-represented and those from Afro-Caribbean families are over-represented. However, the picture relating to children of mixed origin is more confused. In both the Rowe *et al.* (1989) study and that of Bebbington and Miles (1989), such children were by far the most likely to enter care. This was not the case in the particular local authority examined by Barn.

The more detailed analysis provided by Ravinder Barn suggests that although there are many similarities in the background of white and black children who enter care, there are also several important distinctions. Perhaps most significantly, black children were admitted twice as quickly as white children, and their families received less preventative support (Barn, 1993, p. 102).

The growth of fostering

One of the most striking features of post-war child-care policy has been the shift away from residential care to fostering, especially for younger children. This began with the recommendations of the Curtis Committee in 1946, at which time only 29 per cent were 'boarded out' (fostered). To a large extent the emphasis on fostering reflected a rejection of the Dickensian conditions in pre-war residential care – the 'mouldering bastions' referred to by John Stroud. In part too, it was inspired by the influential work of John Bowlby and his stress on the harmful consequences of maternal deprivation. Fostering was seen as a form of surrogate motherhood. Increasingly, though, local authorities' preference for fostering over residential placements was driven by financial considerations (House of Commons Social Services Committee, 1984).

More recently, there have been significant changes in the nature of foster care, which have further contributed to its growing popularity as a placement. In particular, the development of specialist short-term and intermediate foster care placements mean that fostering is frequently used to supplement and support parental care rather than substitute for it. This form of task-centred fostering has become more 'professional', both in the level of training and support offered to foster carers and also in the financial arrangements involved. It has also led some local authorities (Warwickshire, for example) to dispose of all their residential homes (Cliffe and Berridge, 1991).

As a result of these factors, the proportion of children in foster placements has, despite fluctuations in the 1960s and early 1970s, been on an upward trend in the post-war period. By 1992–3, of children in care, it had reached 65 per cent overall, although this masks considerable local variations and differential rates depending on the age of the child. Almost 90 per cent of children aged under 10 in care, for example, were fostered. Considering this remarkable shift towards fostering, there is very little research evidence on the success or otherwise of this form of placement, particularly from a child's perspective. We know almost nothing about how children view foster care, or its impact on them. What research there has been has tended to focus on the extent to which placements break down and the factors that contribute to this instability.

On the whole, breakdown rates have remained at a fairly high, and constant, level throughout the period under consideration here (Trasler, 1960; Berridge and Cleaver, 1987). Although figures do not always differentiate between the various forms of fostering, rates of breakdown range from 20 per cent for short-term placements to 30–40 per cent for long-term fostering. This has prompted one commentator to suggest that fostering 'involves high risks (both for caretakers and children) but can produce high pay offs' (Colton, 1988, p. 33). If the pay-offs are to be realised for children, it is important that foster care is not simply viewed as a cheap alternative to residential provision. To be successful, it needs a level of professional input and support which very few local authorities have hitherto achieved (Sellick, 1996).

Residential care

Residential care has been very much the 'Cinderella' service as regards the placement of children since 1945. Kahan (1993) has suggested that, unlike boarding education – which still enjoys high status and considerable popularity with affluent parents, 'residential care has been dogged by ghosts of long past Poor Law policies . . . which bear little resemblance to modern children's homes'. The growing popularity of fostering, described above, has meant that residential care is frequently viewed as being a last resort. The service has long suffered from poor morale, high turnover and inadequately trained staff. On top of this, revelations in the late 1980s and early 1990s of widespread physical and sexual abuse by residential care staff added to the general feeling of crisis and despair.

Precise data on the number of children in residential care at any one time is difficult to come by. This sector is characterised by a 'mixed economy of care', with a relatively large number of private and voluntary homes. The difficulty of tracking, let alone managing, the diverse range of institutions operating in the residential child-care market was a theme that recurred in a number of inquiries into residential care in the early 1990s (see, for example, Utting, 1991; and Warner, 1992). Two things are clear, though. First, the proportion of children in care/accommodation who are placed in residential settings has declined substantially over the post-war period and at the time of writing is less than 20 per cent. Second, the number of children who pass through residential care is considerably greater than would be indicated by the annual snapshot figures. The study by Rowe *et al.* (1989), for example, in the mid-1980s suggests that, for older children and teenagers in particular residential provision continues to play a significant part in their experience of care/ accommodation.

Moreover, and surprisingly perhaps, there is a fair amount of evidence that children and young people frequently express a preference for residential care over fostering (see especially Berridge, 1985; Aldgate, 1989). It is particularly valued for its emotional neutrality, particularly by those who have experienced traumatic family disruptions. In Colton's terms, residential care is a 'low risk, low dividend' alternative (Colton, 1988) but this may be just what is required by a child whose life has been scarred by rejection and instability.

One consequence of the emphasis on fostering in child-care policy has been the fact that residential care has increasingly been left to cope with the most troubled and troublesome children and young people. Furthermore, it has been expected to do so without much in the way of support and encouragement from senior management within social service departments. The inquiry reports into abuse in children's homes (for example, Utting, 1991; Levy and Kahan, 1991; Kirkwood, 1993) repeatedly highlight the fact that the abuse occurred when the homes in question were virtually abandoned and floating adrift from line management structures.

It is barely credible that in the 1990s less than 1 in 20 care staff in children's homes in England and Wales hold social work qualifications (Dept of Health, 1992). Berridge and Brodie have contrasted the situation in other professions, where we would expect that the more complex the work the more skilled the practitioner, with that in residential child-care where 'the most damaged and problematic young people have traditionally been dealt with by those social work staff who are among the most poorly trained, least well educated and worst paid (Berridge and Brodie, 1996, p. 181).

The experience of children in care accommodation

Providing an overall assessment of the quality of the care/accommodation experience for children in the post-war era is not easy. There has been a notable lack, both in the policy process itself, and in research, of the child's own perspective. The development in the 1970s of a number of pressure groups representing the interests of children in care, such as 'The Voice of the Child in Care' and the 'National Association of Young People in Care' (NAYPIC), together with more general organisations such as the Children's Legal Centre, ensured that children's voices began to be heard. Even so when the government published its summaries of the findings of research studies on the experience of children in care, the direct experience of children was still largely absent (Dept of Health and Social Security, 1985; Dept of Health, 1991).

Despite this omission, what emerges from the research is, in a number of important respects, a rather negative picture of children's welfare while in care. To begin with, it is clear that if being in care is intended to provide children with greater stability in their lives, it generally fails to do so. One message, as the Department of Health rather blandly concludes, is that 'research on a range of topics shows how difficult it is to provide a stable and positive experience for children or young people who are being looked after by local authorities for more than a brief period' (Dept of Health, 1991, p. 18).

The second lesson that can be derived from the research is that children's links with their birth family are generally the most important source of continuity and stability in their lives. This is so in two respects. First, it appears that contact with their family of origin is one of the main factors that promotes stability in children's placement while in care/accommodation. Second, even when most of their childhood has been spent away from their family, young people tend to drift back home when they leave care. Despite the importance of contact with the birth family for children in care, the evidence of the research from the 1980s is that social work policy and practice has not always recognised this. The failure of the social workers, and sometimes their reluctance, to help children maintain contact with their families is one of the consistent findings of the research studies of the 1980s.

The Children Act 1989 attempted to remedy this problem by imposing a duty on local authorities to promote contact whenever it is in the child's interest. It should be emphasised that contact is the right of the child and not of the parents. The fact that the Department of Health summary of research indicates that contact is generally beneficial to children placed away from home should not be taken to mean that it is always so.

The third main lesson from the 1980s research is that children and young people in the care system suffer from educational under-achievement. This may not in itself be surprising, given the high level of deprivation which, as we have seen, characterises children who come into care/accommodation. What is perhaps more disturbing is the low priority apparently given to children's education once they are in the care system. Drawing on a series of research studies the Department of Health's message is that 'care is not usually in itself a primary cause of educational failure. It is rather that children bring their educational problems with them into care and too often the care experience does little to ameliorate these deficiencies' (Dept of Health, p. 9)

Although this last comment is specifically referring to education, it could just as appropriately be taken as a comment on the deficiencies of the care system in general. The cumulative evidence of a wide range of research and inquiry reports tends to suggest that, all too often, being in care/accommodation has merely perpetuated the pattern of instability, poor parenting and, sadly, even the physical and sexual abuse suffered by children before admission. There is no doubt that the drafting of the Children Act 1989 was heavily influenced by this same research evidence. The emphasis in that Act on partnership with birth families, listening to children, and above all on the paramount importance of children's welfare may well serve to improve child-care policy and practice in the future. Certainly, one optimistic sign in the aftermath of the 1989 Act is the establishment by the Department of Health of the 'Looking After Children' project. This is intended to focus local authority social service departments more centrally on the accommodated child through a process of regular developmental monitoring (Ward, 1995).

Adoption

Adoption offers children one route out of care. The number of children adopted each year is now small (just 6751 in 1993 compared to nearly 25 000 in the late 1960s). This is particularly so if we consider only those who are adopted from care/accommodation (about half the total). Nevertheless, it is an issue that is highly contentious. Although it is not the only method by which a child can be placed in a permanent substitute family – both long-term fostering and residence orders can achieve this objective – adoption goes much further in that it involves the complete and absolute transfer of parental rights and responsibilities to a new family. Indeed, it is this draconian impact on the rights of birth parents that has led some analysts to suggest that if adoption has a future at all it should be a severely limited one (Ryburn, 1996).

The consultative Adoption Bill published in 1996 is unequivocally titled 'Adoption: A Service for Children'. The reality has not always been so clear-cut. Indeed, one of the notable features of adoption in its relatively short existence – it was only introduced into English and Welsh law in 1926 – has been the extent to which it has changed its character to meet new demands and to reflect different circumstances. In the post-Second World War era, in particular, a crucial shift occurred in the 1970s. As Tony Hall has suggested:

> In the late 1960s adoption was still widely regarded as a service for childless couples; a way of providing 'healthy white babies' for couples wanting a 'normal' family of their own. Ten years later it had become a service not for parents but for the children themselves. (Hall, 1984, p. xiv)

The change came about largely for demographic reasons. At its peak in 1968 there were over 16 300 adoptions by strangers (that is, other than step-parent adoptions), over 93 per cent of which involved babies and children under the age of 5. By the 1970s the number of 'healthy white babies' available for adoption had dropped substantially because of improved access to contraception and changing attitudes to lone parenthood. It was also a response to the research study *Children Who Wait* (Rowe and Lambert, 1973), which demonstrated that there was a large number of potentially adoptable children in residential and foster care. The change was facilitated by an alteration in the law governing adoption as a result of the 1975 Children Act. This widened the grounds on which the courts could dispense with parental consent to adoption and increased the potential for contested adoptions.

As a result, the work of adoption agencies, and particularly the local authorities, is now mainly focused on finding placements for children in care/accommodation, many of whom will be older and perhaps with emotional or behavioural problems, or with a disability. Increasingly, adopted children may continue to have contact with members of their birth family. Nevertheless, despite the fact that adoption has become considerably more child-centred since the 1970s, with much more emphasis on finding adopters for 'hard to place' children, parental rights have continued to exert a powerful restraining influence. It is notable, for example, that in adoption law the child's welfare is the *first* and not the *paramount* consideration as in other aspects of child-care law. A consultative Adoption Bill published in 1996 aims to bring adoption law into line with the Children Act 1989 in this respect.

There was an uncomfortable transition period in adoption policy and practice when the service was still primarily trying to meet the needs of childless couples and did so by substituting black babies for the diminishing number of white ones. The policy of placing children 'trans-racially' was soon challenged, both by research evidence which suggested that it led to problems of racial identity (Gill and Jackson, 1983) and by black community groups. Most adoption agencies now accept that children's needs are best met by recruiting adopters (and foster carers) who match the children's cultural and ethnic background and have consequently adopted what has come to be known as a 'same race' placement policy. This approach received a measure of endorsement, despite a largely hostile political climate, in the Children Act 1989, where local authorities are required in any decision concerning a child in its care/accommodation 'to give due consideration to the child's religious persuasion, racial origin and cultural and linguistic background' (s. 22.5).

An emerging trend during the 1980s that runs counter to the prevailing 'same race' placement policy of most UK adoption agencies, and which may change the nature of adoption again, is inter-country adoption. The number of babies adopted from overseas, although still very small compared to other northern European countries such as The Netherlands, Sweden and Denmark, has been growing steadily and looks likely to increase more rapidly in the late 1990s. Inter-country adoption is an issue that raises a host of difficult moral and sociopolitical questions which we do not intend to explore here. It is fair to say, however, that it has been mainly driven by the needs of childless adults in affluent Western countries. The majority of adoption agencies in the UK are very uneasy about it, not only because it undermines domestic 'same race' placement policies but also because it may deflect energy and resources from finding adopters for 'hard to place' children in the UK. We may once again find that adoption changes its character in the process.

Conclusion

The Children Act 1989, in common with all preceding child-care legislation in England and Wales, seeks to maintain a balance between the welfare of children and the rights of parents. There is little doubt that it does mark a shift in a more child-centred direction. However, it is progress of a 'two steps forward, one step backwards' kind, for while the 1989 Act makes the child's welfare paramount and requires courts and local authorities to ascertain the wishes and feelings of the child, it also places more emphasis on parental responsibility and family autonomy than did previous legislation. Moreover, as we have seen, the wider context within which local authority child-care is operating in the 1990s is one of resource constraints and internal markets. This has led to a minimalist approach to child-care policy which is increasingly concentrated on only the most serious child protection cases.

We have noted that the Children Act 1989 is limited in that most decisions affecting children are outside its scope. It can be contrasted, for example, with the Children Act (Scotland) 1995, which states that:

A person shall, in reaching any major decision which involves his fulfilling a parental responsibility . . . or in his exercising a parental right . . . have regard so far as practicable to the views (if he wishes to express them) of the child concerned, taking account of the child's age and maturity. (Section 6)

Similar provisions exist in the legal framework which governs child-care policy in all the Scandinavian countries. In comparison, child-care legislation and policy in England and Wales places much more emphasis on family privacy and autonomy. The commitment in the Children Act 1989 to respect for children may be genuine and a welcome development, but it is not rooted in a pervasive culture of listening to children.

Further reading

Packman (1975) provides a valuable account of child-care policy for 1945–75. Fox Harding (1991) is a useful overview of the various perspectives that have influenced child-care law and policy. Hill and Aldgate (1996) is a wide-ranging symposium (including useful articles on Scotland and Northern Ireland) examining child-care policy following the 1989 Act. Parton (1985) provides analysis of the 'rediscovery' of abuse in the 1970s and discusses the policy responses. Barn (1993) analyses black children's care experiences, based on detailed case study material. The Children Act Report (annually since 1992) contains useful data on care policy and discussion on progress in implementing the 1989 Children Act.

9

The Century of the Child?

The well-being of children requires political action at the highest level. We are determined to take that action. We ourselves make a solemn commitment to give high priority to the rights of children. (United Nations World Summit for Children, September 1990)

Introduction

When Margaret Thatcher joined other world leaders in endorsing this positive and unequivocal conclusion of the World Summit for Children at New York in September 1990, she almost certainly believed that it was aimed at the developing countries alone and held little relevance for the UK. However, our review of British social policy since 1945 indicates that there is little room for complacency in Britain. Indeed, unless there are extensive changes in British cultural attitudes towards children and major changes to contemporary social policies as well as in policy-making institutions, the prospects for any marked improvements to the lives of many children appear remote. The rhetoric of the world summit, of itself, will not remedy current deficiencies.

If children lack power, without even the smallest of voices in the policy process, they are also, as Penelope Leach points out, not only the largest minority group but the one that is 'most subject to discrimination and least recognised as being so' (1994, p. 172). Unless this situation can be reversed and all children start to be valued, respected and taken seriously in both public and private arenas, any idea that the twentieth century has been 'the century of the child' will remain a hollow one.

In the preceding chapters we have reviewed six areas of social policy that have a clear and direct bearing on the lives of children; and we have done this from the historical perspective of the whole post-war period since 1945. This period coincides with the establishment of the post-Second World War 'welfare state' which has afforded far more comprehensive and generous programmes of social welfare than anything previously available. Our analysis has therefore covered the heyday of the welfare state, so the general question arises as to how effective post-war social policy has been in improving the lives of children during the decades since the end of the Second World War.

Before attempting to answer this question, two qualifications need to be borne in mind. In the first place, the areas of social policy discussed are by no means the only fields of state activity that affect children. Indeed, in terms of the broad effects of government policies it is not wholly clear what exactly constitutes 'social' as distinct from other spheres of state policy. For example, for reasons of space it has not been possible to include here any detailed examination of economic, taxation and transport policies – all of which have significant implications for children's well-being, even if they are not normally thought of as being areas of central concern in social policy.

The other qualification concerns the limitations of what the state can in fact do to ensure the well-being of various groups within the population. Politicians of the Right have in recent times been only too eager to point out how little the state can accomplish, and to avow that state provision inhibits and distorts the effective operation of consumer choice articulated by the economic market, thus creating a culture of dependency and weakening individual autonomy and the ability of people to help themselves. We reject this interpretation of state welfare. The view adopted here is that welfare provision by the state has been a historical necessity and remains a fundamental basis for economic progress, and for individual well-being and social cohesion. Thus we concur fully with J. K. Galbraith's assessment that 'there are some things the market system does not do either well or badly. In the good society, these are the responsibility of the state' (1994). The protection and promotion of the interests of children is, we suggest, pre-eminently one of these 'things'; and we believe therefore that the proper welfare of children can only be assured by policies underpinned by the resources of government. Having said this, we are at the same time fully aware that social welfare provision, however important a contribution this may make, is ultimately no substitute for good parenting, and that children have needs well beyond those purely material ones about which the state and other formal organisations can do something.

The issue posed here, however, is not the justification for collectively financed social policies, nor the limitations of state-provided welfare, but a question of how adequate and effective post-war social policies have been in meeting children's welfare needs. The conclusion arrived at from this review of social policies is that current policies fail to meet children's needs in important respects, and that many British children are, in effect, denied in substance those rights proposed in the 1989 UN Convention on the Rights of the Child. As the Children's Society (1996) comments in its formulation of six 'Justice Objectives' (which we quoted at the beginning of Chapter 5), 'They are very basic rights, but not all children in Britain have them.'

The main purpose of this final chapter is thus twofold: to ask how children might be given greater prominence in the policy-making process; and, relatedly, to discuss a number of institutional changes that would at least enable a start to be made towards the achievement of this objective. But first, to understand the present situation, we need to preface discussion of these issues by locating post-war social policy in the broader context of a welfare state that has experienced significant changes since 1945.

Children of the 'welfare state', 1945–79

British social policy since the end of the Second World War falls into two distinct phases which in the case of Britain can be distinguished not only economically but also politically. The first thirty years after 1945 saw unparalleled economic expansion, full employment and steadily rising living standards among all sections of the population – a phenomenon experienced in all the major Western industrial societies.

The establishment of the welfare state in the aftermath of the war and its subsequent expansion mirrored such general economic progress. Thus, in the United Kingdom, welfare spending as a proportion of national income rose from 10 per cent during the 1930s to about 20 per cent by the mid-1970s; a post-war increase that is even more spectacular considering how such growth developed from a base of only 6 per cent in 1946 (Hills, 1993, p. 8). In consequence, as variously noted in previous chapters, major *real* increases in public expenditure were achieved in nearly all the main areas of social welfare during these years. Moreover this expansion of welfare spending was built on a 'very considerable political consensus' between the two main political parties over the appropriate roles and responsibilities of government (George and Miller, 1994, p. 6).

As regards children, a dominant motif of the era, as we noted in Chapter 1, was investment in the future. This was firmly argued by Winston Churchill when he suggested that there was no better investment for a nation than putting milk into babies. Such sentiments were echoed, too, in the widespread support for Beveridge's social security proposals, in particular for a scheme of family allowances. 'The post-1945 society was marked,' suggests Hendrick, 'for a time at least, by a sense of confidence in democracy, in the potential for progress, and by a faith in the family as the ideal humanitarian and disciplinary environment' (1994, p. 15). And he concludes, 'the new social services and the desire to build a more egalitarian democracy than had existed in the inter-war period represented years of hope, of a belief in the possibility of change. Children were given roles in this scenario – not large or significant roles in and for themselves, but none the less positive roles' (ibid., p. 285).

Rising real incomes, full employment and smaller families brought an unsurpassed degree of stability and prosperity to the lives of most British families. Social policies to improve the nation's housing, its health services and to expand its educational provision contributed importantly to national well-being. In all this, children were important beneficiaries.

From a 'universalist' to an 'affordable' welfare state

The first post-war phase – *les trente glorieuses* – came to an end in the mid-1970s following the first oil price shock. Britain's Labour government presided over a period of rapid inflation, and was forced to introduce cuts in its welfare programmes to obtain a loan from the IMF.

Labour's difficulties in office during the 1970s over welfare spending coincided with a growing disenchantment among many

Conservative politicians over the very existence of the welfare state. Thus the New Right, from having been of relatively marginal influence within the Conservative Party during the 1950s and 1960s, was to become, with the election of Margaret Thatcher as its new leader in 1975, the party's driving ideological force.

By the late 1970s, therefore, not only did growing economic difficulties foreshadow some retrenchment of welfare spending, but a major political party had committed itself to restraining welfare spending and generally to 'rolling back the frontiers of the state'. The election of the first Thatcher government in 1979 thus presaged important social policy changes and inaugurated a second phase of the evolution of the post-war welfare state – from the 'universalist welfare state' of Keynes and Beveridge to what is now conceptualised as the 'affordable welfare state' of John Major and Tony Blair (George and Miller, 1994, p. 17). The Conservative Party was to go on and win three further consecutive election victories which, with the continuing ideological dominance of the New Right, gave considerable consistency and a strong political sense of purpose to social policy in the 1980s and 1990s.

Although there have been extensive innovations and changes since 1979 inspired by the ideas of the New Right, the welfare state *per se* is far from being dismantled. So while there have been important changes, these have been within the existing structures of welfare provision. This has also been true of other Western countries, though not of former Communist societies, in which welfare programmes have been severely curtailed as a consequence of the collapse of their command economies and the resulting economic dislocation (Klein, 1993, p. 7). Thus, concludes Ramesh Mishra, after twenty years of more adverse economic circumstances the welfare states in Western countries remain in essentially good health: 'The general verdict is that the welfare state remains more or less intact. By and large the changes that have occurred have been marginal' (Mishra, 1993, p. 18).

It is none the less recognised that there have been differences of approach among countries to welfare spending in the post-1973 climate of tightening economic circumstances. Social-democratic regimes (for example, in Austria and Sweden) are cited as having sought to maintain high levels of employment to protect social welfare programmes, while neo-conservative regimes in the USA and the UK have been ideologically committed to cutting back on welfare expenditure, so that while welfare spending has been held in check everywhere, any reduction has been greater in the latter countries. However, Mishra, while acknowledging a variety of approaches and adopted solutions to the economic difficulties since the 1970s, argues: 'we cannot say that mainstream social programmes of social welfare have been substantially retrenched anywhere . . . the mixed economy and especially substantial state programmes of social welfare look like being around for the foreseeable future' (Mishra, 1993, pp. 23–5).

This conclusion is certainly borne out by recent British experience. Thus while public expenditure on welfare has not grown in the UK as it did before the 1970s, it has none the less remained at comparatively high levels since 1979. Analysis of public expenditure thus shows that welfare spending rose to over 20 per cent of GDP by 1981, since when 'it has levelled out' (Hills, 1993, p. 8).

However, in spite of the maintenance of high levels of welfare expenditure since 1979 in Western countries there is one crucial ingredient missing – full employment. In the context of the rapid economic changes of recent decades that have been identified as representing a process of 'globalisation' or 'the internationalisation of capital', a return to the full employment of the early post-war decades is unlikely to be achieved in the future. The 'universalist' post 1945 welfare state, which included the maintenance of full employment as one of its essential pillars, therefore, 'has now passed into history' (Mishra, 1993, p. 25).

Children in a changing welfare state

On the face of it, then, it appears that welfare expenditure throughout the post-war period has been maintained at historically high levels even during the economic difficulties since the 1970s. This implies that children have continued to remain major beneficiaries of comprehensive welfare provision. And close analysis of trends in total welfare spending does show, in fact, that there has been some slight per capita increase over the medium term for children and young people under the age of 18. Yet in the UK, as Sally Holtermann notes, 'these facts about spending coexist with widespread dissatisfaction at the amount that is being spent on children'

(Holtermann, 1996, p. 5). So how, might we ask, is this paradox to be explained?

Before attempting an explanation for this apparent contradiction there are two further related questions that also need to be stated. First, as already noted, in spite of major improvements in many aspects of life for children since the end of the Second World War, the evidence reviewed in earlier chapters shows conclusively that many British children do not enjoy a proper level of well-being, and for some the conditions of life may have in fact deteriorated. So the question arises as to why, given the continued existence of the welfare state, so many children appear to fare so badly. What has gone wrong, and why have children not been better protected by the welfare provision of recent years?

The second and more general question concerns the quality of life of children today. There seems to be a growing recognition or at least an intuitive feeling that the quality of life has been deteriorating in recent years. So, for example, a Gallup survey for the *Daily Telegraph* (3 June 1996) asked a representative sample of adults whether, upon a 'number of key ingredients', they thought the national sense of well-being was improving or worsening. The answers were then compared to those obtained from a similar survey undertaken a generation earlier, in 1968. Not only did the later survey reveal generally a 'mood swing from hope in '68 to the gloom and doom of today', but opinions about a number of specific criteria were found to have become markedly more pessimistic. Thus 51 per cent of respondents think health is worsening, compared to 16 per cent who thought so in 1968; and nearly half the sample (47 per cent) think national standards of knowledge are declining, as opposed to 5 per cent who thought this was the case in 1968.

Public opinion of this kind certainly implicates children, but other commentators specifically identify a declining quality of childhood life. Thus Linda Grant, writing in the *Guardian* (6 January 1996), points out the contradiction between the bewildering choice of consumer goods with which today's young are faced, and their increasing lack of other freedoms: 'Today's pre-pubescents possess some of the most sophisticated skills as consumers in the country. But they have less personal freedom than any previous generation . . . So how will they learn to grow up?' Penelope Leach, in her book, *Children First*, develops a more general critique of the experience of childhood in contemporary Western societies: 'Our society is inimical to children and has therefore devalued parents to such an extent that individual good parenting is not only exceedingly difficult but, ultimately, insufficient' (1994, p. xiii).

All this raises profound issues concerning the nature and the direction of the changes occurring in British society and elsewhere, any discussion of which is beyond the scope of this present work. However, social policies are, as we hope has been amply demonstrated, important determinants of children's opportunities and experiences, and therefore represent important influences, whether actual or potential, on the quality of life enjoyed by the young. Thus we return to the central question of why the contemporary welfare state would seem to be failing so many British children.

The answer, we suggest, lies in a combination of three separate though interrelated sets of circumstances: changed social and economic conditions; social policy failures that have continued throughout the whole of the post-war period; and the effects of Conservative welfare experimentation and restructuring since 1979. We deal briefly with each of these in turn.

Changing social and economic conditions

Underlying contemporary social policy failures to protect children's interests and to ensure a proper measure of well being for a substantial minority of British children, are the widening inequalities since the 1970s. No one can deny that inequalities of income have widened significantly, and whether we identify these widening disparities between different groups as 'poverty' or simply as 'inequalities', it is certainly true that children have been affected disproportionately. Measurable income inequalities – which many recognise as being indicative of relative poverty – have, of course, existed among children during most of the post-war years. However since 1979 growing numbers of households containing children compared with adult-only households have become poorer in relation to average national incomes. We have thus witnessed a twofold widening of inequalities since the 1970s between the better-off majority and the poor, and between those with children and those without.

Two important social changes underlie this growing inequality. One is the increased incidence of family breakdown, divorce and lone parenthood; and the other is the much higher incidence of unemployment since the mid-1970s. Spending on social security programmes has expanded, partly as a response to both these changes. At a casual glance any increased expenditure on social security might appear to have shifted resources in favour of children. But what, in fact, these changes have achieved is that far greater numbers of children have become dependent on subsistence social security benefits. The crucial question thus concerns the adequacy of household income for those dependent on social security benefits; and, as indicated in Chapter 3, contemporary analyses of these find them seriously deficient for sustaining a satisfactory standard of living for households with children.

Continuing social policy failures

Specific social policy failures, as we have seen in previous chapters, have continued in one form or another throughout the whole of the post-war era. However, as the numbers of poor households have multiplied, so such failures have become all the more prevalent and pressing. So, for example, the 'British housing problem' was never wholly solved despite post-war progress. And the inadequacy of social security benefits for families with children has remained a continuing flaw in the social security system. Indeed, as H. Hendrick points out, 'From the rediscovery of poverty in the 1960s . . . the condition of these [poor] children was reiterated in publication after publication' (1994, p. 286). The principal difference between the decades before 1980 and the late 1990s, is that in the latter period much larger numbers of people – especially children – are affected by the same chronic welfare problems.

Social policy changes since 1979

Against a background of widening inequalities between groups of children and the worsening economic circumstances affecting many families, the restructuring of welfare services undertaken since 1979 has, we would argue, on the evidence presented in earlier chapters, been detrimental to the interests of many children. A more market-based provision of welfare can only compound the disadvantages of those already badly situated in other markets, or indeed excluded altogether.

An additional explanation for the apparent contradiction between levels of welfare spending and widespread feelings of the growing inadequacy of the resources devoted to services for children derives from the specific effects of recent reforms. For example, some transfer of resources may well have occurred within a social service, from actual service delivery to an expanded management function, because the real administrative costs of the introduction of internal markets may not have been fully provided for; hence, although total spending levels might have been maintained, none the less cuts in services will have been imposed. Again, individual local authorities may have cut services such as school meals and child care, which are particularly important for children, but which local authorities have no statutory duty to provide, while increasing expenditure elsewhere on services they do have a legal obligation to provide.

Towards greater prominence for children in social policy

It was argued earlier that if we are to achieve child-centred social policies that afford children generally higher priority, we will need to both change the way we view children and increase their access to the policy process. However, in arguing for changes in cultural attitudes towards children and to the institutions that exemplify and perpetuate these self-same attitudes we are immediately faced with a 'chicken and egg' problem – where, indeed, should one start! Tentatively, we begin by examining the obstacles to change posed by contemporary attitudes.

Children as the responsibility of the family

One of the key aspects of the way children are perceived in the UK, and to which attention was drawn in Chapter 1, is the way children are viewed as being primarily the responsibility of their individual family. This is central to the philosophy of the New Right, though it was also an important underlying principle of the post-1945 Beveridge model of welfare and is now reflected in the social policy values espoused by 'New Labour'. There are, however, a number of drawbacks with this emphasis. Not least among these, as we have seen in earlier chapters, is that it results in an unreasonably heavy burden being placed on individual families, one that many are ill-equipped to bear. Unfortunately, the political constituency of those with a direct interest in children is relatively small. So while it may be true that parents are children's best advocates, this cannot compensate for the fact that there are a declining number of them. Even proposals such as Halsey and Young's (1995) to give parents an extra vote to cast on behalf of their children would be unlikely to do full justice to the problem.

Perhaps more convincing are the claims made by David Archard in favour of what he terms 'modest collectivism' and the 'diffusion of parenting' (1993, pp. 164–9). The essence of these ideas is that, while the family would retain its role as the main source of child-rearing, 'responsibility for upbringing should not continually and exclusively fall on the parents. Parenting may be embedded in a network of kin and community' (ibid., p. 167). The most important policy implication of 'modest collectivism' would be a commitment to universal early years child care; while the effect of 'diffused parenting' would, according to Archard, mean that 'children are brought more into the public domain and out of the private shades of the family' (ibid., p. 169).

The United Kingdom is a long way from 'modest collectivism and diffusion of parenting', as any parent who has struggled with a noisy 2-year-old in a crowded restaurant will testify. Even basic necessities such as children's toilets and baby-changing facilities are in short supply; and bystanders are far more likely to be coldly indifferent than to offer themselves as surrogate parents. However, it is certainly true that the campaigning work of organisations such as the National Childbirth Trust are slowly improving facilities in public places. But there is as yet little evidence of parenting becoming 'embedded in the community', apart from parents supporting each other by, for example, sharing 'school runs' and babysitting – and not forgetting the considerable part played by the extended family in child-care arrangements.

Rights for children?

A second and possibly more fruitful avenue for promoting change in attitudes towards children in Britain is the development of children's rights. The importance of a rights perspective was discussed in Chapter 1, so at this point we would simply reaffirm the view that, whatever the substantive benefits conferred on children by specific rights such as the right to health or education, the overriding importance of rights lies in the fact that they represent a recognition of children's social value. As Jeremy Roche puts it:

> A commitment to children's rights requires a respect on the part of the majority (adult) traditions to the different lives led by our children and their different, and at times awkward, voices in the private as well as public world. (1996, p. 37)

Some grounds for optimism in relation to the question of children's rights can be derived from the growing intellectual acceptance of the concept (see Franklin, 1995), together with the increasing number of institutions beginning to work in this area: for example, the Children's Legal Centre, the Children's Rights Development Unit, and the National Association of Young People in Care, as well as, of course, longer-established charities such as the National Children's Bureau, Save the Children, and the Children's Society. In fact, the origins of the children's rights movement can be traced back as far as 1924, when Eglantyne Jebb succeeded in having the Declaration of the Rights of the Child adopted by the League of Nations. But it has been the UN Convention on the Rights of the Child that has mainly been responsible for boosting recent interest and promoting a wider acceptance of children's rights – at least in the public arena.

The limited successes in enshrining children's rights in public policy, notably in the Children Act 1989, have already been mentioned. But other areas of public policy, including education, are still immune. However, it is perhaps in the private sphere of children's lives that there is most resistance to any influence from the rights movement. In England and Wales certainly, as indicated in Chapter 8, the family is left largely to its own devices. Whether or not it would be enforceable, the symbolic importance of legislation requiring parents to take into account the wishes and feelings of their children would be immeasurable.

Institutional change for the empowerment of children?

The advocacy of both 'diffusion of parenting' and the recognition of children's rights is aimed at cultural change with respect to the way children are perceived in the UK. We shall now examine institutional mechanisms that might contribute to the empowering of children.

As things stand at the time of writing, children lack both economic and political power. In the words of Young and Halsey:

> Two of our greatest institutions have failed to find any proper place for children, and so the children have had no secure place in the capitalist market nor in liberal democracy. (1995, p. 12)

Since 1979, under the influence of New Right thinking, welfare policy in the UK, as noted above, has been dominated by the philosophy of the market. The argument has been that people who use services such as education, health, housing and so on are most effectively empowered not through the democratic process but rather by the mechanism of the market or 'quasi-market'. By exercising the power of 'consumer choice', those who use welfare services, according to this theory, are able to impose their wishes on the providers. Whatever the merits or otherwise of this approach in general terms, it is a blind alley when it comes to empowering children.

We discussed earlier in this chapter the extent to which welfare markets have exacerbated inequalities and made many children substantially worse off. The point here is that welfare markets in fact *exclude* children. When exponents of New Right policies talk enthusiastically about giving power to the consumer in education or health, they mean parents, not children. Children are inevitably going to be peripheral and powerless within a market model of welfare.

For this reason, if for no other, we advocate a return to pre-1979 approaches to welfare and a renewed emphasis on empowering users through democratic politics. For children, this will require new structures and institutions. What some of these might be and how they might operate we shall examine briefly below – almost all are drawn from examples in operation elsewhere.

A Minister for Children

One idea that has received some political support in the UK, having appeared in the 1992 Labour Party election manifesto, is the creation of a 'Minister for Children'. Such a post exists in a number of

European countries, including Norway. Details as to how such a ministry might operate are set out by Joan Lestor (1995). She insists that, to be effective, the proposed minister should be of cabinet rank, and the Ministry should have its own civil service establishment and dispense a sizeable budget.

This reform would certainly ensure that issues of child welfare would enjoy a much higher profile than at present when responsibility for the young is diffused across a whole range of government departments – often in competition with each other! It would also facilitate a more strategic approach to policy-making for children. So, for example, its responsibilities could include the development of a 'national plan' for children. Indeed, Joan Lestor argues that the simple process of gathering together the data relating to children that exists in a scattered fashion within government departments (the kind of information presented in this book) would in itself be a catalyst for change:

> It is my view that much of the information about children's lives makes uncomfortable reading; and that once government gives it official recognition, pressure will be put on it to set targets – in child homelessness for example – and to develop policies which work directly to meet those targets and respond to the needs of children. (Ibid., p. 103)

An 'ombudsman for children'

An alternative, or preferably complementary, innovation would be the establishment of a 'commissioner' or 'ombudsperson' for children; this idea is described more fully in Rosenbaum and Newell (1991). Briefly stated, the role of the Commissioner would be to act as an advocate for children; and such a role would entail taking up individual children's grievances as well as promoting the interests of children generally by scrutinising legislation and lobbying governments. The first children's ombudsperson to be appointed in Norway has given a flavour of her work and provided pointers for how it might operate in the UK (see Flekkoy, 1995).

Child impact statements

A less radical and less satisfactory innovation would be the introduction of a system of 'child impact statements' whereby any new legislation or regulations would have to be scrutinised for their impact on children. This measure could, of course, be employed usefully alongside the reforms outlined above and would provide an additional means of raising the profile of children across all government departments.

The role of local government

So far we have considered possible institutional changes at the level of national government. However, in the case of most of the services we have been reviewing in this book, local government continues to play an important, if diminishing, role. There is therefore a powerful case to be made that children's welfare (and also their empowerment) is best served by a strong and active role for local government. Not only is local government closer to the communities it serves, it has a better record of responding to the needs of powerless minority groups. So, for example, about a dozen local authorities in the UK have appointed 'children's rights officers'; and while most of their work has tended to be on behalf of children in care/accommodation, they have at least the potential to take a more wide-ranging and proactive role as local advocates of children's rights (see Ellis and Franklin, 1995).

The Youth Council Initiative

One interesting example of how the active participation by children and young people themselves in the policy process can be encouraged at the local level, is the 'youth council initiative'. One interesting manifestation of this is the work of the Devon Youth Council, as described by Penny Townsend (1996). This particular youth council, with a membership of 150 drawn mainly from affiliated youth organisations, is an active political force within the Devon County Council area. Similar bodies also exist in a number of other countries in both Eastern and Western Europe, although they are still as yet very thin on the ground in the UK. Townsend is enthusiastic about their value, and claims that the Devon Youth Council 'has managed both to change the policy and practice of local authorities and to retain a structure responsive to the needs of young people' (ibid., p. 108).

Structures such as children's or youth councils are enormously important in giving older children 'a voice'. But 'listening' to children does not have to begin with the teenage years, or even when children first learn to speak. Jacqui Cousins (1996) has pointed to the importance of listening to infants, and even babies. Perhaps the real challenge in making policy more child-centred lies with the professionals who work with children and young people. Though often a far from easy task, and one for which many could be better trained, practitioners need to learn to communicate with children in a way which respects them as people.

Conclusion

As we hope has been amply demonstrated in this book, any meaningful realisation of basic rights for children requires important attitudinal and institutional changes. However, we should not pretend that there are not immense difficulties to be overcome if a significantly higher social policy priority for children is to be achieved. Some of the more immediate obstacles to the implementation of genuinely child-centred social policies have been identified in this text, but there are other problems and issues that are well beyond the scope of this present work to address. These surely must include the British constitution which allows the executive, representing 'the Crown in Parliament', to enjoy seemingly near-dictatorial powers; and an electoral system whereby extensive policy changes are implemented by a government representative of only a minority of voters and against the clear preferences of the majority. Such reasons include too the social unrepresentativness of a large number of politicians – by virtue of race, gender, schooling and social class. This latter point cannot be stressed too much. Coteries of predominantly male politicians, often educated in exclusively male educational institutions, well-insulated by gender and money from the trials and tribulations of day-to-day child care, are the people who formulate policies involving public expenditure decisions that affect the life chances of children. In these circumstances it is all too easy to see how a government can brush aside the claims of children, however legitimate and pressing these may be.

The final conclusion of this book therefore must be that the challenge to redirect contemporary social policies in ways more conducive to children's well-being is but a part – though perhaps the most urgent and compelling part – of a broader need to democratise the archaic and ailing institutions of the United Kingdom. This is the challenge that faces all of us as we approach the end of 'the century of the child'. They are after all *our* children.

Further reading

Lowe (1993) and Timmins (1995) provide post-war histories of the welfare state. Arguments over the future of welfare are reviewed by Hills (1993). Recent welfare changes are discussed in George and Miller (1994), Savage *et al.* (1994), and in Jones (1993). Leach (1994) makes a reasoned plea for a better deal for children.

Bibliography

Abbott, P. and C. Wallace (1992) *The Family and the New Right* (London: Pluto).

Abel Smith, B. and Townsend, P. (1965) *The Poor and the Poorest* (London: Bell & Son).

Abercrombie, N., A. Warde, K. Soothill, J. Urry and S. Walby (1994) *Contemporary British Society* (2nd edn) (Cambridge: Polity Press).

Alcock, P. (1987) *Poverty and State Support* (Harlow: Longman).

Alder, M. and G. Raab (1988) 'Exit, Choice and Loyalty: the impact of parental choice on admission to School in Edinburgh and Dundee', *Journal of Education Policy*, vol. 3, no. 2, pp. 155-80.

Aldgate, J. (1989) 'Foster Families and Residential Care for Older Children', *Children and Society*, vol. 3, no. 1.

Alexander, G. (1995) 'Children's Rights in their Early Years: From Plaiting Fog to Knitting Treacle' in Franklin (1995).

Alexander, R. (1992) *Policy and Practice in Primary Education* (London: Routledge).

Allsop, J. (1995) *Health Policy and the NHS* (2nd edn) (London: Longman).

Alston, P., S. Parker and J. Seymour (1992) *Children, Rights and the Law* (Oxford: Clarendon Press).

Anderson, R., J. Britton, A. Esmail, J. Hollowell and D. Strachan (1995) 'Respiratory Disease and Sudden Infant Death Syndrome', in Botting (1995).

Anning, A. (ed.) (1995) *A National Curriculum for the Early Years* (Buckingham: Open University Press).

Archard, D. (1993) *Children: Rights and Childhood* (London: Routledge).

Archbishops of Canterbury and York (1990) *Faith in the Countryside – Report of the Archbishops' Commission on Rural Areas* (Worthing: Churchman Publishing).

Atkinson, R. and P. Durden (1994) 'Housing Policy since 1979: Developements and Prospects', in Savage, Atkinson and Robins (1994).

Audit Commission (1996) *Counting to Five: Education of Children Under Five* (London: HMSO).

Baggott, R. (1994) *Health and Health Care in Britain* (London: Macmillan).

Bainham, A. and S. Cretney (1993) *Children: The Modern Law* (London: Family Law).

Baker, J. (1986) 'Comparing National Priorities: Family and Population Policies in France', *Journal of Social Policy*, vol. 15, no. 4.

Balchin, P. (1995) *Housing Policy* (London: Routledge).

Baldwin, S. and J. Falkingham (1994) *Social Security and Social Change* (London: Harvester/Wheatsheaf).

Ball, S. J. (1990) *Politics and Policy Making in Education* (London: Routledge).

Ball, S., R. Bowe and S. Gewirtz (1994) 'Market Forces and Parental Choice: Self-Interest and Competitive Advantage in Education', in Tomlinson (1994).

Banting, K. (1979) *Poverty, Politics and Policy* (London: Macmillan).

Barker, T. and M. Drake (eds) (1982) *Population and Society in Britain 1850–1980* (London: Batsford).

Barn, R. (1993) *Black Children in the Public Care System* (London: Batsford).

Barnes, P. J. and M. T. Newhouse (1994) *Conquering Asthma* (London: Manson Publishing).

Bebbington, A. and J. Miles (1989) 'The Background of Children Who Enter Local Authority Care', *British Journal of Social Work*, vol. 19, no. 5.

Bennett, N. and J. Kell (1989) *A Good Start?* (Oxford: Basil Blackwell).

Benzeval, M., K. Judge and M. Whitehead (1995) *Tackling Inequalities in Health* (London: King's Fund).

Berger, B. and P. Berger (1983) *The War over the Family* (London: Hutchinson).

Berger, N. (1990) *The School Meals Service* (Plymouth: Northcote House).

Berridge, D. (1985) *Children's Homes* (Oxford: Basil Blackwell).

Berridge, D. and I. Brodie (1996) 'Residential Child Care in England and Wales: The Inquiries and After', in Hill and Aldgate (1996).

Berridge, D. and H. Cleaver (1987) *Foster Home Breakdown* (Oxford: Basil Blackwell).

Bevan, A. (1952) *In Place of Fear* (London: Heinemann).

Beveridge, W. (1942) *Social Security and Allied Services* (The Beveridge Report), Cmd 6404 (London: HMSO).

Blackburn, C. (1991) *Poverty and Health* (Milton Keynes: Open University Press).

Blenkin, G. and A. V. Kelly (1994) *The National Curriculum and Early Learning* (London: Paul Chapman).

Bonnerjea, L. and J. Lawton (1987) *Homelessness in Brent* (London: Policy Studies Institute).

Bonnett, M. (1994) *Children's Thinking – Promoting Understanding in the Primary School* (London: Cassell).

Botting, B. (ed.) (1995) *The Health of our Children – OPCS Decennial Supplement* (London: HMSO).

Botting, B.and R. Crawley (1995) 'Trends and Patterns in Childhood Mortality and Morbidity', in Botting (1995).

Bradshaw, J. (1990) *Child Poverty and Deprivation in the UK* (London: National Children's Bureau).

Bradshaw, J. and H. Holmes (1989) *Living on the Edge: A Study of the Living Standards of Families on Benefit in Tyne and Wear* (London: Child Poverty Action Group).

British Medical Journal (BMJ), see Smith (1991).

Brown, J. (1984) *Children in Social Security* (London: Policy Studies Institute).

Brown, J. (1988) *Child Benefit: Investing in the Future* (London: Child Poverty Action Group).

Bruce, T. (1987) *Early Childhood Education* (London: Hodder & Stoughton).

Bruner, J. (1980) *Under Five in Britain* (London: Grant McIntyre).

Burghes, L. (1980) *Living from Hand to Mouth* (London: FSU/CPAG).

Burnett, J. (1986) *A Social History of Housing* (2nd edn) (London: Methuen).

Burns, L. and A. Smith (1994) *The End of Bed and Breakfast?* (London: Shelter).

Burrows, L. and P. Walentowicz (1992) *Homes Cost Less than Homelessness* (London: Shelter).

Butler, K., B. Carlisle and R. Lloyd (1994) *Homelessness in the 1990s – Local Authority Practice* (London: Shelter).

Campbell, T. (1992) 'The Rights of the Minor as Person, as Child, as Juvenile, as Future Adult', in Alston (1992).

Cannan, C. (1992) *Changing Families: Changing Welfare* (London: Harvester/Wheatsheaf).

Central Advisory Council for Education (1967) *Children and their Primary Schools* (The Plowden Report) (London: HMSO).

Central Statistical Office (1974) *Social Trends* (London: HMSO).

Central Statistical Office (1994) *Social Focus on Children* (London: HMSO).

Central Statistical Office (1995a) *Social Trends – 1995 Edition* (London: HMSO).

Central Statistical Office (1995b) *Fighting with Figures* (London: HMSO).

Central Statistical Office (1996) *Social Trends – 1996 Edition* (London: HMSO).

Challis, L. (1980) *The Great Under Fives Muddle* (University of Bath).

Cherry, G. (1988) *Cities and Plans* (London: Edward Arnold).

Children's Society, The (1996) *A Little Voice* (London: The Children's Society).

Child Poverty Action Group (1995) *Poverty*.

Children Act Report (annual) (London: HMSO).

Chitty, C. (1992) *The Education System Transformed* (Manchester: Baseline Books).

Clark, M. (1988) *Children Under Five; Educational Research and Evidence* (London: Gordon and Breach).

Clarke, F. (1992) 'Sent Up the Stairs', *ROOF*, November/December.

Clarke, L. (1992) 'Children's Family Circumstances: Recent Trends in Great Britain', *European Journal of Population*, vol. 8.

Cliffe, D. and D. Berridge (1991) *Closing Children's Homes* (London: National Children's Bureau).

Cloke, P. (ed.) (1992) *Policy and Change in Thatcher's Britain* (Oxford: Pergamon Press).

Cohen, B. (1988) *Caring for Children* (Brussels: Commission of the European Community).

Cohen, B. (1990) *Caring for Children: The 1990 Report* (London: Family Policy Studies Centre).

Cohen, R. *et al.* (1992) *Hardship Britain: Being Poor in the 1990s* (London: Child Poverty Action Group).

Coleman, D. (1988) 'Population', in Halsey (1988).

Coleman, D. and J. Salt (1992) *The British Population* (Oxford University Press).

Collier, J. A. B. and J. M. Longmore (1989) *Oxford Handbook of Clinical Specialities* (2nd edn) (Oxford University Press).

Colton, M. (1988) 'Substitute Care Practice', *Adoption and Fostering*, vol. 12, no. 1.

Colton, M., C. Drury and M. Williams (1995) 'Children in Need: Definition, Identification and Support', *British Journal of Social Work*, vol. 25.

Commission for Racial Equality (1989) *From Cradle to School* (London: CRE).

Commission on Social Justice (1994) *Social Justice: Strategies for National Renewal* (London: Vintage).

Conway, J. (1988) *Prescription for Poor Health* (London: London Food Commission, Maternity Alliance, SHAC and Shelter).

Conway, J. and P. Kemp (1985) *Bed and Breakfast – Slum Housing of the Eighties* (London: SHAC).

Cooper, D. (1994) 'Making a Meal of It', *Search*, no. 21, Winter (Joseph Rowntree Foundation).

Cousins, J. (1996) 'Empowerment and Autonomy from Babyhood', in John (1996a)

Craig, J. (1994) 'Replacement Level Fertility and Future Population Growth', *Population Trends*, no. 78, Winter (OPCS).

Daniel, P. and E. Burgess (1994) *The Child Support Act: The Voice of Low Income Parents with Care* (London: Welcare).

David, T. (1990) *Under Five – Under Educated* (Buckingham: Open University Press).

David, T. (1993) *Educational Provision for Our Youngest Children: European Perspectives* (London: Paul Chapman).

Davie, R., N. Butler and H. Goldstein (1972) *From Birth to Seven* (London: Longman and The National Children's Bureau).

Davis, J., R. Grant and A. Locke (1994) *Out of Site, Out of Mind – New Age Travellers and the Criminal Justice and Public Order Bill* (London: The Children's Society).

Dearing, R. (1993) *The National Curriculum and its Assessment* (The Dearing Review) (London: School Curriculum and Assessment Authority).

Dept for Education and Employment (1995) *The English Education System* (briefing paper).

Dept of Education and Science (DES) (1978) *Special Educational Needs* (The Warnock Report) (London: HMSO).

Dept of Education and Science (1990a) *A Survey of the Education of Children Living in Temporary Accommodation: April–December 1989*, HMI Report: Reference 178/90/NS.

Dept of Education and Science (1990b) *Starting with Quality* (Rumbold Report) (London: HMSO).

Dept of Education and Science (1991) *A Survey of Educational Provision for Traveller Children in Essex – a Report by HMI: Reference 8/91/DS*.

Dept of Education and Science (1992) *Curriculum Organisation and Classroom Practice in Primary Schools* (London: HMSO).

Dept of the Environment (1961) *Homes for Today and Tomorrow* (The Parker Morris Report) (London: HMSO).

Dept of the Environment (1977) *Housing Policy – A Consultative Document*, Cmnd. 6851 (London: HMSO).

Dept of the Environment and Welsh Office (1995) *Our Future Homes – Opportunity, Choice, Responsibility* (White Paper) Cm. 2901 (London: HMSO).

Dept of Health (1990) *Playgroups in a Changing World* (London: HMSO).

Dept of Health (1991a) *Patterns and Outcomes in Child Placement* (London: HMSO).

Dept of Health (1991b) *The Health of the Nation – A Consultative Document*, Cm. 1523 (London: HMSO).

Dept of Health (1992) *The Health of the Nation – A Strategy for Health in England*, Cm. 1986 (London: HMSO).

Dept of Health (1993) *Circular LAC (93) 1* (London: HMSO).

Dept of Health (1995) *NHS – The Patient's Charter* (London: HMSO).

Dept of Health (1995) *Child Protection: Messages from Research* (London: HMSO).

Dept of Health and Ministry of Agriculture, Fisheries and Food (1995) *National Diet and Nutrition Survey – Children aged one and a half to four and a half* (London: HMSO).

Dept of Health and Social Security (1974) *Report of the Committee on One Parent Families* (Finer Report) (London: HMSO).

Dept of Health and Social Security/Dept of Education and Science (1978) *Co-ordination of Services for Children Under 5* (London: HMSO).

Dept of Health and Social Security (1985) *Social Work Decisions in Child Care* (London: HMSO).

Dept of Health and Social Security (1988) *Report of the Inquiry into Child Abuse in Cleveland* (London: HMSO).

Dept of Social Security (1990) *Children Come First* (London: HMSO).

Dept of Social Security (1994) *Households Below Average Incomes: A Statistical Analysis 1979–91* (London: HMSO).

Dingwall, R., J. Eekelaar and T. Murray (1983) *The Protection of Children* (Oxford: Basil Blackwell).

Dobson, B., A. Beardsworth, T. Keil and R. Walker (1994) *Diet, Choice and Poverty* (London: Family Policy Studies Centre).

Donaldson, J. (1994) *Living with Asthma and Hay Fever* (Harmondsworth: Penguin).

Dorling, D. (1993) 'Children in Need', *ROOF*, September/October.

Douglas, J. W. B. (1964) *The Home and the School* (London: MacGibbon & Kee).

Dowler, E. and C. Calvert (1995) *Nutrition and Diet in Lone-Parent Families in London* (London: Family Policy Studies Centre).

Dunleavy, P. (1981) *The Politics of Mass Housing in Britain 1945–1975* (Oxford: Clarendon Press).

Durward, L. (1990) *Traveller Mothers and Babies – Who Cares for Their Health?* (London: Maternity Alliance).

Early Years Curriculum Group (1989) *The Early Years Curriculum and the National Curriculum* (Stoke-on-Trent: Trentham Books).

Eekelaar, J. and R. Dingwall (1990) *The Reform of Child Care Law* (London: Routledge).

Elfer, P. and G. Beasley (1991) *Registration of Childminding and Day Care: Using the Law to Raise Standards* (London: HMSO).

Ellis, S. and A. Franklin (1995) 'Children's Rights Officers: Righting Wrongs and Promoting Rights', in Franklin (1995).

Elshtain, J. (1982) *The Family in Political Thought* (Amherst: University of Massachusetts Press).

European Community (1992) *Council Recommendations of 24th June on Common Criteria concerning Sufficient Resources and Social Assistance in Social Protection Systems* (Brussels).

Fagin, L. (1984) *The Foresaken Families: The Effects of Unemployment on Family Life* (Harmondsworth: Penguin).

Family Welfare Association (1995) *Guide to the Social Services* (83rd edn) (London: FWA).

Farmer, E. and M. Owen (1995) *Child Protection Practice: Private Risks and Public Remedies* (London: HMSO).

Farson, R. (1978) *Birthrights* (Harmondsworth: Penguin).

Feinberg, J. (1966) 'Duties, Rights and Claims', *American Philosophical Quarterly*, vol. 3, no. 137.

Ferri, E. and D. Birchall (1986) *A Study of Support and Training for Childminders* (London: National Children's Bureau).

Field, F. (1982) *Poverty and Politics* (London: Heinemann).

Finch, J. (1989) *Family Obligations and Social Change* (Cambridge: Polity Press).

Flekkoy, M. (1995) 'The Scandinavian Experience of Children's Rights', in Franklin (1995).

Fletcher, H. (1991) 'Childhood Asthma: Strategies for Primary and Community Health Care', in Wyke and Hewison (1991).

Ford, J. and E. Kempson (1995) 'No Way Out', *ROOF*, July/August.

Forrest, R. and D. Gordon (1993) *People and Places – a 1991 census atlas of England* (Bristol: School for Advanced Urban Studies (SAUS)).

Fox Harding, L. (1991) *Perspectives in Child Care Policy* (London: Longman).

Fox Harding, L. (1996) *Family, State and Social Policy* (London: Macmillan).

Franklin, B. (1989) 'Children's Rights: Developments and Prospects', *Children and Society*, vol. 3.

Franklin, B. (ed.) (1995) *The Handbook of Children's Rights: Comparative Policy and Practice* (London: Routledge).

Freeman, M. (1992) 'Taking Children's Rights More Seriously', in Alston (1992).

Freeman, M. (1995) 'Children's Rights in a Land of Rites' in Franklin (1995).

Frost, N. (1990) 'Official Intervention and Child Protection: The Relationship between State and Family in Contemporary Britain', in Violence Against Children Study Group, *Taking Child Abuse Seriously* (London: Unwin Hyman).

Galbraith, J. K. (1994) 'The good life beckons', *New Statesman and Society*, 28 January 1994.

Garnham, A. and E. Knights (1994) *Putting the Treasury First: The Truth about Child Support* (London: CPAG).

George, V. and S. Miller (eds) (1994) *Social Policy Towards 2000* (London: Routledge).

Gil, D. (1975) 'Unravelling Child Abuse', *American Journal of Orthopsychiatry*, vol. 45, no. 3.

Gill, O. (1992) *Parenting Under Pressure* (Cardiff: Barnardo's).

Gill, O. and B. Jackson (1983) *Adoption and Race* (London: Batsford).

Gilligan, C. (1982) *In a Different Voice* (Harvard University Press).

Gittus, E. (1976) *Flats, Families and the Under-Fives* (London: Routledge).

Glennerster, H., M. Matsaganis, P. Owens and S. Hancock (1994) *Implementing GP Fundholding* (Buckingham: Open University).

Golding, P. (1986) *Excluding the Poor* (London: CPAG).

Gray, J. (1995) 'Hollowing the Core', *Guardian*, 8 March.

Greenland, C. (1986) *Preventing CAN Deaths* (London: Tavistock).

Greve, J. with E. Currie (1990) *Homelessness in Britain* (York: Joseph Rowntree Memorial Trust).

Griffiths, R. (1983) *The NHS Management Inquiry Report* (London: DHSS).

Hafen, B. (1977) 'Puberty, Privacy and Protection: The Risks of Children's Rights', *American Bar Association Journal*, vol. 63, p. 1383.

Hair, P. E. H. (1982) 'Children in Society 1850–1980', in Barker and Drake (1982).

Hall, A. (1984) 'Foreword', in P. Bean (ed.), *Adoption: Essays in Social Policy, Law and Sociology* (Oxford: Basil Blackwell).

Halsey, A. H. (ed.) (1988) *British Social Trends since 1900* (London: Macmillan).

Halsey, A. H. and M. Young (1995) *Family and Community Socialism* (London: Institute for Public Policy Research).

Ham, C. (1992) *Health Policy in Britain* (3rd edn) (London: Macmillan).

Hammarberg, T. (1995) 'Preface', in Franklin (1995).

Hansard, 22 March 1988.

Harris, M. (1984) 'How unemployment affects people', *New Society*, 19 January 1984.

Haskey, J. (1994) 'Stepfamilies and Stepchildren in Great Britain', *Population Trends* (OPCS), no. 76, Summer.

Health Visitors' Association and the General Medical Services Committee (1989) *Homeless Families and Their Health* (London: HVA and GMSC).

Hegarty, S. (1993) *Meeting Special Needs in Ordinary Schools* (2nd edn) (London: Cassell).

Henderson, P. (ed.) (1995) *Children and Communities* (London: Pluto Press).

Hendrick, H. (1994) *Child Welfare: 1870–1989* (London: Routledge).

Hewitt, P and P. Leach (1993) *Social Justice, Children and Families* (London: Institute for Public Policy Research).

Heywood, J. (1959) *Children in Care* (London: Routledge & Kegan Paul).

Hill, M. and J. Aldgate (eds) (1996) *Child Welfare Services* (London: Jessica Kingsley).

Hills, J. (1990) *The State of Welfare: The Welfare State in Britain since 1974* (Oxford: Clarendon Press).

Hills, J. (1993) *The Future of Welfare – A Guide to the Debate* (York: Joseph Rowntree Foundation).

Hills, J. (1995) *Inquiry into Income and Wealth*, vol. 2 (York: Joseph Rowntree Foundation).

Holman, R. (1980) *Inequality in Child Care* (London: Family Rights Group/ CPAG).

Holt, J. (1975) *Escape from Childhood* (Harmondsworth: Penguin).

Holtermann, S. (1995) *All Our Futures* (Barkingside: Barnardo's).

Holtermann, S. (1996) 'The Impact of Public Expenditure and Fiscal Policies on Britain's Children and Young People', *Children and Society*, vol. 10.

Home Office (1960) *Report of Committee on Children and Young Persons* (Ingleby Report), Cmnd. 1191 (London: HMSO).

House of Commons Committee on Education and Science (1986) *Achievement in Primary Schools* (London: HMSO).

House of Commons Social Social Services Committee (1984) *Children in Care* (London: HMSO).

House of Commons Social Security Committee (1993) *Report on the Operation of the Child Support Act* London: HMSO).

Howard, E. (1902) *Garden Cities of Tomorrow* (1965 edn) (London: Faber).

Hygiene Committee of the Women's Group on Public Welfare (1942) *Our Towns* (London).

Iliffe, S. (1983) *The NHS: A Picture of Health* (London: Lawrence & Wishart).

Ivatts, J. (1988) 'Housing Policy', *Social Policy and Administration*, vol. 22, no. 3, December.

Ivatts, J. (1992) 'The School Meals Service', *Social Policy and Administration*, vol. 26, no. 3, September.

Jackson, S. (1993) 'Under Fives: Thirty Years of No Progress', *Children and Society*, vol. 7, no. 1.

Jephcott, P. (1971) *Homes in High Flats* (Edinburgh: Oliver & Boyd).

John, M. (ed.) (1996a) *Children in our Charge: The Child's Right to Resources* (London: Jessica Kingsley).

John, M. (ed.) (1996b) *Children in Charge: The Child's Right to a Fair Hearing* (London: Jessica Kingsley).

Jones, C. (ed.) (1993) *New Perspectives on the Welfare State in Europe* (London: Routledge).

Jones, H. (1981) *A Population Geography* (London: Harper & Row).

Joseph, K and J. Sumption (1979) *Equality* (London: John Murray).

Kahan, B. (1993) 'Children Living Away From Home', *Children and Society*, vol. 7, no. 1.

Kelly, A. V. (1994) *The National Curriculum – A Critical Review* (London: Paul Chapman).

Kerr, M. (1989) *The Right to Buy* (London: DoE, HMSO).

Kids Club Network (1990) *A Patchwork of Provision* (London).

King, M. and J. Trowell (1995) *Children's Welfare and the Law: The Limits of Legal Intervention* (London: Sage).

Kirkwood, A. (1993) *The Leicestershire Inquiry 1992* (Leicestershire County Council).

Klein, R. (1993) 'O'Goffe's Tale', in Jones (1993).

Krausz, E. (1971) *Ethnic Minorities in Britain* (London: MacGibbon & Kee).

Kumar, V. (1993) *Poverty and Inequality in the UK – The Effects on Children* (London: National Children's Bureau).

Labour Party (1996) *Early Excellence: A Head Start for Every Child* (London: Labour Party).

Land, H. (1975) 'The Introduction of Family Allowances' in Hall, Parker, Land and Webb (eds.), *Change, Choice and Conflict in Social Policy* (London: Heinemann).

Land, H. (1979) *The Family Wage* (University of Liverpool).

Lansdown, G. (1992) 'Children and Rights' in *Children Now* (London: National Children's Bureau/The Children's Society).

Lansdown, G. (1995) *Taking Part: Children's Participation in Decision-Making* (London: Institute of Public Policy Research).

Lasch, C. (1977) *Haven in a Heartless World* (New York: Basic Books).

Laslett, P. (1977) *Family Life and Illicit Love in Earlier Generations* (Cambridge University Press).

Lawson, J. and H. Silver (1973) *A Social History of Education in England* (London: Methuen).

Lawton, D. (1975) *Class, Culture and the Curriculum* (London: Routledge & Kegan Paul).

Le Gros Clark, F. (1948) *Social History of the School Meals Service* (London: Council of Social Service).

Leach, P. (1994) *Children First* (Harmondsworth: Penguin).

Lestor, J. (1995) 'A Minister for Children', in Franklin (1995).

Levitt, R., A. Wall and J. Appleby (1995) *The Reorganised National Health Service* (5th edn) (London: Chapman & Hall).

Levy, A. and B. Kahan (1991) *The Pindown Experience and the Protection of Children* (Staffordshire County Council).

Lewis, J. (1980) *The Politics of Motherhood* (London: Croom Helm).

Lewis, J. with the National Asthma Campaign (1995) *The Asthma Handbook* (London: Vermilion).

Lister, R. (1990) *The Exclusive Society: Citizenship and the Poor* (London: CPAG).

London Borough of Brent (1985) *A Child in Trust* (Jasmine Beckford Inquiry Report).

London Borough of Greenwich (1967) *A Child in Mind* (Kimberley Carlile Report).

London Borough of Lambeth (1987) *Whose Child?* (Tyra Henry Report).

Lord Butler (1971) The Art of the Possible (London: Hamish Hamilton).

Lowe, R. (1988) *Education in the Postwar Years – A Social History* (London: Routledge).

Lowe, R. (1993) *The Welfare State in Britain since 1945* (London: Macmillan).

Lowndes, G. A. N. (1955) *The British Educational System* (London: Hutchinson).

Lowry, S. (1991) *Housing and Health* (London: BMA).

Lyon, C. and N. Parton (1995) 'Children's Rights and the Children Act 1989', in Franklin (1995).

MacGregor, B. D., D. S. Robertson and M. Shucksmith (1987) *Rural Housing in Scotland* (Aberdeen University Press).

Mack, J. and S. Lansley (1985) *Poor Britain* (London: Unwin).

Maclure, J. S. (1979) *Educational Documents* (London: Methuen).

Macnicol, J. (1980) *The Movement for Family Allowances 1918–45* (London: Heinemann).

Macpherson, S. (1987) *Five Hundred Million Children – Poverty and Child Welfare in the Third World* (Brighton: Wheatsheaf).

Malpass, P. and A. Murie (1994) *Housing Policy and Practice* (4th edn) (London: Macmillan).

Mason, D. (1995) *Race and Ethnicity in Modern Britain* (Oxford: University Press).

McPherson, K. and Coleman, D. (1988) 'Health', in Halsey (1988).

Mead, L. (1986) *Beyond Entitlement: The Social Obligations of Citizenship* (New York: Free Press).

Melhuish, E. (1991) 'Research on Day Care for Young Children in the UK' in Melhuish and Moss (1991).

Melhuish, E and P. Moss (eds) (1991) *Day Care For Young Children: International Perspectives* (London: Routledge).

Middleton, S., K. Ashworth and R. Walker (1994) *Family Fortunes* (London: CPAG).

Millar, J. (1993) 'Foreword', in A. Garnham and E. Knights (eds), *Child Support Handbook 1993–94* (London: CPAG).

Millar, J. and P. Whiteford (1993) 'Child Support in Lone Parent Families: Policies in Australia and the UK', *Policy and Politics*, vol. 21, no. 1.

Miller, A. (1987) *For Your Own Good: The Roots of Violence in Child-rearing* (London: Virago).

Miller, M. (1990) *Bed and Breakfast – Women and Homelessness Today* (London: Women's Free Press).

Ministry of Health (1945) *Circular 221/45* (London: HMSO).

Mishra, R. (1993) 'Social policy in the postmodern world', in Jones (1993).

Mohan, J. (1995) *A National Health Service?* (London: Macmillan).

Moore, J. (1989) *The End of the Line for Poverty*, speech delivered 11 May 1989.

Morris, J. and M. Winn (1990) *Housing and Social Inequality* (London: Hilary Shipman).

Mortimore, P., P. Sammons and L. Stoll (1983) *School Matters: The Junior Years* (Wells: Open Books).

Moss, P. (1987) *A Review of Childminding Research* (London: Thomas Coram Research Unit).

Moss, P. (1991) 'Day Care Policy and Provision in Britain' in Moss and Melhuish (1991).

Moss, P. and E. Melhuish (1991) *Current Issues in Day Care for Young Children* (London: HMSO).

Moss, P. and Owen, C. (1990) 'Use of Pre-School Day Care and Education 1979–86', *Children and Society*, vol. 3.

Murphy, M. and A. Berrington (1993) 'Household Change in the 1980s: A Review', *Population Trends* (OPCS), no. 73, Autumn.

Murray, C. (1984) *Losing Ground: American Social Policy 1950–80* (New York: Basic Books).

National Commission on Education (1993) *Learning to Succeed* (London: Heinemann).

National Conference – the Partnership Project (1991) *see* Save the Children (1991).

National Union of Teachers (1994) *Crumbling Schools* (London: NUT).

NCH Action for Children (1995) *Fact File '95*.

Newell, P. (1995) 'Rights,Participation and Neighbourhoods', in Henderson (1995).

Newson, J. and E. (1969) *Patterns of Infant Care* (Harmondsworth: Penguin).

Newsom, J. and E. (1989) *The Extent of Parental Physical Punishment in the UK* (London: Approach).

Newton, J. (1994) *All in One Place* (London: CHAS).

Noble, C. J. (1987) *School Meals since the 1980 Education Act – The Need for Nutritional Guidelines*, Unpublished M.Phil. thesis, University of Surrey.

Northern Gypsy Council (1993) *The Gypsy Survey 1993 – From Myth To Reality* (Northumberland: The Partnership Group).

Office for National Statistics (1996) *Population Trends*, no. 84, Summer (London: HMSO).

Office of Population Censuses and Surveys (1989) *Survey of Disability GB* (London: HMSO).

Office of Population Censuses and Surveys (1993) *1991 Census – Summary and Review: Local Authorities* (London: HMSO).

Office of Population Censuses and Surveys (1995) *Birth Statistics 1993*, Series FM1 no. 22 (London: HMSO).

Office for Standards in Education (OFSTED) (1996) *The Education of Travelling Children*, Reference: HMR/12/96/NS.

Office for Standards in Education (OFSTED) (1996) *The Annual Report of Her Majesty's Chief Inspector of Schools 1994/95* (London: HMSO).

Oldfield, N. and A. Yu (1993) *The Cost of a Child: Living Standards for the 1990s* (London: CPAG).

Oppenheim, C. (1990) 'Count Me Out: Losing the Poor in the Numbers Game', *Poverty*, no. 76.

Oppenheim, C. (1993) *Poverty – The Facts* (London: CPAG).

Oppenheim, C. and L. Harker (1996) *Poverty – The Facts* (3rd edn) (London: CPAG).

Osborn, A. and J. Milbank (1987) *The Effects of Early Education* (Oxford: Clarendon Press).

Owen, D. (1994) 'Spatial variations in ethnic minority group populations in Great Britain', *Population Trends* (OPCS), no. 78, Winter.

Packman, J. (1975) *The Child's Generation* (Oxford: Basil Blackwell).

Packman, J. (1993) 'From Prevention to Partnership: Child Welfare Services across Three Decades', *Children and Society*, vol. 7, no. 2.

Packman, J. and B. Jordan (1991) 'The Children Act; Looking Forward, Looking Back', *British Journal of Social Work*, vol. 21.

Page, D. (1993) *Building for Communities – A Study of New Housing Association Estates* (York: Joseph Rowntree Foundation).

Pahl, J. and M. Vaile (1986) *Health and Health Care Among Travellers* (Canterbury: Health Services Research Unit, University of Kent).

Pahl, J. (1989) *Money and Marriage* (London: Macmillan).

Parker, H. (1989) *Instead of the Dole* (London: Routledge).

Parton, N. (1985) *The Politics of Child Abuse* (London: Macmillan).

Parton, N. (1995) 'Neglect as Child Protection: The Political Context and the Practical Outcomes', *Children and Society*, vol. 9, no. 1.

Pascall, G. (1986) *Social Policy – A Feminist Analysis* (London: Tavistock).

Philo, C. (1995) *Off the Map – The Social Geography of Poverty in the UK* (London: CPAG).

Piachaud, D. (1979) *The Cost of a Child* (London: CPAG).

Platt, S. (1987) 'The New Rural Clearances', *ROOF*, July/August.

Plowden Report (see Central Advisory Council for Education, 1967).

Power, A. (1987) *Property Before People – The Management of Twentieth-Century Council Housing* (London: Allen & Unwin).

Power, C. (1995) 'Health Related Behaviour', in Botting (1995).

Power, S., D. Halpin and J. Fitz (1994) 'Underpinning Choice and Diversity? The Grant-Maintained Schools Policy in Context', in Tomlinson (1994).

Power, S., G. Whitty and D. Youdell (1995) *No Place to Learn – Homelessness and Education* (London: Shelter).

Pugh, G. (1988) *Services for Under Fives: Developing a Co-ordinated Approach* (London: National Children's Bureau).

Pugh, G. (1989) 'Services for Under Fives', in S. Morgan and P. Righton, *Child Care Concerns and Conflicts* (London: Hodder & Stoughton).

Pugh, G. (1992) *Contemporary Issues in the Early Years: Working Collaboratively for Children* (London: Paul Chapman).

Quortrup, J. (1994) *Childhood Matters* (Aldershot: Avebury).

Raleigh, V. and R. Balarajan (1995) 'The Health of Infants and Children Among Ethnic Minorities', in Botting (1995).

Ranade, W. (1994) *A Future for the NHS?* (London: Longman).

Rathbone, E. (1924) *The Disinherited Family* (London: Edward Arnold).

Rathbone, E. (1949) *Family Allowances* (London: George Allen & Unwin).

Robinson, R. and J. Le Grand (eds) (1993) *Evaluating the NHS Reforms* (London: King's Fund Institute).

Robson, W. A. (ed.)(1948) *Social Security* (3rd edn) (London: George Allen & Unwin).

Roche, J. (1996) 'Children's Rights; A Lawyer's View', in John (1996a).

Rogers, A. and B. Clements (1985) *The Moral Basis of Freedom* (Exeter: Victoria Books).

Rona, R. J. and S. Chinn (1984), 'Parents' Attitudes Towards School Meals for Primary School Children in 1981', *Human Nutrition: Applied Nutrition*.

Rosenbaum, M. and P. Newell (1991) *Taking Children Seriously: A Proposal for a Children's Rights Commissioner* (London: Gulbenkian Foundation).

Rowe, J., M. Hundleby and L. Garnett (1989) *Child Care Now* (London: BAAF).

Rowe, J. and L. Lambert (1973) *Children Who Wait* (London: Association of British Adoption Agencies).

Rowntree, B. S. (1901) *Poverty: A Study of Town Life* (London: Nelson).

Rowntree, B. S. (1918) *The Human Needs of Labour* (London: Nelson).

Royal College of Physicians (1992) *Smoking and the Young* (London: RCP).

Royal College of Physicians (1994) *Homelessness and Ill Health* (London: RCP).

Royal Society of Arts (1994) *Start Right: The Importance of Early Learning* (London: RSA).

Rutter, J. (1994) *Refugee Children in the Classroom* (Stoke on Trent: Trentham Books).

Ryburn, M. (1996) 'Adoption in England and Wales; Current Issues and Future Trends', in Hill and Aldgate (1996).

Sanderson, M. (1987) *Educational Opportunity and Social Change in England* (London: Faber).

Savage, S. P., R. Atkinson and L. Robins (1994) *Public Policy in Britain* (London: Macmillan).

Save the Children, West Midlands Education Service for Travelling Children, Walsall Health Authority, National Gypsy Council (1991) *National Conference April 1991 – Partnership 2000*.

Schaffer, F. (1972) *The New Town Story* (London: Paladin).

Scottish Office (1992) *The Report of the Inquiry into the Removal of Children from Orkney in February 1991* (London: HMSO).

Seebohm, F. (1968) *Report of the Committee on Local Authority and Allied Personal Social Services*, Cmnd. 3703 (London: HMSO).

Sellick, C. (1996) 'Short Term Foster Care', in Hill and Aldgate (1996).

Sexty, C. (1990) *Women Losing Out – Access to Housing in Britain Today* (London: Shelter).

Shelter (1994) *Homelessness – What's the Problem?* (London: Shelter).

Short, J. R. (1982) *Housing in Britain – The Post-War Experience* (London: Methuen).

Simon, B. (1985) *Does Education Matter?* (London: Lawrence & Wishart).

Simon, B. (1991) *Education and the Social Order 1940–1990* (London: Lawrence & Wishart).

Sinclair, R. (1996) 'Children and Young People's Participation in Decision Making: The Legal Framework in Social Services and Education', in Hill and Aldgate (1996).

Smith, A. (1776) *The Wealth of Nations*.

Smith, R. (1991) *The Health of the Nation – The BMJ View* (London: BMJ).

Smith, T. and M. Noble (1995) *Education Divides – Poverty and School in the 1990s* (London: CPAG).

Statham, J. *et al.* (1990) *Playgroups in a Changing World* (London: HMSO).

Stearn, J. (1986) 'An expensive way of making children ill', *ROOF*, vol. 11, no. 5, September/October.

Stroud, J. (1960) *The Shorn Lamb* (London: Longman).

Tansey, G. and T. Worsley (1995) *The Food System* (London: Earthscan).

Thatcher, M. (1972) *Let Our Children Grow Tall* (London: Centre for Policy Studies).

Times Educational Supplement (1996) 'Fall Out as Vouchers Create Free for All', 25 October.

Times Educational Supplement (1996) 'Vouchers do Little for Parental Choice', 1 November.

Timmins, N. (1995) *The Five Giants – A Biography of the Welfare State* (London: HarperCollins).

Titmuss, R. M. (1950) *History of the Second World War – Problems of Social Policy* (London: HMSO and Longmans, Green & Co.).

Titmuss, R. M. (1958) *Essays on the Welfare State* (London: George Allen & Unwin).

Tizard, J., P. Moss and J. Perry (1976) *All Our Children* (London: Maurice Temple Smith).

Tomlinson, S. (ed.) (1994) *Educational Reform and Its Consequences* (London: Rivers Oram Press/IPPR).

Townsend, P. (1979) *Poverty in the UK* (London: Penguin).

Townsend, P. (1996) 'Too Many Rights Don't Make a Wrong: The Work of the Devon Youth Council', in John (1996b).

Townsend, P. and Davidson, N. (eds) (1992) *Inequalities in Health – The Black Report* (London: Penguin) (see also Whitehead, M.).

Trasler, G. (1960) *In Place of Parents* (London: Routledge & Kegan Paul).

Ungerson, C. (1994) 'Housing: Need, Equity, Ownership and the Economy', in George and Miller (1994).

UNICEF (1989) *The State of the World's Children 1989* (Oxford University Press).

United Nations (1990) *World Summit for Children.*

United Nations Convention on the Rights of the Child (1989).

Utting, D. (1995) *Family and Parenthood* (York: Joseph Rowntree Foundation).

Utting, W. (1991) *Children in the Public Care* (London: HMSO).

Viet-Wilson, J. (1994) *Dignity Not Poverty* (London: Institute for Public Policy Research).

Vilien, K. (1993) 'Provision for Pre-School Children in Denmark', in David (1993).

Vostanis, P., S. Cumella, E. Gratton and C. Winchester (1996) *The Impact of Homelessness on the Mental Health of Children and Families* (Birmingham: University Department of Psychiatry).

Walker, C. (1993) *Managing Poverty: The Limits of Social Assistance* (London: Routledge).

Ward, C. (1993) *New Town, Home Town – The Lessons of Experience* (London: Gulbenkian Foundation).

Ward, H. (1995) *Looking after Children: Research into Practice* (London: HMSO).

Warner, M. (1989) *Into the Dangerous World* (London: Chatto).

Warner, N. (1992) *Choosing with Care* (London: HMSO).

Warnock Report (see Dept of Education and Science, 1978).

Waterhouse, L. and J. McGhee (1996) 'Families', Social Workers' and Police Perspectives on Child Abuse Investigations', in Hill and Aldgate (1996).

Watson, J. L. (1977) *Between Two Cultures* (Oxford: Basil Blackwell).

Webster, C. (ed.) (1993) *Caring for Health: History and Diversity* (Buckingham: Open University Press).

Which? (1992) 'School Dinners – Are They Worth Having?' September.

Which? (1995) 'Is your doctor a fundholder?' June.

Which? (1995) 'Air Pollution – The big smoke' July.

Which? (1995) 'Who needs private health care?' August.

Which? (1995) 'Should you buy Private Medical Insurance?' September.

Whitehead, M. (1992) *Inequalities in Health – The Health Divide* (London: Penguin).

Widgery, D. (1988) *The National Health: A Radical Perspective* (London: Hogarth Press).

Wilkinson, R. G. (1994) *Unfair Shares* (Barkingside: Barnardo's).

Williams, F. (1989) *Social Policy: A Critical Introduction* (Cambridge: Polity Press).

Williams, P. (1992) 'Housing', in Cloke (1992).

Wilson, C. and R. Woods (1991) 'Fertility in England: A Long-Term Perspective', *Population Studies* (OPCS), vol. 45, no. 3.

Wilson, E. (1977) *Women and the Welfare State* (London: Tavistock).

Woodhead, M. (1989) 'School Starts at 5 . . . or 4 Years Old?', *Journal of Social Policy*, vol. 4, no. 1.

Woodroffe, C. and M. Glickman (1993) 'Trends in Child Health', *Children and Society*, vol. 7, no. 1.

Woodroffe, C., M. Glickman, M. Barker and C. Power (1993) *Children, Teenagers and Health* (Buckingham: Open University Press).

World Health Organisation (1995) *Bridging the Gaps* (Geneva).

Wragg, T. (1995) *The Ted Wragg Guide to Education* (Oxford: Butterworth–Heinemann).

Wyke, S. and J. Hewison (eds) (1991) *Child Health Matters* (Milton Keynes: Open University Press).

Young, M. and A. H. Halsey (1995) *Family and Community Socialism* (London: IPPR).

Young, M. and P. Willmott (1962) *Family and Kinship in East London* (Harmondsworth: Penguin).

Index

1 Unless otherwise indicated, all references to a subject are to aspects of that subject relevant to children.
2 Page numbers in **bold** type indicate an illustrative figure or table.